Real Essays for College & Grad School

Anne McKinney, Editor

PREP PUBLISHING

FAYETTEVILLE, NC

PREP Publishing
1110½ Hay Street
Fayetteville, NC 28305
(910) 483-6611

Copyright © 2012by Anne McKinney

Cover design by Chris Pearl

Library of Congress Cataloging-in-Publication Data

Real essays for college & grad school / Anne McKinney, editor.
     p. cm. -- (Real-resumes series)
     ISBN 978-1475094039; 1475094035
     1. College applications--United States. 2. Universities and colleges--United States--Graduate work--Admission. 3. Universities and colleges--United States--Admission. 4. Exposition (Rhetoric) I. Title: Real essays for college and grad school. II. McKinney, Anne, 1948- III. Series.

    LB2351.52.U6 R42 2000
     378.1'616--dc21
                                            00-026978
                                                    CIP

Printed in the United States of America

By PREP Publishing

Business and Career Series:

RESUMES AND COVER LETTERS THAT HAVE WORKED

RESUMES AND COVER LETTERS THAT HAVE WORKED FOR MILITARY PROFESSIONALS

GOVERNMENT JOB APPLICATIONS AND FEDERAL RESUMES

COVER LETTERS THAT BLOW DOORS OPEN

LETTERS FOR SPECIAL SITUATIONS

RESUMES AND COVER LETTERS FOR MANAGERS

REAL-RESUMES FOR TEACHERS

REAL-RESUMES FOR STUDENTS

REAL-RESUMES FOR CAREER CHANGERS

REAL-RESUMES FOR SALES

REAL ESSAYS FOR COLLEGE & GRAD SCHOOL

Judeo-Christian Ethics Series:

SECOND TIME AROUND

BACK IN TIME

WHAT THE BIBLE SAYS ABOUT...Words that can lead to success and happiness

A GENTLE BREEZE FROM GOSSAMER WINGS

BIBLE STORIES FROM THE OLD TESTAMENT

Fiction:

KIJABE...An African Historical Saga

Table of Contents

PART FOUR: MBA PROGRAMS AND BUSINESS SCHOOLS

PART FIVE: COLLEGES AND UNDERGRADUATE SCHOOLS
INCLUDING THE IVY LEAGUE AND MILITARY ACADEMIES

PART SIX: MEDICAL SCHOOL, PHYSICIAN'S ASSISTANT PROGRAM, DENTAL SCHOOL, VETERINARY SCHOOL, AND RESIDENCY PROGRAM

PART SEVEN: MISCELLANEOUS OTHER ESSAYS AND PERSONAL STATEMENTS FOR SCHOLARSHIPS, INTERNSHIPS, FELLOWSHIPS, AND OTHER PURPOSES

A WORD FROM THE EDITOR:
ABOUT REAL ESSAYS FOR COLLEGE & GRAD SCHOOL

Welcome to Real Essays for College & Grad School. This book is designed to help you make your dreams come true and gain admission to as many academic programs as possible.

The essays which accompany your application for college or grad school can count up to 60% in the admissions decision, according to some admissions directors. As you approach the task of creating your own essays, you will find it helpful to see real samples and real essays used in situations similar to yours.

Here is our advice about how to use this book. Don't look only at the section for medical professionals if you are seeking admission to medical school or dental school. Many of the essays in the other sections could provide valuable insights. Often essay questions occur in different forms in essays for college, graduate school, and professional programs. For example, there is often a question which gives you an opportunity to explain a weak period in your past. ("Do you feel your undergraduate GPA is an adequate reflection of your ability to excel in a rigorous degree program?" is such a question.)

Essay questions are an attempt by the admissions committee to "get to know you." As you approach an essay question, remember that the goal of the admissions committee is to "get to know you." You should view the question or questions posed as an opportunity for you to showcase your talents and "put your best foot forward."

Essay questions are an attempt by admissions committees to see "what's different" about you from the masses of other qualified candidates.
Too often, applicants approach essay questions as though they are trying to "measure up" to other qualified candidates. The approach you should take, instead, is to choose an approach to the essay which will permit you to show off your differences from other qualified candidates. Remember that admissions committees are trying to choose classes made up of human beings who are varied in strengths, talents, abilities, and goals. Don't be afraid of coming across as a unique human being. That kind of essay might just get you into the colleges and universities of your choice! Good luck!

Part One

Using the Internet: A Practical Way to Use it for Getting into College

Using the World Wide Web to get into college is a smart bet. Hundreds of college books crowd bookstore shelves, and few offer any specialized information about the school you want to attend. But you're in luck! Most colleges and universities operate websites, with instant access to admissions officers, educational costs, and applications. We do recommend that you visit the official college websites and contact the admissions office before you apply. As important as the web can be as a resource, it is always best to develop a working relationship with the admissions counselors and financial aid officers.

1. Official College Sites

If you know the name of the school to which you would like to apply, then use a basic search engine like the ones listed below. Simply type the name of the school, for example, University of North Carolina at Chapel Hill, and wait for the results. The best way to distinguish a college's website is by the address ending. Official sites usually end in ".edu"—for example, Harvard University is www.harvard.edu—making it easy to remember. Add a bookmark on your computer, and you can easily access the college site.

When you enter these "official" college sites, just click your mouse on New Students or Admissions Information. You will find admissions facts and figures, an admission application, student testimonies, the e-mail address for the admissions office, links to academic departments, images of the campus, and much, much more. The college websites are virtual catalogs, sharing many similarities with the colorful brochures that clog your mailbox.

But as a student or parent, you may want to know more about the college, about day-to-day life on campus or course descriptions. Often this information is available on the college's own site, and the trick is to use the right keywords when conducting a search within the site. Try the following: "Course Descriptions, Student Newspaper, Faculty Evaluations, Class Schedules, Student Clubs."

Here are several general search engines that are useful for basic college searches.
- **www.altavista.com**
- **www.infoseek.com**
- **www.excite.com**
- **www.lycos.com**
- **www.northernlight.com**
- **www.snap.com**
- **www.yahoo.com.**

2. Professional Associations on the Web

Professional associations, college alumni groups, fraternities and sororities, and ethnic associations can be useful tools when researching colleges. These associations maintain sites that let you know which colleges maintain chapters on campus. Many sites have access to alumni who can describe their experiences in college.
- **www. alumnet.com**

College Alumni Groups

- www.hillel.org
Hillel Site
Hillel is the foundation of the campus Jewish community. A nonprofit organization that supports Jewish life on campuses worldwide. It contains information for prospective students beginning the admissions process and links to colleges with Hillel chapters.

- www.naacp.org
NAACP Site

- www.greeks.com
National and Local Fraternities and Sororities

3. How to Get Into College Sites
A productive Internet search begins with learning what information exists on-line. Once you know about the diverse services and sites, you can decide what kind of information you require. Most college advice sites offer a wide array of options for students and parents. We do not recommend one site over another, but suggest that each person find a site or search engine that suits them best. The Internet will only be as useful as you make it.

Commercial ventures offer services that will assist students looking for the right college, the right program, and the right costs. College search engines and on-line application sites enable today's students to find colleges, talk with admissions counselors and submit applications. Multimedia and interactive virtual tours make campuses accessible to students who could not otherwise afford plane tickets.

The following websites provide college search engines, planning guides, and links to colleges and universities. There are many different features provided at the sites. Some provide on-line applications, downloadable college applications, and fee-based application services. Most offer free memberships, or at the very least free tips and advice.

- www.campustours.com
This provides a search engine that allows a student to search for a college alphabetically or by state. It includes links to individual college websites, virtual tours of most colleges, links to scholarship information and financial aid, and daily profiles of individual schools.

- www.collegeboard.org
The site offers on-line SAT registration. It also features a planning guide for parents and students beginning the college admissions process. The site provides tips on how to find an excellent college match and how to finance college tuition. An on-line store is available for the purchase of test preparation materials.

- www.collegexpress.com
This website provides advice how to find a good college match and succeed in the application process. The services on this site include a college search engine, college profiles, financial aid information, a section for parents, information on college athletics and student life, and special scholarship contests.

- **www.collegequest.com**

Collegequest.com offers a free membership to users who register. This site includes a search engine, an organizer that manages your college list and personal information, in-depth profiles from the *Peterson's Guide* and *Yale Daily News*, over 1,000 on-line applications, scholarship search, financial aid advice, and articles from campus newspapers.

- **www.embark.com (formerly collegeedge.com)**

Students registering as a member of this site gain free access to tools that allow you to find, apply to, finance, and get prepared for the college and educational program of your choice. The search engines can be customized for the individual user's interests in schools, regions, and programs. The site also features a career search that allows the student to consider employment options, scholarship and financial aid searches, and contests.

- **www.nced.ed.gov/ipeds/cool**

This site is a part of the National Center for Education Statistics. COOL stands for College Opportunities On-Line, and it is a search engine that allows you to look up schools by geographic region, type, program, and Title IV eligibility. Searches offer detailed information about the school, phone numbers, tuition/fee information, and enrollment statistics.

- **www.powerstudents.com**

A website devoted to sharing first-hand student experiences as a learning tool. The site is divided into network areas that focus on High School, College, Graduate School, Career, and Parents. The site includes interactive forums, bulletin boards, chat rooms, and email. It also features the Inside Guide, a perspective of institutions by students from individual colleges.

- **www.scholarstuff.com**

Here is a general purpose website that provides access to undergraduate and graduate programs worldwide. It has links to sites devoted to financial aid, test preparation, study abroad programs, student travel, and job searches.

- **www.usnews.com**

The Magazine *U.S. News and World Report* publishes an annual ranking in the Fall of "The Best Colleges" and "The Best Graduate Schools." Both issues give national rankings, best values rankings, and regional rankings. There is also information on specialty schools and service academies. *U.S. News* also provides a college search engine, a college personality quiz, a cost estimator that calculates college expenses, and a scholarship engine.

3. College Entrance Exam Review Sites
- **www.collegeboard.org.**

This site offers on-line registration for the SATs. It posts deadlines for registration, the test dates, and the registration fees. In addition, it contains test taking tips, strategies, and information about test preparation.

- **www.ets.org**

The body is the Educational Testing Service. The site provides information to students and to parents about the standardized tests administered by ETS. It includes links to college website databases, jobs and careers, tips for returning students and international students, information for students with learning disabilities, practice test questions, computer-based testing. This site links directly to the CollegeBoard which manages test registration.

- **www.kaplan.com**

The Kaplan site features information on how to prepare for the standardized tests required by most four year colleges, graduate schools, law school, medical school, and professional licensing exams. Registration and detailed information about the Kaplan program is available at this site. It also features college search databases and career advice. Scholarship funding is available to offset the high cost of enrollment in the Kaplan program.

- **www.powerprep.com**

This site offers free, downloadable software that assists you with SAT and ACT preparation. Users have access to separate SAT and ACT laboratories that contain a variety of tools and resources. This site contains a college search engine, financial aid advice, and a high school timeline.

- **www. prepusa.net**

PREP USA is an educational program that instructs students in preparing for the SAT, ACT, PSAT and TOEFL. The site gives information about where to find the nearest PREP USA location, how to enroll in the programs, and the costs of the services. The courses generally are less expensive than either the Kaplan or Princeton Review Courses.

- **www.review.com**

The Princeton Review site offers user information about standardized tests, college admissions, college searches, and career programs. The focus of the site includes people seeking admission to a four-year college, professional school, law school, or any graduate program. The site also provides free membership to the site, but not to the Princeton Review courses.

- **www.wordcommand.com**

Users of this site can register for the free delivery of a daily vocabulary word to their email boxes. The words selected by WordCommand frequently appear on standardized exams such as the SAT, ACT and GRE. The site also provides pricing information and product description of the WordCommand software program.

4. On-line Applications
- **www.commonapp.org**

You can download a free copy of the Common Application form at this site. The form is available in both Windows and Macintosh versions. The Common Application is a recommended admissions form used by nearly 200 independent colleges and universities. The application is updated every academic school year, according to the specifications and interests of the participating schools.

- **www.collegelink.com**

Collegelink.com is an application service that has access to most schools' customized applications. This site takes you step-by-step through filling out the application form, and it allows you to print a draft version for review. You then submit it to the Collegelink center for processing. The first application is processed free of charge. Any additional applications cost $5 each.

- **www.collegeview.com**

This site features the AppZap® program that allows you to download customized electronic college applications for the school(s) of your choice. Once you complete the AppZap form, you can send it over the Internet or submit it directly to the school via the post office. This site also contains multimedia virtual tours of many colleges and universities as well as an extensive college information database. Additional features are a financial aid section, electronic applications, guidance office, bulletin boards, a career center, and a campus bookstore. The site also allows users to request information from schools.

- **www.weapply.com**

As part of the Princeton Review website, weapply.com provides access to Apply!, the independent electronic application product. Apply! is used by more than 500 colleges and universities for admission to their undergraduate programs. The site lists the participating institutions, including the schools that accept Apply! through electronic submission. Apply! generates exact replicas of each school's own application forms. The forms are available on-line or on CD-Rom or disks, and a high school guidance counselor can order them for free.

- **www.xap.com**

This site features an on-line admissions form to colleges who have agreed to accept the xap forms. More than just an application consortium, the site also contains a search engine that matches a student's interests with a group of colleges. It also provides users with a college planner, financial aid applications, cost estimators, and virtual campus tours.

5. Financial Aid and Scholarship Information
- **www.ed.gov**

The U.S. Department of Education site contains information about Stafford loans, Pell Grants, and other federally funded aid programs. It offers access to an electronic version of the Free Application for Federal Student Aid (FAFSA), and users can submit the information over the Internet. All students seeking federally funded aid, as well as some state aid, must submit this form.

- **www.ed.gov/prog_info/SFA/StudentGuide/**

The U.S. Department of Education publishes The Student Guide annually, which is a comprehensive resource on student financial aid. Available in paper as well as electronic form, the guide contains information about grants, loans, and work-study. The Student Guide tells you about these three different aid programs, and it advises you on how to apply for them.

- **www.fastweb.com**

Fastweb.com is a scholarship search site that offers a free membership. The service conducts scholarship and college searches based on your interests and qualifications. The site also includes advice on college costs, admissions, financial aid, career planning, and job searching. A free on-line mailbox is available to receive and store daily scholarship information.

Using the Internet

- **www.finaid.org**

FinAid is a free public service site that holds an extensive collection of information about student financial aid on the web. This site offers students advice on loans, scholarships, military aid, financial aid applications, and other types of student aid.

- **http://www.salliemae.com:80/index.html**

The Student Loan Marketing Association, better known to people as Sallie Mae, provides answers to basic financial aid questions and information on low cost lenders. The site contains a scholarship service and advice on how to plan and pay for college. The highlighted feature is an on-line financial aid calculator that you can use to estimate tuition expenses, loan options and total college debt.

- **www.estudentloan.com**

Here is another site you might investigate for scholarship possibilities!

- **http://www.Scholarships.com LLC**

This organization offers a free database of more than 600,000 scholarships.

- **http://www.FastWeb.com**

This is one of the oldest and largest of the scholarship databases.

- **http://www.college.ucla.edu/up/SRC/SS.htm**

Here is a UCLA link to free scholarship Web sites.

Part Two: Law School
Essays and Personal Statements

In the following pages you will see examples of letters and essays written especially for law school.

In essays and personal statements viewed as part of an application process, you are often asked to reveal your philosophy, values, ideas, and goals. Although these samples are provided to give you some ideas and insights, it's very important to be yourself!

Usually an essay is a tool for conveying autobiographical information. In this section, you will see an essay used as part of the application process for law school which presents autobiographical information in an effort to explain slow academic progress. This letter is called a personal statement and is a formal part of the application process for many graduate schools. Personal statements often provide an opportunity to explain erratic periods in your past.

In essays and personal statements, you are trying to create a memorable image of yourself, and you are attempting to create, in words, a "picture" of who you are and who you want to be. Avoid cliched expressions which will make you appear the same as everybody else. Use words and phrases, based on your unique life experiences and circumstances, that will make you "come alive" and appear unique.

Personal Statement and Biographical Sketch
James Allen Collins
North Georgia University School of Law

PERSONAL STATEMENT AS PART OF AN APPLICATION TO LAW SCHOOL

Often an essay is an opportunity to "explain" a reckless or irresponsible period in one's life. This individual is seeking admission to law school at middle age, and he provides an intensely personal glimpse into who he is, where he's been, why he's done some of the things he's done, and what he wants to do now.

I respectfully ask the admissions committee to consider the following factors when evaluating my undergraduate academic record. After graduation from high school, I was financially unable to enter college. I worked in a local factory while continuing to work on the family farm. I came from a family of eight children and grew up in rural eastern Georgia. Most of my life—through age 16—we were sharecroppers. During my sophomore year in high school, my father obtained an entry-level civil service job. We then moved to our own family farm which my parents had bought when my father returned from World War II. This was the first opportunity we had to farm our own land rather than to sharecrop. The income from my father's job and our farm still barely kept us above the poverty level. I'm not sure that it did.

I am the third oldest child and the oldest son. When my father began working in the public job, I took over the running of the family farm. My parents believed strongly in education and sacrificed a great deal to see that we were provided with a quality education. We also sacrificed for each other. My oldest sister graduated from high school and went to work to help provide for us. When my next sister graduated, she was able to attend college a semester later. I enrolled at Georgia State University two years later with no outside financial aid. I worked part time and full time. I had six younger siblings who were still in school and who ranged in age from elementary through high school. I felt guilty, and my grades suffered. After dropping in and out of school several times, I decided to stay out of school and help the younger children. I knew that I would eventually return to college. In many respects, I'm glad that I made the decision to stay out of school and concentrate on helping support the family.

When my father died, my younger siblings needed my financial and moral support even more than before. Besides helping my family, I experienced a lot of personal growth during my absence from college. I completed the automotive mechanics course at the local community college and worked as a mechanic at a local dealership. I also repaired and serviced vehicles for many of the elderly and needy people in the community free of charge, because they needed the assistance. I still do some of this type of work when time permits.

After I entered military service, I experienced much of life that I never would have been able to experience otherwise. Besides serving my country, I also had the opportunity to provide for and help shape the lives of many individuals. I found a lifetime mate with like ideals and similar interests and who is also unselfish and dedicated to serving humanity. This time when I returned to college, I was able to work without the distractions of worrying about my family's basic needs. Five of the eight children in my family have earned bachelor's or advanced degrees and the other three have technical degrees and have done very well in their courses. I made the Dean's List each of my last four semesters even though I had a lot of earlier incompletes and failing grades to overcome. I am a hard worker and can excel in a rigorous curriculum.

WHAT IS YOUR PROFESSIONAL ORIENTATION?

My Professional Orientation

I have a passionate desire to work in the public service sector of criminal law. Though America is by far the greatest country in this world, we have a long way to go. I know first hand that we don't all start out in life on an equal footing. As a minority I know that I have a responsibility to help level the field. I have experienced first hand the obstacles and road blocks that too often impede the pursuit of the basic rights of all humans. I know what it's like to be under-represented or not represented at all. I know what it's like to overcome adversity. I know that adversity builds character. It also makes one a better advocate. Unless you really understand what it's like to be in another's situation, you cannot be the best advocate. I grew up financially strapped, but I know that lack of funds does not necessarily hinder one's success. I was born with an ear condition that left me deaf in one ear. It probably could have been corrected had we been able to afford proper treatment. Despite this setback, I overcame and often excelled.

There are many people with a lot to offer our society if given the slightest of opportunities. I began my military career as an enlisted man. I knew first hand what those at the lower ranks and pay grades must endure. When I became a non-commissioned officer and later a commissioned officer, I could better serve and lead because of understanding and being able to see all sides. Too many times I've been an "only" or "one of the few." I've been the "only" Chinese NCO in my section. I've been the "only" Chinese company commander in a battalion. I've been "one of the few" minority commissioned officers on a post. I've been the "only" Chinese profit center manager in a company I worked for, and later "one of the few" in each of these situations. I've tried to be a good advocate. I've personally helped many Chinese, Blacks, whites, and other nationalities to succeed, despite the odds against them, and to realize their full potential—even though some of them would have been considered more "fortunate" than I. I've seen that many times some individuals in positions of authority place their personal agenda above the rights of others.

I want to be in a position to help insure "justice for all." I know that passion and commitment alone are not sufficient to do what I want to do. I need a legal education and a law degree to be equipped with the knowledge and credentials necessary for me to make a positive impact on our criminal justice system.

I am drawn to North Georgia School of Law because I know of its strong reputation in areas of advocacy. I personally know many North Georgia lawyers who set the standard for others to emulate. My personal lawyer is a North Georgia graduate. North Georgia is my undergraduate alma mater. I believe this fine institution's areas of expertise are an excellent fit for my goals.

ESSAY IN APPLICATION FOR ADMISSION TO LAW SCHOOL

This essay is intended to convey his passion for and commitment to the area of law which he wishes to study.

What is your professional orientation?

PERSONAL STATEMENT OF MICHAEL MCHALE
Northeastern University

What is your professional orientation?

**PERSONAL STATEMENT
WHAT IS YOUR
PROFESSIONAL
ORIENTATION?**

I am particularly interested in specializing in environmental law, and this interest evolved in college and has strengthened since then. As you will see from my resume, since graduating from college I have worked in Tahoe Resort Company which is just 50 miles from Tahoe. As one of 28 professional ski patrollers, I participate in a wide variety of tasks related to keeping the mountains skiable and safeguarding guests.

While working in this winter paradise, I have become knowledgeable of environmental issues regarding wildlife endangerment, air pollution, overpopulation, and diminishing scarce resources as well as problems posed by hazardous wastes and toxic substances. Just recently I have seen first-hand the dangers posed by population growth as I have observed problems caused by the doubling of Tahoe County's population in the last five years. Furthermore, the population is expected to double again in five years; air pollution originating from Tahoe just 40 minutes away is noticeable; and species of wildlife such as mountain lions and black bears and even deer, which used to be abundant here, are scarce. I want to be a part of shaping and defending environmental policies in the US, and I believe my talent for working with people would make me an effective legal consensus builder between those who want to save all the land and those who want permission to build anything.

A lawyer from Washington State who befriended me when we discussed these issues recently said that he would gladly assist me in obtaining an internship with the Bureau of Land Management or the EPA during one of the summers after I enroll in law school.

I have a passionate desire to work in public service in the environmental area, and I believe that having a passion for something—such as I do for the environment— is a critical factor in becoming an effective advocate. I know, however, that passion and commitment are not sufficient by themselves to do what I want to do. I need a legal education and a law degree in order to be equipped with the knowledge and credential necessary for me to make a positive impact on environmental policy within the U.S. Again, that is why I am drawn to Northeastern University: I know of its strong reputation in the areas of environment law and advocacy, and I believe this fine institution's areas of expertise are an excellent fit with my strategic goals.

WHY SHOULD YOU BE SELECTED TO ATTEND LAW SCHOOL?

I am a hard worker with proven ingenuity and resourcefulness.

Using the resume I am enclosing with my application, I can demonstrate that I am a resourceful hard worker. I have worked since I was 15 years old in jobs that included setting up a business "from scratch" when I was a junior in high school. In that business called Your Helping Hand, Inc., I applied my entrepreneurial instincts as my best friend and I contracted with loggers for oak logs which my partner and I split, stacked, dried during the summer months, and then delivered during the winter months in a business from which we grossed $8,000 annually.

I have acquired excellent work habits.

From that experience I learned valuable lessons about what it takes to form a successful partnership. During the summers and college breaks, I also held jobs as a trim carpenter and as an aide/landscape technician in a large construction company. Through those jobs I learned that the productivity of every person in an organization is important; for example, it was my work as a landscape technician which was often the general public's "first impression" of a new development, and a poor outside appearance would have discredited even the finest inside operation. My favorite jobs, however, and those which most related to my professional interests, were those in which I cultivated a love for the outdoors and a reverence for nature.

I offer a respect for the outdoors and a desire to be a steward.

In the summer of 1995 I was a senior counselor at a well respected camp for boys called Camp Verity, and since graduating from college I have worked in Vail, Colorado, as a Professional Ski Patroller, a job which has required extensive training in areas related to search and rescue, medical emergency care, and other areas. I have become well acquainted with the day-to-day problems involving the environment and natural resources which I sincerely seek to protect through sensible actions that balance the need for growth with the need for conservation. Equipped with a law degree, I believe I can be a powerful tool for practical problem solving in the area of environmental stewardship in the 21st century.

WHY SHOULD YOU BE SELECTED TO ATTEND LAW SCHOOL?

This essay is intended to emphasize his capacity for hard work and ingenuity. Know the points you are trying to make in your essay. Don't just "drift" from thought to thought in an incoherent pattern.

DEVELOP A SUMMARY OF THE OVERALL GOAL YOU HAVE FOR YOUR LIFE.

DEVELOP A SUMMARY OF THE OVERALL GOAL YOU HAVE FOR YOUR LIFE.

Essays provide an opportunity for the admissions committee to see how you write, how you think, and how you feel. Don't be afraid of showing your emotion.
Note: This essay was written especially for a school which is strongly religious.

I feel that God is calling me toward a legal career which involves playing a role in shaping family law policy and intervention in the U.S.

I have a great respect for family values and the sanctity of familial bonds, and since earning my B.S. degree in Social Work, I have worked as a family counselor for the City of Detroit. Working with fractured families, families for whom crime is a daily reality, I have become knowledgeable of the legal system in a hands-on way. I have also seen how the law can unintentionally hurt the indigent.

Just recently a family that I have aided over an extended period of time has been able to send their eldest child to college. I have seen first-hand the dangers individuals encounter when they are without representation. I want to be part of shaping and defending children's rights policies in the U.S., and I believe my talent for working with people would make me an effective legal consensus builder between those who want to save family structure and those who want to provide the best environment for children.

A lawyer for a woman whom I have counseled has offered to assist me by providing an internship position with his firm, provided that I am accepted to law school. I have a passionate desire to work in the public service arena, but I know that passion alone is not enough. I know a legal education is the necessary tool I need in order to do the good I envision.

I have examined your university's second and third-year elective courses and feel that they, along with the Christian philosophy that your university endorses, are tailored to my spiritual needs and professional goals.

SPECIAL FACTORS AFFECTING MY UNDERGRADUATE EDUCATION

I would respectfully ask the admissions committee to consider the following factors in evaluating my undergraduate academic record. After receiving a $1,000 academic scholarship to Georgia College and State University, I enrolled and began my academic career in my hometown of Milledgeville, Georgia. I got off to a good start academically and was elected a Senator in Student Government.

Then I made a poor decision to transfer to Georgia Perimeter College in Clarkston, Georgia, because my best friend was there and I wanted to "get away from home." After declaring my major as pre-med, I chose to enroll in some of the most difficult pre-med courses offered and joined a fraternity. My grades suffered as I began to realize that attending medical school was not my choice but the choice my parents had encouraged me to make. That realization was also the birth of my decision to apply to law school after college; I had "grown up" to a new level and had a fresh understanding of my professional goals.

I then transferred to Mercer University-Macon in Macon, Georgia, declared my major in Political Science and Political Philosophy, and went inactive in my fraternity after one semester in order to concentrate on academics. As a senior, I performed with distinction in a graduate-level course in International Law, for which I wrote and orally defended a 50-page paper on Cuban Refugees. Once I found my true academic "fit" and realized my career goal, my grades began to improve, although my GPA is not as strong as I would like it to be.

I ask that the admissions committee examine the attached resume because you will see that I am a hard worker who has held part-time and summer jobs since I was 15 years old. I am very proud of my parents and grateful to them for their parenting of me, but I feel that my uneasy undergraduate years also reflect my desire to seek my own identity apart from my two exceptionally talented parents—my mother owns and manages a large website business, and my father is a successful convenience store entrepreneur. In a way, I grew up under the shadow of two strong and successful business people and I believe my undergraduate years were a struggle to discover my own identity and God-given talents.

Going to law school is not the "easy way out" for me. The "easy way out" would be for me to accept a professional home in either my mother's or my father's company. But I feel strongly that the study of law is what will best equip me personally to combine my analytical skills, public speaking ability, capacity for hard work, and sincere instinct for public service. I am an individual who lives by high principles and morals, and I feel certain I would one day be a credit to the law profession as I make contributions in public sector policymaking.

SPECIAL FACTORS AFFECTING MY UNDERGRADUATE EDUCATION
If you are presented with such a question, view it as an opportunity to explain a weak area in your background.

REVIEW YOUR RESPONSES AND STATE ANY ADDITIONAL INFORMATION THAT MIGHT HELP TO GIVE AN ACCURATE PICTURE OF YOUR PERSONAL, SPIRITUAL, ACADEMIC, AND PROFESSIONAL GOALS.

REVIEW YOUR RESPONSES AND STATE ANY ADDITIONAL INFORMATION THAT MIGHT HELP TO GIVE AN ACCURATE PICTURE OF YOUR PERSONAL, SPIRITUAL, ACADEMIC, AND PROFESSIONAL GOALS.

Here is an essay written for a law school which is strongly religious in orientation.

I am a person who never gives up. Even when I hit a low point in college, wondering what I really needed to be doing with my life, I never felt like quitting for a moment. I am a tough, resilient, persevering individual and, indeed, even my current job as a Paramedic requires utmost discipline at all times. I take my commitments very seriously, and I am seriously committed to undertaking the study of law.

Although my personal, spiritual, academic and professional goals may seem eclectic if viewed from afar, they are closely tied by the underlying desire to achieve, become, and succeed.

My personal goals include bettering my rock-climbing skills and eventually scaling one of the highest peaks in my area. I am also an accomplished runner. I believe firmly in community commitment and volunteer time to teach inner city children self reliance as well as teamwork through learning to function in the wilderness.

Spiritual goals are so often difficult to define. I am firmly committed to growing spiritually and am convinced that God is leading me. My main spiritual goal is to do what is right according to my religious beliefs.

Academically I hope to graduate from your program near the top of my class. I am determined to absorb the law as fully as humanly possible. I also hope to become involved in student organizations that assist the local legal community in providing *pro bono* work for the elderly and impoverished.

Professionally I hope to one day be a leader in the field of law. Although I am currently not sure what area I wish to specialize in, I feel that my competitive spirit and drive to excel will aid in me in any endeavor that I undertake.

DO YOU FEEL THAT UNDERGRADUATE GPA IS A GOOD INDICATOR OF AN INDIVIDUAL'S CAPACITY FOR INTENSE STUDY?

I do not believe my undergraduate GPA is a good indicator of my intellect and capacity for intense study.

I would respectfully ask that the Admissions Committee look at my GPA and consider the fact that I was uncertain of my professional goals during my college years. I entered college at the very young age of seventeen. I was unprepared for the level of self-discipline and academic rigors with which I was faced. I suddenly found that, although I had the self-discipline required to maintain academic viability, I did not possess the desire to achieve my full potential. I felt aimless. I considered leaving college but I possess a tenacious personality not given to quitting. Although I struggled for the first half of my college career, a fact that my grade point average reflects, the second half of my college career was exemplary. As I matured, I was elected president of the college newspaper, The Source. Then, I took a class that changed my life. The class, Courts and Criminal Procedures, was required for my degree in journalism. I quickly became enthralled with the law. I changed my major to pre-law and suddenly found myself excelling academically. I found my strong communication and analytical skills could best be utilized in the legal arena. My initial lack of focus during my undergraduate career had a negative impact on my GPA, but out of that turbulence was born the firm conviction that I belong in the legal arena working to assure that we meet the responsibilities placed reverently on our shoulders by our forefathers when they signed the constitution that governs us to this day. I am a tireless worker with great intellectual acumen, and I regret that my GPA does not clearly reveal that. At age 25, I now have a clear vision of what my goals are and how they may be achieved. I ask the Admissions Committee to look beyond my cumulative GPA and see the fact that I was in the midst of a great personal and professional transition which is explained more fully in the next paragraph.

WHAT HAVE BEEN YOUR GREATEST BLESSINGS AND OBSTACLES?

I am very grateful to my parents and value the strong example they both have provided for me in being moral, hard-working individuals. They provided me with exceptional care, educational opportunities, and spiritual guidance. When I graduated at seventeen, they feared that I would not attend college if I did not enroll immediately. Living up to their high standards has always been important to me, but after beginning my college education, I realized that I should have taken a year to grow and mature before devoting myself to college. It was a hard lesson, but one that taught me that only I know the appropriate direction for my life. My undergraduate GPA reflects this struggle to find out who I was and what I wanted to do with my life. I think that this growth period in my life was essential, if difficult, and provided me with the gift of perspective that I had previously lacked. It enabled me to recognize the perfect fit my talents and goals have with the legal field when I first studied criminal law. I could have dropped out of college when I first encountered difficulties and thereby preserved my GPA. That would have been the easiest thing for me to do, but it would have betrayed my belief in perseverance in the face of uncertainty. My parents cast a long shadow, and I believe I was in their shadow until my sophomore year of college, when I began to find my own shadow and define my own career goals.

DO YOU FEEL THAT UNDER-GRADUATE GPA IS A GOOD INDICATOR OF AN INDIVIDUAL'S CAPACITY FOR INTENSE STUDY?

This essay question could be viewed as an opportunity to wax philosophical or "sound like a lawyer," or it could be used as an opportunity to explain a low GPA in one's past academic record.

WHAT HAVE BEEN YOUR GREATEST BLESSINGS AND OBSTACLES?

DESCRIBE HOW YOUR PROFESSIONAL LIFE HAS PREPARED YOU FOR THE STUDY OF LAW.

DESCRIBE HOW YOUR PROFESSIONAL LIFE HAS PREPARED YOU FOR THE STUDY OF LAW.

As an applicant to the Doctor of Laws degree program at Cornell University School of Law, I am a proven performer in both the academic and professional arena. In 1995 I completed a four-year Bachelor's degree from Wilkes University in Wilkes-Barre, PA, in Paralegal Technology and Methodology, and I was honored by selection as a Representative in two prestigious pleading contests and public law competitions.

Since 1997 I have worked as a paralegal for a Superior Court Judge. With a reputation as an astute thinker and insightful writer, I have assisted in drafting written opinions, a legal document containing an opinion on the legalities of the Middle East Peace Treaty, as well as a pamphlet on racial discrimination at work. From 1995-97, I was a highly respected paralegal and research aide in the prestigious Cameron & Brown law firm, which specialized in preserving the constitutional rights of inmates. We pioneered and established many administrative procedures in the New York state detention system related to parole hearings, transfer hearings, temporary leave hearings, illegal detention procedures, and survey and revision procedures to verify sentencing period time. I worked with attorneys practicing immigration law for refugees as well as with international students, investors, and exporters. I have also performed extensive pro bono work which involved directing and referring victims of criminal acts to government resources, organizing judicial and social clinics, and coordinating the transition of young offenders between correctional centers and their families. While earning my undergraduate degree, I also worked for the U.S. Border Patrol. I can offer outstanding professional references throughout the academic and professional communities in New York and Pennsylvania. In 1999, my husband and I founded a software company in New Canaan, NY, called Braintrust Communications, and I have handled all legal aspects of opening and operating the company. It is my intention to practice law in the U.S. in two main areas:

(1) I wish to acquire specialized expertise in the area of patent law and intellectual property law since the protection of original software is a vital ingredient in the long-term success of Braintrust Communications, the business co-founded by my husband and me.

(2) I also wish to continue to work in the areas of criminal law and human rights law for which I am well respected in New York. I am seeking the overview of the American legal system and instruction in written tasks expected of American law practitioners which the Cornell University program provides, and I believe my experience as a paralegal will be an asset to the program.

DO YOU FEEL THERE IS A CORRELATION BETWEEN UNDERGRADUATE GPA AND SUCCESS IN ADVANCED STUDIES?

Undergraduate GPA is not always a reliable indicator of a person's ability to succeed in areas of advanced study.

I would respectfully ask that the Admissions Committee look at my GPA and consider the extenuating circumstances that accompanied the attainment of this average. My father and mother have worked their entire lives to ensure that they could send their only child to college. My father is a plumber and my mother is a housekeeper. They have never been wealthy but they made my education their priority and their dream. I had no idea when I left for college that my mother had been diagnosed with cancer. She threatened dire consequences to anyone who told her secret to me. She feared that I would drop out of college if I knew, sacrificing my dreams for her as she had always done for me. Eventually my father could no longer care for her alone and I was told the truth. I returned home and transferred to a small local college. I was the primary caretaker of my mother for the two years that she fought cancer. She is now healthy and cancer free, but the burden of caring for my mother through surgeries and chemotherapy took its toll. I could not provide the care my mother deserved and maintain the grades that I know otherwise I would have achieved. I do not regret the exchange made. I feel my care was instrumental in my mother's survival. A nurse or other caretaker could not have provided her with the emotional support necessary to recover from such a devastating illness. The fact that I remained a full-time college student through this period is proof that I am a dedicated hard worker. Given the opportunity to apply myself wholeheartedly to your curriculum, I can assure you that you will find my GPA to be a poor reflection of my analytical ability and communication skills. I appreciate the opportunity that I had to care for my mother as she had always cared for me and now ask that you see this inherent dedication for which I am known would be an incredible asset to your school and the legal community.

WHY ARE YOU ATTRACTED TO THE OHIO STATE SCHOOL OF LAW?

I am attracted to the Ohio State School of Law because of its fine curriculum and its leadership in the area of negotiation and mediation.

I am aware that the Ohio State School of Law is known for its commitment to academic excellence and has a commitment to training lawyers who will help develop a new ethic to guide the legal system through the 21st century.

I am aware of the Ohio Law Society and wish to become actively involved in it. In examining the curriculum, I liked the emphasis on mediation, counseling, and arbitration in the sixth semester, 3rd year, because I feel that many issues can be settled through skillful resolution of disputes using counseling, mediation, and arbitration.

I offer strong talents as a communicator, and I have excelled throughout my life in helping disputing parties "see" each other's point of view. I offer a proven ability to help others find common ground and form consensus, and I would like to play a role in helping the Ohio State School of Law pioneer its concept of finding solutions outside the congested courtroom.

DO YOU FEEL THERE IS A CORRELATION BETWEEN UNDERGRADUATE GPA AND SUCCESS IN ADVANCED STUDIES?

WHY ARE YOU ATTRACTED TO THIS PARTICULAR SCHOOL?
Admissions committees often ask a question like this to make sure that you understand what their "distinctive competence" is in relation to other law schools.

IS YOUR GPA AN ADEQUATE REFLECTION OF YOUR ABILITY?

IS YOUR GPA AN ADEQUATE REFLECTION OF YOUR ABILITY?

I am proud to be the son of migrant workers. My Mexican culture is a cherished part of me. It is a culture that has blessed me greatly and at times been a liability. English is not my first language and schooling during my formative years was always secondary to following the crops. The deficit was difficult to overcome. I did not begin to learn English until I entered the first grade. I became proficient at spoken English fairly rapidly but written English remained a problem for me. Through high school, I studied endlessly and still only managed mediocre grades. I found that I spent so much time trying to translate what was being said that I did not have time to then comprehend it before an examination was given. The problem continued throughout my college career. However, I refused to give up and graduated from college, the first of my parents' twelve children to do so. I used to blame my parents for not teaching me English earlier in life but my struggles in school have taught me more than I would have ever learned if grades had come very easily, and the firm cultural foundation in which my parents grounded me has allowed me to be at ease in any environment. The plight of the migrant farm workers in the United States is a sad one. Legal representation is a luxury not often extended to them. I feel that my dedication to your program would eventually transform me into an excellent lawyer who could fight on behalf of the migrants and their civil rights which are frequently violated. In the words of Lyla Cox, "It isn't the length of the race, but he who finishes that is to be exalted." I am one who finishes those things to which I fervently commit. I hope you will view my GPA as what it is, an inadequate reflection of the value I could add to the profession on behalf of your university and my people.

INDICATE YOUR GREATEST STRENGTHS AND ABILITIES AND DESCRIBE THEIR RELATIONSHIP TO YOUR GOALS.

INDICATE YOUR GREATEST STRENGTHS AND ABILITIES AND DESCRIBE THEIR RELATIONSHIP TO YOUR GOALS.

Throughout junior and senior high school, I was considered a "born leader" and I have used that leadership in positive ways. For example, in my freshman year, I was elected a Senator in Student Government Association. I also have an ease for being in front of the public. For example, in high school I was chosen for the lead in several school plays and I was selected as Master of Ceremonies for the Northern High School annual beauty pageant. I believe in the concept of "a strong mind in a strong body" and I was a distinguished soccer player in high school and was named "All Conference" my junior and senior years. Finally, I offer a high degree of curiosity, natural creativity and resourcefulness, exceptional intellect, and a hard-working nature that are suited to law.

WHAT WOULD YOU CONSIDER YOUR WEAKNESSES TO BE?

WHAT WOULD YOU CONSIDER YOUR WEAKNESSES TO BE?

I have a sensitive nature, and I am working on my ability to accept criticism in a gracious way. I often understand that the criticism is intended to help and guide, but sometimes I allow it to wound me, and I am trying to "toughen up" so that I can withstand even harsh criticism if I need to. Another weakness is that I hate to fail at anything. That does not keep me from trying new things, however, if I decide after careful analysis that it is the right thing to do. Mother Theresa said once, "God did not call me to be successful; he called me to be faithful." I think I know what she means but I still hate to fail at anything.

WHY ARE YOU COMMITTED TO THE STUDY OF LAW?

I am passionately committed to embarking upon the study of law in order to play a key role in advocating victims' rights and practicing criminal law.

After earning my B.S. degree in Political Science, I left college with the intention of applying to law school after working for a year or so to save money. I was drawn to my current job because of my respect for justice, and while working in this environment, I have become passionately dedicated to victims' rights and to the goal of ensuring that the perpetrators of illegal activity are brought to justice. I am currently working as an assistant at the local district attorney's office. The dedication that the professionals at this office have demonstrated has filled me with the deepest respect not only for them, but also for their vocation. I have come to love researching and understanding the law and seeing how it affects victims and criminals firsthand. I am, however, frustrated at my limited involvement in the legal process. I want to be a part of a system that I have seen work. As an advocate for victims and doggedly determined defender of justice, I feel my anticipated reputation as an effective prosecutor and tireless advocate would reflect admirably on your institution should you accept me.

WHY ARE YOU COMMITTED TO THE STUDY OF LAW?

SUMMARIZE THE MOST SIGNIFICANT EXPERIENCES AND ACHIEVEMENTS OF YOUR PROFESSIONAL LIFE.

As the only daughter of hard-working parents, I am proud of the numerous jobs I have held since I was 15 years old. I displayed my business skills in high school when I started a security business with a friend for which we developed and served a regular clientele while grossing $6,000 over the summer. For four summers I worked at this business and in other service jobs. I have also been a Big Sister through the Big Brothers/Big Sisters Program. These experiences have given me invaluable time-management and organizational skills.

SUMMARIZE THE MOST SIGNIFICANT EXPERIENCES AND ACHIEVEMENTS OF YOUR PROFESSIONAL LIFE.

WHAT PROFESSIONAL GOALS WOULD YOU LIKE TO ACHIEVE DURING YOUR LIFETIME?

Equipped with a law degree, I would like to work in the public sector helping to formulate appropriate solutions for problems of air pollution, toxic substances, hazardous wastes, water pollution, threats to wildlife and other natural resources, and balancing building needs with conservationist desires. I would consider at some point in my career running for political office, since I am confident that I have the charismatic personality, public speaking skills, and high personal principles which I feel are needed in someone who is elected to a position of public trust. I want to use the law degree so that I can be a force for shaping public policy in a positive way.

WHAT PROFESSIONAL GOALS WOULD YOU LIKE TO ACHIEVE DURING YOUR LIFETIME?

PERSONAL STATEMENT OF Alex Whein
University of Michigan School of Law

What are the special factors affecting your undergraduate education?

WHAT ARE THE SPECIAL FACTORS AFFECTING YOUR UNDERGRADUATE EDUCATION?

I would respectfully ask the admissions committee to consider the following factors in evaluating my undergraduate academic record. After graduating from college with a degree in Business, I entered the work force. For several years now I have been a successful salesman. I have excelled in this profession but have never felt that it was my true calling. I have an innate desire to help people, especially those that find themselves in situations where they cannot help themselves. I recently sold the product that I represent to a young widow. In the process of negotiating the sale, a friendship developed. This women confided in me the legal proceedings regarding her late husband's estate. Most of his estate had been legally robbed from her by an unscrupulous relative. She was unaware what a skilled attorney could offer her. These are the types of individuals that I want to assist. In my hometown, there is a nonprofit legal service to provide aid to the indigent and elderly. I have contacted this organization and they explained that there would be a position for me should I be accepted to law school.

As a young man in college, my studies were not of great import. I played football and enjoyed campus life, perhaps a bit too much. This is reflected in my GPA. I am now an established businessman with a highly successful wife and beautiful children. I feel my maturity and real-world experience would be an asset to the student body and your university as a whole. I am part of a growing population of returning "nontraditional" students. I would ask that you look at the stability and success that epitomize my current existence and recognize how these traits would translate into an attorney of irreproachable ethics and insight. As a salesman I have developed communication skills of the highest caliber. I have not, nor have I allowed my staff, to engage in dishonest sales practices and thereby set an example in the business community. I am accustomed to hard work and thrive on challenge. I ask you to consider these facts and balance them against a less than reliable gauge of a person's intellect such as a GPA.

WHAT DO YOU HAVE TO OFFER OUR PROGRAM?

WHAT DO YOU HAVE TO OFFER OUR PROGRAM?

As an experienced journalist, I offer a reputation for integrity, honesty, and high moral and ethical principles.

I believe I would enter the law profession not only with a clear vision of how I wish to use my law degree but also with an unwavering conviction that I would not compromise the high principles and values by which I live. In my job as a journalist, I have seen the infringement made upon individual rights increase exponentially. I feel that my talents could be better used fighting to defend the rights that were granted us under the laws that established our great nation: free speech and religious freedom and other concepts that I hold very dear. I am interested in working for the American Civil Liberties Union after graduation from law school, should I be accepted to your venerable institution. My undergraduate degree in Journalism and my GPA does not reflect the amount of dedication and commitment that I gave to school. As a single mother of two young children, attending college at all was an ambitious goal. I worked full time at a hospital on twelve-hour shifts to put myself through school. My children were young but very supportive of all that I was trying to achieve. They understood that I was attempting to make a better life for us. My proudest moment was when I donned my cap and gown and my children cheered as I received my degree. No, my GPA is not stellar. It is possible that I could have achieved a higher GPA but it would have been at the expense of the precious little time that I had with my children at that stage in my life. My children are now older and are again ready to support me as I pursue my dream of receiving my law degree. I work at a very flexible job as a freelance writer and am financially comfortable. The sheer determination that was required to get through a rigorous journalism program at a respected university while caring for my children and working should stand as a testament to what I can achieve if given the opportunity. I hope that you will recognize this and provide me with such an opportunity by accepting my application.

WHAT ATTRACTS YOU TO THE STUDY OF LAW?

I am attracted by the study of law because I perceive of a legal education as a tool which could be used as an instrument of God's plan in the world. I believe God does have plans for the environment in the 21st Century which he will need soldiers like myself to help achieve. Going to law school is not the "easy way out" for me. My prosperous father or my successful mother would love to make a home for me in their respective businesses, but I feel God has another plan. I believe he wants me to become a technical expert where the law is concerned so that I can then bring a God-centered approach to the formulation of environmental policies within our nation, states, and local areas.

WHAT DO YOU EXPECT TO OBTAIN FROM YOUR ACADEMIC EXPERIENCES?

Having studied the curriculum and compared it to the curriculum of other law schools, I feel that your curriculum will provide the solid foundation and overview of the legal system which I seek. With regard to elective courses, I am particularly interested in courses such as LAW 811 Land Use Planning, LAW 768 Environmental Law, LAW 783 Conflict of Laws, LAW 782 State and Local Government, and LAW 150 Administrative Law as well as others. The curriculum offered seems tailored to my interests, and the fact that the curriculum is offered within a strong Christian framework is a strong force beckoning me to apply.

WHAT ATTRACTS YOU TO THE STUDY OF LAW?

WHAT DO YOU EXPECT TO OBTAIN FROM YOUR ACADEMIC EXPERIENCES?

WHAT SKILLS DO YOU POSSESS THAT MAKE YOU MOST SUITED TO THE STUDY OF LAW?

My strong writing skills, public speaking ability, and powers of persuasion are well suited to the practice of law.

I am a strong writer, and in college I demonstrated that strength as I performed with distinction in a graduate-level course in International Law during my senior year in which I wrote and orally defended a 30-page paper on Age Discrimination and the Law.

I am attracted by your institution's emphasis on legal writing, and I feel I possess many natural talents for such specialized, technical writing. From the time I was a youth, I have been known for my excellent public speaking skills, which I refined as a member of the Debate Club during high school. As a member of the this club, I have argued my positions not only with passion and conviction, but more importantly, with factual research.

In high school, I led the Debate Team at state competition and delivered the winning argument regarding the Effectiveness of Transracial Adoption. I am comfortable being in the limelight and have been told many times that I am a gifted public speaker. I also offer the ability to communicate effectively with others one-on-one and in groups, and I feel that "power of persuasion" can be put to valuable use in the practice of law as I attempt to help disputing parties find a way to reach consensus.

Part Three: Master's Degree and PH.D. Programs
Essays and Personal Statements

In this section you will find essays used in applying for graduate schools and Ph.D. Programs.

Many essay questions invite you to provide revealing insights into your life experiences, philosophy, life goals, and most significant personal achievements and failures. The way you write is important, but the subject you choose to write about is also critical. Admissions committees are evaluating both your writing style and the content of your essay. Remember that admissions committees are looking to constitute their classes with unique, resourceful people so choose topics that will help to differentiate you from the dozens or hundreds of other competent, high-achieving individuals applying for a scarce number of spots.

LETTERS OF APPLICATION, ESSAYS, AND OTHER MATERIALS WRITTEN FOR ADMISSION TO GRADUATE SCHOOLS AND PH.D. PROGRAMS

The University of Vermont
Statement of Purpose

Name: _____   Date: _____

Having completed my undergraduate degree and gained practical experience in the working world, the next step in my career progression is to begin my graduate studies. It is my desire to attend graduate school at the University of Vermont and earn a Master's degree in Software Engineering and Systems.

After majoring in English while I lived on my own in my native country of Africa, I came to the United States in 1990 to be near my mother and sister. I studied programming at a local technical college, and then transferred to the University of Toledo and earned my Bachelor of Science in Computer Science, maintaining a 3.8 GPA in my major. After graduation, I applied these skills, overseeing computer operations and programming needs for my family's real estate business.

I authored accounting software, using the C++ language to develop an application that tracks accounts payable and receivable, balances and reconciles the company's bank accounts, and prepares billing statements, late notices, and other accounting documents. I also wrote a Pascal program that keeps track of repair and maintenance orders, maintenance orders completed, and estimates of labor cost and completion time. Using Microsoft Excel, I designed a database for the company's rental properties, with names of current tenants, addresses, and rental income generated. Although I was successful at this type of programming, it did not offer me the intellectual stimulation that I desire from my eventual career.

The University of Vermont's reputation as a truly international institution of higher learning was a major factor in my decision to apply. With students from 130 countries, this cultural diversity made it a natural choice for someone who was not born in this country.

One of my main career interests is to work as a Software Engineer for a government organization, such as the CIA, where my native knowledge of African dialects and culture will be of special benefit. The opportunity to serve as the interface between such an organization and its African counterpart would be the best use of my unique background and abilities. The University of Vermont, with its proximity to the headquarters of these organizations, will provide greater opportunities when I begin to apply for internships.

My practical work experience, undergraduate studies, and personal interests all support my decision to study Software Engineering and Systems. In addition to the requirements for my major, at the University of Toledo, I studied related Mathematics and Computer Information Systems courses to prepare me for advanced studies in this field. This program will develop my knowledge of programming theories and methods, honing skills that will allow me to design software systems to solve real-world problems.

With wide and varied opportunities to participate in software design projects, research, and development, I feel that The University of Vermont will offer me the mental challenges and competitive atmosphere that will allow me to excel in my career.

DESCRIBE THE MOST SIGNIFICANT INFLUENCING FACTORS IN YOUR LIFE AND DISCUSS YOUR GREATEST CONTRIBUTIONS.

It is my belief that positive role models and an innate desire to work with children were the primary forces that influenced me to choose teaching as a career.

I was very fortunate to have had supportive, caring, talented, and devoted teachers as role models when I was a child. The manner in which they presented themselves and their obvious love for teaching inspired me to want to be a teacher.

My innate desire to work with children was another influencing factor. This gift has been reflected in aptitude tests throughout my school career. I have always had a good rapport with children, even from an early age. As a child, I loved to "play school" and "teach" the neighborhood children. Furthermore, I wrote short plays and "directed" my siblings and friends in neighborhood productions. I had a yearning for sharing knowledge with my peers. This passion manifested itself, and I knew that, when it came time to declare my major in college, it would be education.

The greatest contributions I have made in education are those that are not tangible to the touch, but to the minds and hearts of my students. By presenting myself as a positive role model each day in class, I feel I am making an impression that will last a lifetime with these young boys and girls. Kind words, understanding, fairness, and patience have been motivating and contributing factors to success in school for my students.

The giving of my time, talents, and knowledge are also contributions I have made to education. Imparting those essentials to students, parents, and co-workers has contributed to positive growth and learning experiences.

I felt very honored by being selected *Teacher of the Year* by the members of my faculty. It is an accomplishment equated to the "icing on the cake." Being recognized for that which you love to do is truly special and rewarding.

Another specific accomplishment that comes to mind is my being a part of an Inclusion Program last year. Three high-functioning autistic students were "included" in my class. Making these students part of a regular classroom and having them achieve success was a heartwarming accomplishment.

Chairing, organizing, and implementing a behavior management plan for students last year was another accomplishment. Students that consistently followed school rules were allowed to attend "Wonderful Wednesdays" during which they were treated to special entertainment. Those students who needed to work on their behavior were sent to "It's Your Choice" to participate in cooperative lessons to reinforce positive behavior.

Earning a master's degree will help to enhance my performance in the classroom and provide me with the tools I need in order to make greater contributions within the educational arena.

DESCRIBE THE MOST SIGNIFICANT INFLUENCING FACTORS IN YOUR LIFE AND DISCUSS YOUR GREATEST CONTRIBUTIONS.

DESCRIBE YOUR COMMITMENT TO COMMUNITY.

Commitment to my community first lies in giving the students with whom I work the best education available. Secondly, I am committed to the families of my students. Last Christmas, I, along with representatives of several local corporations, provided clothes for one of my students and his siblings. When there is a need such as this, I cannot help but respond.

I am deeply committed to my church, the Calvary United Methodist Church, having taught Sunday School for many years there before becoming an active member of the adult choir. As an active member of the church, I feel a genuine concern and responsibility for our youth. During 1998, I served on the Administrative Board and was the Chairperson for the Council of Children's Ministries, coordinating all children's programs for the year. One of the most successful programs offered was our Wednesday Evening Fellowship; the program included various community service persons from the Red Cross, the local museum, the arts council, the county library, and several area utility companies. I was nominated in 2000 for a three-year term as Chairman of the church's Education Committee and, in that capacity, we have instituted a "Reading is Fun" Program with a nearby elementary school in which children are paired up after school, one day a week, to read with a church volunteer. The aim of this program is to increase the reading competency of at-risk elementary school children. The elementary school with which we are working says it is a tremendously popular program for which there is a waiting list of children anxious to be selected, and we are pleased that it has not been tainted with a reputation as a program for "slow learners."

TELL US ABOUT YOUR PERSONAL BELIEFS.

I believe that teaching is one of the most rewarding and demanding jobs in our nation. As a teacher, you possess the seeds of knowledge for the future. How you choose to sow those seeds determines famine or plenty.

There have been many changes in my philosophy of teaching since my entering the field 19 years ago. I have prided myself in being flexible and creative enough to try different teaching styles. **It appears to me that no matter what style you use, the key to student success is motivation.**

It is known that it is much easier to chase a child than to drag him. This is a philosophy that I support. By showing students respect, giving them choices, and making them feel that they belong, you create an environment that provides important elements for motivation. Motivate a child and you will be well along the way to school success.

One factor which I feel makes me an outstanding teacher is that I accept all children as they come to me in their own unique packages. Physical impairments or learning disabilities do not influence my expectations of each student. I emphatically impress upon my students that they need to strive to do their best always and to meet each challenge with a positive frame of mind.

The rewards I receive from teaching come through everyday experiences:
* the smile on a child's face when he finally learns the multiplication tables;

- the excitement in a child's eyes when she learns how to form a word in cursive;
- the pat on the back from a co-worker for help you rendered;
- the former student who drops by to let you know how much he liked your class;
- the parent who calls to express appreciation for all you did to help his or her child.

DESCRIBE YOUR PERSONAL TEACHING STYLE.

My beliefs about teaching are reflected each day through my personal teaching style. **I am an advocate of cooperative learning and incorporate cooperative lessons in everyday planning.** As previously mentioned, my philosophy centers around motivation as the key to success. I use cooperative lessons to motivate students in my class. Learning is not a solitary activity, and hands-on experiences and the sharing of ideas instill confidence in children. Through cooperative learning, students are able to make choices, share thoughts, and have positive interactions among themselves.

Teaching, rather than telling, is another part of my personal teaching style. The incorporation of the SCIS Program is an effective tool in supporting this philosophy. Rather than giving all the answers, the children are able to explore with me to find the answers. It is a pleasure to chase my students rather than drag them!

WHAT DO YOU THINK ARE THE MAJOR ISSUES FACING PUBLIC EDUCATION?

Violence, teacher accountability, inclusion, testing, and illiteracy are what I consider to be the major public education issues of today. Violence is what I look upon as the most serious problem facing our schools in the new millennium. The spread of violence is on the rise. Its causes are numerous and its effects are devastating.

Unfortunately, more and more children are being abused or exposed to abusive situations in the home. Research has proven that abused children become abusive themselves as they grow older. These children do not know how to deal with their emotions and react impulsively, often causing harm to others.

A wrong message is being sent to our youth through the airwaves. Violence is being portrayed as funny in certain children's cartoons and television programs. Our youth see violence as brave and macho in today's movies. Teens listen to violent lyrics in music. Popular music channels celebrate violence toward women and others.

Our schools are being exposed to more violence because of the formation of gangs. Gangs encourage youth to steal, intimidate, carry and use weapons, become involved in drugs, fight, and sometimes kill.

The effects of violence are being carried over into our schools at an alarming rate. More and more children are coming to school with low self-esteem and psychological problems as a result. Another result of violence is that we are losing more and more youth at the hands of others or because of suicide. How it saddens me to hear that a young life has been so needlessly destroyed.

There is no one clear-cut way to resolve the problem of violence. I do believe there are steps that can be taken to begin the process of turning this problem around.

DESCRIBE YOUR PERSONAL TEACHING STYLE and WHAT DO YOU THINK ARE THE MAJOR ISSUES FACING EDUCATION TODAY? These essays are intended to make this individual come across not just as a competent teacher but as a unique, caring, thinking individual who cares deeply about her work and the impact it has on those whom she teaches.

First, we must have better psychological counseling in our schools for victims of violence. We cannot count on parents to provide the proper mental health care for their children.

Next, as educators, parents, or concerned members of society, we can write television companies, movie studios, and recording artists to express our concerns about violence and the effects their medium has on our youth.

We can provide afterschool programs for our youth to encourage them to stay off the streets and out of trouble. I envision a joint effort with the community in establishing programs in sports, homemaking, art, music, dance, and a multitude of other disciplines that would enrich the lives of our youth rather than take their lives. Through my chairmanship of my church's Education Committee, I have seen how partnerships between neighborhood churches and schools can bear fruit, as demonstrated through the "Reading is Fun" program for 50 at-risk children sponsored by our church and a local elementary school. I also celebrate the efforts of our police chief in teaching martial arts classes to youth who are seeking physical expression of their aggressions.

I believe that it is shortsighted not to include the building of gymnasiums when money is raised through bond issues for the building of new schools or the renovation of existing schools. I would love to see the local school gymnasium become the "hangout" for children after school. I have never seen a child who enjoyed anything more than throwing, kicking, or playing with a ball. Gymnasiums at our schools could do much to keep children off the street. Children need inexpensive physical outlets for their considerable youthful energies.

Finally, the continuation of programs such as D.A.R.E. and the proliferation of other enrichment programs are a must. We need more programs like this in our schools to properly educate youth concerning the consequences of drug involvement and acts of violence.

HOW WOULD YOU IMPROVE THE TEACHING PROFESSION?

I feel that one of the best ways I can strengthen and improve the teaching profession is **to strengthen and improve myself** both professionally and personally. Presenting myself as a professional and positive role model to the public exhibits success and strength.

Continuing education through staff development, workshops, conventions, and professional magazines keeps me informed and updated with key issues and new trends in education. It has always been a habit of mine to share information, ideas, and materials with my co-workers. Through this type of sharing, we can gain strength and grow professionally. Teachers are, by definition, mentors for other teachers.

Participating in professional organizations is another way to improve and strengthen the teaching profession. These organizations provide educators many opportunities to promote education in the community and have a say in the decision-making process within the profession. I believe I am doing my part to strengthen the profession through my role as building representative for two professional organizations.

Serving as mentors to student teachers and beginning teachers is a major way in which we can strengthen our profession. In this complex and fast-paced age in which technological advances place a strain on all of us just to "keep up," I think it is imperative that we all find opportunities to share our knowledge and discoveries with others.

One thing I like about teaching is that it is cooperative rather than competitive. If we were in the business world, our peers might well be our competitors and we would be well advised to safeguard our insights and our knowledge. I enjoy working in an environment in which I can share my knowledge.

WHAT DO YOU FEEL IS THE BEST FORM OF ACCOUNTABILITY?

It is sad, but true, that most of the public views standardized test scores as the basis for teacher accountability. I do not accept this viewpoint and take issue with those who feel that one test at the end of the school year measures all that has been taught. Furthermore, a test score is not always a true indicator of what a child has or has not attained.

In my opinion, **teachers should be accountable for student success.** Realistically, however, we know that some children will never score well on tests; therefore, I believe we need to reassess the tool or tools we use to measure success.

Student portfolios may be better indicators of what has been achieved throughout the year and give a more accurate representation of student growth. Portfolios would reveal documentation of the day-by-day achievements of the students and help the teacher better assess students' needs. Teachers should then be held accountable for ensuring that students achieve success at their own developmental level.

PERSONAL STATEMENT OF KATHRYN DIANGELO

PERSONAL STATEMENT AS PART OF AN APPLICATION TO GRADUATE SCHOOL IN PURSUIT OF A MASTER'S DEGREE

An essay is an opportunity to provide an intensely personal glimpse into who you are, where you've been, why you've done some of the things you've done, and what goals you envision for the future.

I was born in New York, New York, to working class parents. My father worked at a factory and my mother stayed home to raise us. I took for granted the fact that she picked up me and my two sisters from school in the afternoons, stood over us as we did our homework at the kitchen table, and was involved in our school activities. I believe I have been "called" into the teaching profession, and I believe that God has given me abilities and talents that make me special as a teacher, but I did not realize that I wanted to be a teacher until I was working in a well paid job after college graduation.

In 1996 I graduated from Michigan State University with a B.S. in Biology and a minor in Chemistry. While in college, I was known as a campus leader and was appointed administrative aide of my 50-resident dorm. I was also elected Freshman Class Treasurer. Although I came from a family that loves me, I never had any encouragement from my family to attend college, and I am the only one of my sisters to this date who has graduated from college. I have always known that I wanted to "make something of myself," and I figured out that a college degree would help me do that. I met my husband, John, when I was a sophomore at MSU, and I found in him a "soul mate" who also wanted to achieve things in life. John was from a broken home but he had the attitude that "you are what you make of yourself." His confidence in himself and his confidence in me has been a major motivating force in my life.

After we graduated from Michigan State University, I found that there were many employers who wanted to hire young people with degrees in science. My B.S. degree in Biology with a minor in Chemistry helped me land a job at Parker Laboratories for $37,000 a year. I happily accepted the job and thought I was "set."

Although I excelled in my job at Parker Laboratories and was told I had a bright future with the company, something was missing. I couldn't quite put my finger on what was missing, but when I began to analyze what I wanted professionally, I began to realize that I am happiest when I am around children. I had worked with children in a work-study program at the Child Care Center at MSU while earning my college degree, and I had thoroughly enjoyed feeling needed and feeling that I was making a difference in the lives of sensitive, fragile young people. Knowing that a career move to teaching would require a cut in salary as well as other adjustments, I cautiously discussed my feelings with my husband, and he wholeheartedly encouraged me to "follow my heart" and give teaching a chance. In January of 1998 I was hired as a 6th grade teacher at Fallworth Elementary School as a lateral-entry teacher, and I taught all subjects in a self-contained classroom. In my second year at Fallworth, I was singled out by the principal for the Professional Development Award, and that honor signified to me that someone else besides me could see that I had gifts and talents that were well suited to teaching! That honor gave me the encouragement I needed to complete teacher certification courses, and I became certified to teach math and science.

Since receiving that first award recognizing my teaching accomplishments, I have added the Dedicated Educator Award, the PTA Appreciation Award, and the Teacher of the Year Award. I am humbled and gratified by these honors, and I am even more convinced now that I have been called to teach middle school children. My greatest contributions and accomplishments in education are the lives I have helped to shape and the minds I have taught. I believe that I cannot teach a mind unless I first shape an attitude—so I always approach teaching with the attitude that I must first communicate to my students that I respect them and that I want their respect in return. I do demand excellence in all things, but I am a role model for the excellence I ask them to strive for, and they can always see me working hard and "practicing what I preach."

I have learned that middle school children are LOUD because they want to be listened to, so I bring a respectful, listening style of teaching into my classroom. I am a self-disciplined person who believes that, without discipline, one cannot accomplish much in life, so I strive to instill in my students the desire to set high goals and be disciplined in achieving them.

One example of the effectiveness of my style is a teaching assignment I had recently at Caison Middle School. The principal asked me to take over a class of "trouble-makers" which had lost two teachers in rapid succession. I agreed. Within a few months, I had built a relationship with those 7th graders, and students previously branded as troublemakers were setting high goals and achieving them. I take a very hands-on approach to the teaching of science, and middle school students love doing things and working with their hands rather than just studying theories from books.

I believe the best teachers are also cheerfully involved in activities outside the classroom. At Caison Middle School, I am very involved with the Junior Beta Club, which is essentially a junior honor society. We have bake sales and other events that help us sponsor the Academic Banquet each year which honors scholastic excellence.

I have been extensively involved, also, in community activities. I was Chairperson for the Committee to Elect Tom Smith for Commissioner of the town of Battle Creek. This was his first campaign for political election, and I was honored that he chose me to head his campaign. We performed extensive telemarketing, encouraged people to register to vote, helped transport people to the polls, conducted numerous educational events to explain the issues and explore voter concerns, and developed informational mailings. I was personally thrilled to see Tom elected for a variety of reasons, not the least of which is that he cares deeply about education and will aggressively support any initiatives which place priority on our children's educations and on their future.

I am also active in my church. As an active adult volunteer with the Youth Department at Kensington Baptist Church, I am constantly interacting with youth of all ages, from middle school up to high school. I coordinate a number of youth activities ranging from Bible studies to banquets, and I organize youth for church activities including reading Bible verses and helping with the choir. I also serve as a **church deaconess** and am extensively involved with the church's **missionary activities,** both in our own country and abroad. I have also played a key role in the **tutorial program** sponsored by the church in conjunction with Battle Creek County Schools. The program takes a different form and caters to different age groups each year, but this year the tutorial program is serving up to 45 children who are brought to the church after school one day a week for one hour after school. Through the program, volunteers are provided who assist the students in small groups in math, reading, and writing. I personally tutor the children involved in this program, and I have seen what a difference it can make in a child's life to know that "someone cares."

On numerous occasions, and without pay, I have tutored high school students in chemistry. I serve as **Executive Secretary** and also as a **Lady Attendant** for Michener's Funeral Home, and I derive satisfaction from helping the bereaved to cope with their loss and find some peace. I have extensively volunteered my time to **Girl Scout Troop 92** working with cadets and helping young girls develop high moral standards.

In summary, I can only say that I believe that teaching is a lifestyle, not just a job. I am proud that people look at me and think "teacher." I hope my greatest accomplishment is that the students I have taught have genuinely felt the love and respect which I had for them. **I believe great teaching starts with an attitude, just as I believe that all learning must begin with a good attitude.** It is the attitude which I try to shape and influence before I attempt to transmit content, and children always feel that I *want* to be in the classroom with them. Education cannot be separated from love and respect.

WHAT ARE YOUR TEACHING PHILOSOPHIES AND BELIEFS?

I have five main teaching beliefs.

1. **Respect the student.** I take the view that I cannot teach the brain until I break through the child's attitude. I have learned in teaching that an outwardly belligerent child is often using unruly behavior as a mask for his feelings of insecurity, so I respect the fact that the troublemakers are often experiencing problems and troubles both in and out of school. I use humor, warmth, eye contact, and listening to "get through" to students who are accustomed to "turning off" other teachers through their antagonistic behavior. On numerous occasions, I have seen students respond to the respect I show them by "chilling out" and calming down in my class. It is not uncommon for many middle school children to behave like ladies and gentlemen in my class and then go down the hall to another class and become a troublemaker. While respecting the student, I always create an environment in which the process of learning is itself respected by both teacher and students.

2. **Have fun in the learning process.** My students accuse me sometimes of "getting crazy" because they know I am open to field trips, science experiments, and many other types of experiences that bring concepts "to life." Middle school children are extremely physical creatures, and I try to channel their tactile behavior and physical aggression into hands-on learning experiences that will help them acquire a love for learning and "see" concepts in a different way.

3. **Be positive.** I try never to fall into the trap of responding to negative behavior with negative reactions myself. This is not always easy, especially when middle school children try to "act up." But I feel I often talk loudest through my actions, and I try to return negativism with a positive response. Children are often amazed by this response, but they do notice. A positive attitude is infectious, and I try to spread a positive attitude.

4. **Respect the learning environment (i.e., maintain discipline).** Learning cannot be accomplished in an uncontrolled environment, so one thing I communicate aggressively but positively to my students is that we will respect the learning environment.

I communicate clearly my expectations of high performance standards and good manners to each other in the classroom, but I communicate my expectations in a positive, enthusiastic manner without being condescending to students and without putting them down.

5. **Be enthusiastic.** Ask any student, and he or she will tell you the difference between a "good" teacher and a "bad" teacher: The good teacher wants to be in the classroom, and the good teacher is enthusiastic about his subject area.

My rewards in teaching

I chose teaching as a profession and made a career change from a job that paid me better in money. However, I enjoy the "pay" I receive through teaching when I see a child's eyes light up because he or she has learned, or when I see an antagonistic or indifferent attitude in a child become ruled by a positive, enthusiastic attitude. I left a well-paid job in industry for a teaching career, and I haven't looked back once and regretted my decision. I love teaching, and I feel well compensated in many areas. I abandoned a career in which I would have focused on corporate profitability for a career which gives me an opportunity to make a lasting difference in people's lives. I take very seriously the fact that how I treat a child may impact significantly on his or her ability to lead a productive and satisfying life. When I am entrusted with a child's mind, I am not only attempting to fill that mind with a certain amount of math and science knowledge. I am also attempting to help a sensitive and fragile human being develop an attitude of respect for learning and a love of learning so that my student will literally "fall in love" with learning and its rewards. Many students whom I have taught call me frequently because they know that I am approachable, that I am their friend, and that I care about them.

My beliefs are reflected in my teaching style.

My teaching style reflects my belief that, you must first influence the attitude before you can teach the mind. Many children whom I have taught have been transformed from outcasts into high achievers because their attitudes changed! I have seen that behavior problems are frequently a mask for fear and insecurity, and I have become even bolder in my philosophy that I must first influence the attitude and then teach the brain. Children must feel self confident before they can set high goals for themselves. So many children in today's society have no leadership or guidance in the home. Often they are in single-parent homes, where frequently the older siblings care for the younger ones, and it is not uncommon for many children in our region to go home to empty houses and then have parents who work at night. When they come to school, they are seeking love and affection and affirmation as much as anything else, and I am ready and willing to give them that love and affirmation! Of all the products that I could be associated with in the scientific community, I cannot think of one that would give me the joy that I receive from the opportunity to train a young mind and influence a young person in the development of his moral and ethical standards. I am proud to be a teacher and, on a daily basis, I try to be worthy of this high calling which I consider teaching to be! In an era of so much cynicism and indifference, I feel fortunate indeed to have found my "calling" in life—to be a teacher.

IF YOU WERE TO OBTAIN A PH.D. IN EDUCATIONAL ADMINISTRATION, WHAT WOULD BE THE KEY ISSUES FACING PUBLIC EDUCATION WHICH YOU WOULD ADDRESS?

There are many major public education issues today about which I feel strongly including:

1. **Accountability is lacking.** There is need for strong accountability in teaching and education, which I feel the ABC plan is addressing adequately.

2. **Support for education is lacking.** There is a lack of support for education and a lack of emphasis on education given to the children of lower-economic families.

3. **Parents are often lacking.** The fact is that many children in our society are latchkey children and are almost literally raising themselves, with parents working nearly all the time and unable to spend much time with their children. Since I myself am an African-American, I hope I will be perceived as objective when I say that I have especially noticed that the classes of "troublemakers" I have taught have been composed of African-American children. As a member of that race and culture, I feel I could do much to speak to that community and to reach out to that community's churches, families, and network to try to motivate them to help their children acquire strong personal values and an attitude of self-discipline.

4. **Unfortunately, violence is not lacking.** The sad fact is that so many children choose violence and fighting as a way of resolving their problems, and that truth is that our schools are not as safe as they should be. While there are many issues affecting public education about which I feel strongly, I would choose the issue of safety in schools as the issue I would like to address.

Our schools need to be a safe place!

It is vital to the educational process that we ensure a safe and orderly environment in order for quality teaching and learning to occur. It is no secret that many teachers, students, and parents are concerned that the school environment is not safe enough. We need a shared vision of a safe and effective school that would serve as a beginning point for planning. All schools should strive to increase or improve the order, discipline, and safety of the school environment, which will result in a more positive school climate or culture. I realize there may be different kinds of safety problems in elementary, middle, and high schools, so I would urge that a study group be convened at each school made up of students and teachers who could study the unique safety problems at that school.

My basic approach in choosing safety as a major public education issue is that I feel safety is as much an attitude and a value as it is anything else. It is a respect for safety and the nonviolent handling of problems that I feel should receive greater emphasis in our schools. The particular approach I would like to see taken in emphasizing safety is to use safety as way of promoting nonviolence and nonaggression. The type of "Safety First" program I have in mind is a way of teaching children values and helping them acquire a more disciplined approach to solving their problems than hitting someone or lashing out in anger.

Safety at elementary schools. I feel an emphasis on safety at the elementary school level would promote character development in young children by stressing that fighting and physical assaults will not be tolerated. I would also like to see safety stressed in all school-related activities such as fund raisers, since there have been a few instances when children crossing busy highways to sell fundraiser products have been killed. Safety First is as much a program to teach young children to handle their problems non-aggressively as it is a program about fire or building safety.

Safety at middle schools. In middle schools, there are major problems related to violence and intimidation, so the safety emphasis in middle schools would include a major emphasis on no fighting. Again, the emphasis on safety and on finding nonviolent and nonphysical avenues of solving problems is a way of helping middle school children learn values of self-discipline and self-control. I believe we must be firm in disciplining children who fight and who assault other children, but I believe the standard "detention" should be married up with educational programs—perhaps in video form—to help children understand concepts related to self control and anger control.

Safety in high schools. Hopefully a safety program at the middle school level would have acquainted youth with concepts related to self discipline and anger control, but safety violations may have to be dealt with more aggressively at the high school level. Our court systems use community service instead of jail time as a way of punishing/rehabilitating violent offenders in some situations, and I believe we could require our high school students who use violence and fighting to perform some community service as a form of retribution for their crimes. I do not think anyone "wins" when high school students do not graduate from high school, so I would use permanent expulsion as the totally last resort with our high school students who use violence and physical aggression against their peers.

In summary, I believe greater emphasis on safety in our schools is really a way of championing strong personal values of nonaggression and nonviolence as a means of solving problems.

Strengthening and improving the teaching profession

I came to teaching from the scientific community, where research and development are paramount and where "finding a better way of doing things" is always of utmost importance. In teaching as well, I strongly believe in "R & D" and in continuously reaching out to find new approaches. I have learned much from the staff development training I have taken, and I believe continuous training is a vital part of strengthening and improving the teaching profession.

I would, however, like to see some more funding provided for teachers who wish to participate in extensive training programs. If teachers could have access to a wider range of grants and fellowships in their pursuit of teaching excellence, I believe more teachers would take advantage of opportunities during the summers to improve their teaching techniques and subject knowledge. I would also like to see teachers rewarded for their initiatives in pursuing teacher training opportunities outside the classroom.

I believe I can personally strengthen and improve the teaching profession by my dedication and personal example. **I am a firm believer in the fact that a great deal can be accomplished by single individuals full of passion and purpose.** I am honored to be a part of the teaching profession and I am excited about making even more of a difference in the lives of children once I obtain my Ph.D.

This essay is a vehicle for discussing the issues about which she feels most passionate.

DESCRIBE YOUR TEACHING PHILOSOPHY AND THE VIEWS YOU WOULD ESPOUSE AS THE LEADER OF A SCHOOL SYSTEM ONCE YOU EARNED A PH.D.

Teachers are the professionals in our society who are most likely to influence the values, morals, and attitudes of the next generation. I take very seriously this privilege and this responsibility, and I believe I can strengthen and improve the teaching profession through my emphasis on "the whole child" and my belief that teachers must interact each day with the "whole child"—not just the child's brain but his or her emotions, insecurities, values or lack of them, and attitude. My approach is to educate the "whole child" and I believe I can make a significant contribution to the teaching profession by helping junior teaching professionals understand this concept and learn how to implement the proven techniques in the classroom I have found successful.

Accountability in the teaching profession: I support the ABC model.

I wholeheartedly endorse the ABC school-based accountability model which has been introduced to improve accountability in the teaching profession. Good teachers want to be accountable, and I believe the ABC model is a viable approach that will strengthen teaching. Here are three reasons why I support the ABC model.

1. Student performance on end-of-grade tests is measured. The **"A" stands for Achievement Levels,** and the ABC model identifies performance levels ranging from insufficient mastery to superior mastery, based on student performance on end-of-grade tests. It is vital that we identify where each student is in the learning process so that we can develop a suitable plan for raising performance.

2. Learning the basics of reading, writing, and arithmetic is measured.

The ABC Plan emphasizes **"The Basics," "B."** I believe the model is correct in emphasizing key skill areas of reading, writing, and mathematics. I look forward to the day when each student will master a foreign language before graduating from college, but we cannot get to that level of performance until students master the basics.

3. Each school's performance is measured. Finally, the ABC plan provides a **Composite Score, "C,"** so that each school can measure its aggregate performance and compare its performance to sister schools. I believe it is vital that each school knows how it is doing as a unit in order for teacher and student performance to improve.

The ABC Plan works.

After some experience with the ABC plan, I believe it provides methods for establishing standards and using accountability measures in the classroom that can facilitate and strengthen learning. I have personally been a major advocate behind the scenes of this new accountability system, and I have observed that many teachers who were resistant to this approach have come to see its value. This ABC plan was piloted in 10 states during the recent school year, and experiences in those states influenced the model. I have observed that the ABC plan as implemented in our state has provided the teaching staff with key areas to target. I would like to see a strong ABC Committee at each school made up of teachers, administrators, and PTA officers who would meet at least quarterly to review the requirements of the ABC plan and find resourceful ways to administer it. For example, such a committee might decide that more tutoring of at-risk students would be beneficial, so the PTA could assist in locating the needed volunteer resources. Parents are certainly needed to proctor the End-of-Grade tests, so again the committee could assist in finding volunteers who could assist with implementation of the ABC Plan. In summary, I would like to see the ABC plan recently introduced into our school system embraced and strengthened by both parents and teachers alike who share a common belief that quality education and mastery learning is our goal.

IF YOU WERE ELECTED SUPERINTENDENT OF THE YEAR, WHAT WOULD YOUR MESSAGE BE?

It is difficult for me to choose the main message I would communicate as Superintendent of the Year, because I feel passionate about both (1) the issue of accountability in the teaching profession and (2) the issue of school safety. I believe I could do much good communicating with teachers about the value of the ABC and about my own positive experiences with it. The ABC plan is in its infancy and is in need of enthusiastic advocates, and I believe I could be a major spokesperson for the benefits of this accountability model. Teachers need to view the ABC plan in a positive light, and I am positive I could "sell" the ABC plan to teachers.

However, I feel very strongly about the issue of school safety, and since I must identify the **one** issue I would choose as my main message, I choose school safety.

One thing all parents, teachers, and students can agree on is that our schools are not safe environments. It is inappropriate that students ever have to experience fear in a school environment, and I wish to be a powerful spokesperson for improving school safety. I have a three-point plan which I would recommend to all schools. My motto would be, "My Choice: Non-Violence!"

First, I would advocate the establishment of a committee at each school made up of students, parents, and educators who would be called the School Safety Committee. This committee would meet monthly during the school year, and students would be elected to serve on it. General safety issues would be discussed, and a subcommittee of this School Committee would function as a Disciplinary Court which would provide a "court of last resort" for students who are threatened with severe disciplinary action or expulsion. I believe many of the answers to school violence problems will be provided by the students, and this committee would get students involved in solving the problem.

Second, during my year as Superintendent of the Year I would encourage schools to choose suitable methods of emphasizing nonviolent methods of dispute resolution. From the student altercations I have seen, violence is used as a primitive method of solving a problem, so I would ask teachers to help students refine their problem-solving skills by learning techniques of mediation, negotiation, and arbitration. I would hope I could seek the assistance of the American Arbitration Association in sponsoring workshops and perhaps essay contests which celebrate nonviolent problem solving. I would choose Martin Luther King Day as a special opportunity to celebrate nonviolence in dispute resolution, and I believe Dr. King would heartily approve.

Third, I would emphasize to all communities and to parents the importance of their involvement in students' lives. The whole community must be involved in educating a child and in supporting the main themes espoused in the school environment.

DESCRIBE YOUR WORK AND ACCOMPLISHMENTS IN A PROGRAM OF SIGNIFICANCE WITH PUBLIC SCHOOLS

AN EXCITING NEW APPROACH—COMBINED EDUCATION

I had the pleasure of working as a change agent implementing a new educational approach within the Webster County School System, and that experience gave me new insight into my ability to formulate and implement change of a significant nature within the public school system.

Historically, students with moderate to severe disabilities have been educated in settings separate from non-handicapped peers.

During the past several years, parents and educators have advocated including students with moderate to severe disabilities in general education classrooms within their neighborhood schools. This concept is known as **combined education** and is being addressed nationally in public schools. **Combined education** is not a mandate but is an attempt to further meet the mandate of educating handicapped students to the maximum extent appropriate with non-handicapped peers.

From 1996-2000, I was involved in the committee that would study and implement **combined education** in the county schools. We realized that inclusion would require thoughtful planning and much staff development for all educational personnel and parents. We recognized that changing attitudes would be the first hurdle.

The first step--choosing a model. The first step was to determine a model to follow. After researching various models, our committee selected the Murphy Teaching Model which we had observed being implemented in Maine schools. The Murphy Teaching Model is "an educational approach in which general and special educators work to jointly teach heterogeneous groups of students in general education classrooms. Both teachers are simultaneously involved in instruction.

The second step--selecting an expert. We chose an expert to direct us through this change process. Dr. Howard Jennings, Associate Professor at Columbia University, was selected to be the lead consultant and to train our teachers. He is nationally recognized in the field of special education and combined classrooms.

The next step in implementing change was to sponsor top-quality staff development, and our process was to begin with a small number of "voluntary" schools. We had two high schools, two junior high schools, and two elementary schools during the first year of implementing the change.

The principals were designated as the first professionals to have staff development. As the instructional leaders of their schools, they had to be supportive of combined education if it was to be successful.

Staff development was then provided to teams of regular education and special education teachers.

After staff development, the model was implemented within the schools. The students with mild to moderate disabilities were selected to participate. These students were receiving special education from a traditional "pullout" model—one to three hours daily, rather than the more severely handicapped students who received most of their special education in a separate special education classroom. These were the students who would most likely obtain high school diplomas and would greatly benefit from instruction in a general education setting.

There were two options available to the teachers:

(1) Team teaching: The regular education teacher and the special education teacher jointly plan and teach the academic subject content to all students.

(2) Complementary instruction: The general education teacher maintains primary responsibility for teaching subject content and the special education teacher provides instruction in specific strategies to students who might benefit.

The school had the flexibility of selecting the option that would best meet their students' needs. Most of the schools initially used the team teaching option, primarily because the special education teachers wanted to be actively involved in instruction. Their greatest fear was that they would become "assistants."

Results and conclusions: Informal data was collected at the end of that year so that results could be measured.

Result 1: We discovered that grades and test scores increased while attendance and discipline problems decreased!

Result 2: We found that at-risk students and non-handicapped students had benefited as well as the handicapped students.

Result 3: The most positive findings were reports from the students of increased self-esteem. They liked remaining in the classroom; being "pulled out" made them feel different.

Result 4: Students also liked achieving at grade level curriculum and they liked having two teachers, because there was always a teacher to answer questions and assist them.

Result 5: Although some parents had been hesitant initially, parent reports were very positive at the end of the year.

These "pilot" sites were used for other schools in the school system to visit. The county teaching model was expanded into most of the schools over the next few years. This county has become a model site for other school systems to visit.

At the present time, many of the moderate-needs students are receiving their special education through the Murphy Teaching Model. However, there are students whose needs were not met in this setting, and those students are provided their special education needs through the traditional "pullout" program.

DESCRIBE YOUR WORK AND ACCOMPLISHMENTS IN A PROGRAM OF SIGNIFICANCE WITH PUBLIC SCHOOLS.

WHY DO YOU WANT TO PURSUE A DOCTORATE?

WHY DO YOU WANT TO PURSUE A DOCTORATE?

My desire to obtain a doctorate is not new. Indeed, pursuing a doctorate has been my goal since earning my M.A. in Elementary Education. Now, I feel the timing is right, and, furthermore, it would be a great honor to earn the terminal degree in my field from an institution where I earned both my B.S. (magna cum laude) and my M.A.. My commitment to education is well illustrated in my career. After earning my B.S. degree (major Psychology, minor English), I excelled as part of the Adult Basic Education and Human Resources Development Instructor with Adirondack Community College. Subsequently I taught sixth grade at Carter Elementary School. From 1990-97, I taught fourth grade at Edison Elementary School. From 1997-present, I have served as Assistant Principal at Liberty Elementary School, and I have made major contributions through my administrative ability, creativity, and true love for children. I am especially proud of two programs: we have implemented a Success-Only Math Lab which has improved mathematics skills, and we have pioneered a unique In-School Suspension Program aimed at lessening negative and inappropriate behaviors.

My goal after receiving the doctoral degree is to apply my administrative skills and teaching ability in leadership positions at local, county, or state levels. After earning the doctorate, I would seek a position in which I could play a significant role in helping children (and teachers) by designing and implementing educational policy. I would seek to serve in positions such as Principal, Superintendent of Schools, as well as in policy-making roles at the state and federal levels. I believe my diverse experience outside the academic world would help me in refining our public educational systems after I receive my doctorate, and I also believe that I could enrich a doctoral program through my experience in teaching and other areas. For example, I have been a member of the Youth Services Advisory Board (an appointed position by the county commissioners) and was a co-chair of the Student Service Team for four years. As I believe my extensive memberships and affiliations demonstrate, I have always reached out to serve on community organizations which aim to help children both inside and outside the classroom. These memberships and involvements have equipped me with rich insights which I believe could make me a vital and valuable part of the doctoral program. I am a strong believer in involving as many community agencies as possible in the educational process, and I generously devote my time to serving on such committees as a member and leader.

I love education, and I am proud to be dedicating my life to this great field. For that reason, I am always very proud and deeply honored when I earn the respect of my colleagues, as I did when I was named "Teacher of the Year" at Carter Elementary School.

If accepted into the doctoral program, I would consider it a great honor which would permit me to imagine, discover, and conceptualize creative concepts in education and student services which could be implemented in this century. I believe that the success of our nation depends upon high standards of educational excellence. I support high standards for student behavior and achievement; excellence in teaching; a positive school environment; and vigorous parental involvement. I believe teaching is a social as well as an academic process and cannot be separated from the total character and tasks of society. The more a student feels that school is an institution in which he can grow and work in connection with the natural tasks such as life requires, the happier and more productive he/she will be, and the more our society as a whole will benefit.

It is my deep desire to be of service to our state and nation that motivates me to seek the doctoral degree. There is nothing that thrills me more than to see our public schools graduate students who are ready for employment and who are equipped with the self confidence to face life enthusiastically.

I am confident that I could enthusiastically, intelligently, and resourcefully contribute to the goals of public education, and I believe the world could be a better place for us all if I were equipped with the doctorate and with the additional knowledge and tools it would give me so that I can work at the highest levels of professional activity for the benefit of our schools and the students we educate.

When admissions committees evaluate essays, they are trying to find the people who could contribute the most to the profession and they are trying to discover the individuals who will become renowned members of the profession. If you have an idea that you will one day be a credit to the institution to which you are applying, say so!

ESSAY DESCRIBING MY PURPOSE IN PURSUING A DOCTORATE

Pursuing a doctorate has been my goal since earning my M.ED. in Special Education. I had an opportunity in 1998 to attend a workshop at Adrian University and was impressed with the positive atmosphere and open learning environment. After investigating the credentials and background of the faculty, I became convinced that Adrian University was the perfect place for me to pursue my doctoral studies.

ESSAY DESCRIBING MY PURPOSE IN PURSUING A DOCTORATE

Compare this essay to the one on the previous page so that you can assess for yourself the difference in style and subject chosen to write about.

If accepted into the doctoral program, I am planning on taking leave from my current job as Director of Exceptional Children's Programs with Baldwin County Schools where I currently supervise 85 teachers, teacher assistants, speech pathologists, and psychologists while also writing federal grants and developing innovative new training opportunities for educators. While earning my doctorate, I plan on completing a textbook on special education strategies for parents which I have been writing for more than seven years. Two publishers have already indicated their interest in reading the manuscript. My credentials in the special education arena are top-notch, and it is my desire to strengthen my knowledge and skills related to special education through my pursuit of a doctorate.

My goal after receiving the doctoral degree is to apply my knowledge in a staff or managerial policy-making position at the national level. While specializing in the field of exceptional children's programs, I have acquired an ability to adapt quickly to the fast pace of change in the way exceptional children's needs are met within school systems and by individual teachers in classrooms. I offer considerable experience as a "change agent" within public school systems. I believe my expert knowledge of exceptional children's programs and needs could be a valuable addition to your doctoral program and could provide enriching insights for the other doctoral candidates.

If you look at my vitae, I believe you will see that your doctoral program is the obvious next step in my professional life so that I can contribute to an even greater extent to public school education in our state and nation. As a doctoral candidate, I would offer a "track record" of committed service to education along with expert knowledge of the area of exceptional children's programs administration. I began my teaching career as a teacher of 3rd and 4th grade students in Maine and, in that first teaching position, I encountered the problem of having students who were nonreaders. That experience in my "rookie" year of teaching caused me to make a commitment to gain more specialization as a teacher so that I could help children who were not learning. After obtaining my M.ED in Special Education, I taught in exceptional children's programs and have been involved in the supervision of exceptional children's programs in Baldwin County Schools and Caldwell County Schools.

As we face the challenges of the 21st century, I foresee greater and greater cultural and educational diversity in our classrooms. This is already happening! With a reputation statewide as an expert in the field of exceptional children's programs, I am intimately acquainted with the increasing tendency toward more inclusion of handicapped children in regular classrooms. That reality means, very simply, that teachers cannot teach a heterogeneous student population in the same way that they would teach a homogeneous population.

I have a sincere desire to help teachers figure out the best way to teach as they find themselves working in these increasingly complex and diversified classroom environments.

It is my strong professional belief that teacher preparatory programs will eventually be moving away from training teachers as **either** regular teachers **or** special education teachers. As more and more children with special needs are being included in regular classrooms, I believe teacher preparatory programs at the college and university level eventually will be training teachers to work with diverse populations—at-risk, handicapped, multi-cultural, and other specialized groups. While this trend in combined education will eventually dramatically impact university teacher preparatory programs, the changes caused by combined education will even more immediately require sensitive and capable administrators who have the vision and knowledge to help teachers, students, and parents respond to the new challenges of combined classrooms.

In summary, it is my deep desire to be of service to our nation that motivates me to seek the doctoral degree. There is nothing that thrills me more than to see our public schools graduate students who are ready for employment and who are equipped with the self confidence to face life enthusiastically—both of which can be produced by a quality public school education. As a practical person with 15 years of experience in teaching and administration, I believe the doctoral program will enhance my skills as a practitioner and enable me to continue to manage growth and change within the highly exciting and fast-paced world of public education.

IS YOUR G.P.A. AN ADEQUATE PREDICTOR OF YOUR ABILITY TO BE SUCCESSFUL IN THE PH.D. IN SOCIAL WORK PROGRAM?

IS YOUR G.P.A. AN ADEQUATE PREDICTOR OF YOUR ABILITY TO BE SUCCESSFUL IN THE PH.D. IN SOCIAL WORK PROGRAM?

I do not believe that GPA or standardized tests are always an accurate reflection of an individual's ability. If GPA and standardized test scores were accurate barometers of ability, then my scorings in undergraduate school would hardly predict the successful and rewarding career I have enjoyed since graduation. As a young student, it is often difficult to see the applicability of many aspects of classroom learning to real-world environment. I struggled with this throughout college as reflected by my GPA.

My undergraduate were filled with a misplaced certainty that I was wasting time before getting my hands dirty in the real-world. I wanted to "do," not study. I am now filled with the humility and insight that I must glean every kernel of knowledge offered by the best and the brightest at your university. Experience has brought maturity and a sense of mission to my life. After extensive real-world experience, I see the functionality of conceptual classroom study. I see clearly now that "street smarts" and "book learning" are companion tools for problem solving in life.

Since my undergraduate days, I have been out in the real world and have gotten my hands dirty. I have found that I enjoy working in the trenches with at-risk youth. But I have learned that I still have a lot to learn about how to help them, and it is that realization that has brought me to the doorstep of your institution, application in hand. I strongly desire to become one of the 12 handpicked doctoral candidates for your Ph.D. program. I know I can be a credit to the program. My extensive work with at-risk children in homes for youth offenders will enable me to provide insights as a Ph.D. candidate which other doctoral candidates might not have, and I am confident that my experience will enrich the doctoral program at your university.

I believe that the ingredients for success in graduate school include excellent analytical and problem-solving abilities, superior written and public speaking skills, and relentless persistence to succeed in spite of all obstacles. I also believe that a professional in any field pursuing a doctoral degree must possess the highest ethical and moral standards and be someone in whom the public can place absolute confidence. I am an individual who lives by high personal principles and strong moral values, and I also possess the strong analytical and communication skills required by your rigorous program.

My innovative approach to problem-solving has been apparent in my chosen career since my graduation from undergraduate school. I have excelled in troubled youth intervention and treatment in an area where many fail. After military discipline programs failed with hard-core gang members, I tried art. One young man who was facing hard prison time graduated from my program and is now a successful artist in Houston. If art failed, I have tried gardening and animal care. Through determined love, I have shown these children how to care about something in a world that they had previously felt was beyond caring for them. This determination to succeed, no matter what, is what I feel will make me a successful doctoral candidate.

I have seen how effective intervention programs can be, and I am now frustrated that I cannot implement more far-reaching programs. Without a doctoral degree I can go no farther in the current infrastructure of intervention programs. I have a passion for my work and will work tirelessly to succeed in your program. I have seen firsthand that each youth who does not find himself in an effective intervention program is a youth lost to the system. That I find unacceptable. By accepting my application to graduate school, the board is not only investing in me as an individual but in some of tomorrow's most troubled youth.

I would like to make you aware that attending graduate school is an exceedingly difficult choice for me. It means that I must leave to others the administration of the programs which I have developed. It also means that fewer youth will be helped than would be helped if I remained in my current position because, due to budget constraints, my position will not be replaced until my graduation from the doctoral program. I must give up the day-to-day rewards of working side-by-side with kids who have the potential to be tomorrow's leaders or tomorrow's "most wanted." The choice I have made, however, is the strategic one. I must help the many even if it sacrifices a few due to my absence.

IS YOUR G.P.A. AN ADEQUATE PREDICTOR OF YOUR ABILITY TO BE SUCCESSFUL IN THE PH.D. IN SOCIAL WORK PROGRAM?

Armed with the doctoral degree, I feel that I could help develop a nationwide network of intervention programs that will be much more effective and far-reaching than those currently in place. I have received grant aid for this network conditional to my graduation from your doctoral program. My passion to help our nation's children will undoubtedly prove to be an excellent motivating factor throughout your program, and I humbly ask the admissions committee to favorably review my application for admission.

WHAT SPECIAL PROJECT IN EDUCATION HAVE YOU COMPLETED?

WHAT SPECIAL PROJECT IN EDUCATION HAVE YOU COMPLETED?

One of the most successful projects in our school was "Give me a book and I'll read it." This was a project which I conceived of, planned, and implemented which was designed to increase the entire student body's interest in literacy. While applying my skills as a writer of grant proposals, we were able to utilize grant money to purchase two book titles for each grade level. The books were used to teach reading and writing using an integrated approach according to the goals and objectives of the Arkansas Standard Course of Study and End-of-Grade tests.

A primary objective of the project was for each child to have two books, one of which was left at school and the other sent home. The purpose of this objective was to enable each child to establish or add to his/her own personal library. By accomplishing this goal of helping the child start or add to a personal book collection, we hope the child will be inspired to develop a love of reading and to see books as a daily companion.

As a result of this project, we have motivated our parents to become actively involved with our "We're a Family of Readers!" Program. In this family reading program, parents establish and maintain the habit/discipline of reading at least fifteen minutes each night with their children and the reading time is documented on a reading log form which is turned in to the child's teacher. In evaluating the program, we have found that children who have a "reading buddy" at home enjoy the one-on-one attention they receive during the special reading time. The time spent reading with the child seems to be a form of "leadership by example" in which the child sees clearly that reading is viewed as an important activity by an adult whose behavior is noticed and often gets copied by the child. We have often discovered that shared reading time enhances the self-esteem of children because they feel special that this reading time is set aside by the parent. The child seems to feel important because the parent makes the time to read alone with the child each day.

DESCRIBE YOUR LEADERSHIP STYLE IN 30 WORDS OR LESS.

DESCRIBE YOUR LEADERSHIP STYLE IN 30 WORDS OR LESS.

A believer in leadership by example, I excel in utilizing encouragement and praise to motivate teachers. I create an atmosphere which encourages creativity, teamwork as well as personal accountability, and a striving for excellent results. I emphasize the cultivation of personal qualities that include self respect and respect for others.

DESCRIBE HOW RELATIONSHIPS BETWEEN COMMUNITY AND SCHOOLS AFFECT EDUCATION.

DESCRIBE HOW RELATIONSHIPS BETWEEN COMMUNITY AND SCHOOLS AFFECT EDUCATION.

It is my belief that the purpose of education is to provide the best education possible for all students. In order for teachers and administrators to do an excellent job in educating children, we must not only let the community know our school's mission but also inform the community about specific ways in which it can be a part of that mission. As the principal of Seven Hills Elementary School, I make an assertive effort to share all the school's activities with the community.

As a guest speaker, I have communicated the school's mission to the Duquenes Kiwanis Club, many churches in the community and surrounding areas, Boy Scout troops, Business and Women's Clubs, the Kiwanis Community Center, and several groups at local universities. Frequent speaking engagements in the community give me an opportunity to personalize the school while discussing in detail our goals, objectives, philosophies, and purposes. I ardently believe in "getting the word out" to various community groups about the extent to which our teachers and assistants are involved with students' learning and the positive results we are getting. In each speech I give, I always provide specific examples of how the community can get involved in order to help individual children while assuring that excellent educational standards are maintained for the benefit of local employers and the community at large.

One way I encourage the community to get involved is through our Mentor-Tutor Program, which is the highlight of our school's volunteer program. This program is comprised of parents, grandparents, professors, and students from Northwestern University (Education Department, Computer Department, Law School, Medical School, and The Student Union). We use our volunteers to provide one-on-one instruction for the students. Presently we have nearly 50 volunteers participating in this program, and they have volunteered hundreds of hours since the program began.

Our Adopt-a-School Partners are members of the greater community, as well as our parents. They sponsor student incentive programs such as Terrific Kids, Students of the Week, Students of the Month, Writers of the Month, Perfect Attendance, and Honor Rolls. All of these programs inspire our students to have high expectations and achieve recognitions in areas that promote student interest and emphasize their purpose for being in school. As principal, I emphasize to my teaching staff the idea that children learn by example and that children learn more from what we do than from what we say. Therefore, I believe it is imperative for parents and other caring community people to be visibly involved in school activities, and we are delighted at the excellent participation of the community in our Adopt-a-School Partners Program.

Our students are caring and responsible students who want to help our less fortunate citizens. Our student body as a whole has participated in local service projects and national service projects. For example, the fifth grade students have organized food drives at Thanksgiving for the Department of Social Services in Brighton County. They have also sponsored a nonperishable items' drive for victims of Hurricane Andrew in Florida. Grades three through five participate in the Children's Hospital Math-a-Thon each year. Our students have raised approximately $2,500 for the past three years for the Children's Hospital Project.

In summary, we are very fortunate to have excellent parental support and involvement in all facets of our school: tutors, volunteers, service projects, fund raisers, family reading program, Fall Carnival, Heritage Day, award assemblies, and other programs. The parents' high level of participation allowed us to receive the Golden Key Award for Parental Involvement in my first year as principal at Seven Hills Elementary School. I can say without overstating anything that "Seven Hills is truly a community school."

DESCRIBE HOW RELATIONSHIPS BETWEEN COMMUNITY AND SCHOOLS AFFECT EDUCATION.

DESCRIBE WHAT YOUR PHILOSOPHY AND PRACTICES WOULD BE AS AN EDUCATION ADMINISTRATOR.

It was the spring, and I had just finished my masters program. Our staff at that time had received notice from the Central Office that we would be transferred to Dark Mouth Elementary School in the fall. The transfer added more staff members and an assistant principal position. Until that point in time, I earnestly believed that my mission in life was to be the very best teacher I could be for the boys and girls in my class.

DESCRIBE WHAT YOUR PHILOSOPHY WOULD BE AS AN EDUCATION ADMINISTRATOR.

This principal must answer some probing questions in order to determine his philosophy if he were in charge of a school system.

At that point in my life, when I and other teachers were anticipating a transfer to Dark Mouth Elementary School, my principal came to me and shared a vision that he said he and my peers had for me: becoming an assistant principal. He told me that it was the unanimous feeling of my peers that I should take my respected teaching expertise to an even higher level of education—to the job of assistant principal— where I could combine my teaching background with my leadership and management skills in order to make a major impact on students, staff, and other teachers. I was overwhelmed and touched by the reality that my principal and peers had such high regard for me and shared this vision of where I should be professionally so that I could "make a difference" in education for all of us. I humbly agreed to take the job of assistant principal.

My mission in life now is to positively impact the lives of students, staff, and parents through my job as a principal. All of my efforts as a principal I appreciatively dedicate to my former principal and to the former staff and teachers at Mason Heights Elementary School who placed their faith in me. Without their expression of faith in me, I might not have taken that step toward assistant principal and principal. This is what we do as teachers, too: we encourage, embolden, motivate, inspire, and help people to see and achieve their potential. I thank God that I am a teacher and I thank teachers for just being teachers.

I regard the job of principal as one in which I am constantly solving problems and finding new opportunities to positively impact the lives of students, teachers, and parents. As principal, I am privileged to have an opportunity to share my commitment to education with others; I communicate to teachers and other staff the philosophy that we are all accountable because we share as a team the same vision and goals.

As an offshoot of my belief that we are all accountable for our results, I continuously seek to find practical ways of measuring our successes as well as our shortcomings. I believe strongly that teaching professionals will be more likely to work to achieve goals that they themselves have helped to establish, so I assume a "hands-on" management style as teacher and foster an atmosphere in which teachers' opinions are listened to and respected. Together, we set goals that are ambitious and achievable, and then we develop the specific plans to achieve our goals. Once we achieve our goals, I believe in publicizing our success stories, so we are a marketing-oriented school that aggressively seeks to communicate to parents, students, and the community the strides we are making in helping students develop to their fullest academic, physical, and mental capacity.

One of my main jobs as principal is to listen. I believe that listening is often the "forgotten part" of the communication process, and I make an effort to make myself available to listen to students, teachers, parents, and community members. Some of my best ideas for new programs and for modifications of existing programs have come about because I have taken the time to listen. **The contribution I would like to make in this field is to be an instructional leader who loves to select, develop, and empower outstanding teachers and assistants who can ensure accountability.** I believe this will be best accomplished by utilizing strategies and techniques in teaching designed to improve student outcomes which have been developed through teamwork.

DESCRIBE A SITUATION WHICH SHOWS HOW YOU RESOLVE SPECIFIC ADMINISTRATIVE PROBLEMS IN EDUCATION.

Our school is in a small community and everyone knows almost everyone else in the school. I try to avoid changing a student to another teacher's class once the rosters are posted, unless there is a situation where the child's year will be impacted in a negative way unless this is accomplished. For example, one day the parents of one student asked me to change their child from one teacher's class to another because of personality differences which were affecting the child in an adversely emotional manner. I listened to the parents, empathized with them about their perceived differences in the classrooms, and discussed my reasons for not making it a general rule to change classroom assignments. However, I told them that I would make the change based on the students' emotional distress, which was documented by a doctor's note.

In the situation which I am describing, it was not only important to make the right decision, but it was also important to implement the decision in a sensitive manner. I told the parents that I must first inform the teachers and share some things with them because our job is to provide opportunities for the best possible education for each child. I held private sessions with each teacher involved, and I communicated to each one in a tactful, sensitive manner so that no one's feelings were hurt and no professional pride diminished. The teachers involved both understood that they had my complete confidence and full support, and they were both supportive of making a change that seemed in the child's best interests.

The rules of confidentiality were observed, and I have carefully monitored the situation since the change in classroom was made. All parties seem happy, and I believe this change was necessary. This was a situation in which it would have been wrong, in my opinion, to "stick by the rules" and refuse to adjust a situation which was becoming dysfunctional. I feel strongly that I made the right decision and implemented the decision correctly, and I would not alter in any way the way I handled this particular problem.

DESCRIBE A SITUATION
WHICH SHOWS HOW YOU
RESOLVE SPECIFIC
PROBLEMS IN EDUCATION.

IMAGINE YOURSELF AS THE SUPERINTENDENT OF A SCHOOL SYSTEM ONCE YOU GRADUATE WITH YOUR PH.D. HOW WOULD YOU IMPROVE STUDENT ACHIEVEMENT?

IMAGINE YOURSELF AS THE SUPERINTENDENT OF A SCHOOL SYSTEM ONCE YOU GRADUATE WITH YOUR PH.D. HOW WOULD YOU IMPROVE STUDENT ACHIEVEMENT?

One of the major issues facing educators today is accountability for principals and teachers for improved test scores on End-of-Grade tests. I would use my position as a superintendent to inform teachers, students, parents, and the community about students' progress in the following ways:

1. Review the goals and objectives of the Standard Course of Study by grade level.

2. Review the benchmarks and proficiencies for each grade level in reading, writing, and mathematics.

3. Analyze test data to determine strengths and weaknesses on grade level.

4. Implement strategies to maintain strengths and to improve weaknesses of skills in the curriculum.

5. Evaluate our gains from year to year for each grade level.

6. Target students in grades K-2 who are at-risk in language development skills. Target students in grades 3-6 who make a level 1 or level 2 on End-of-Grade tests.

7. Implement a whole language reading program for kindergartners, "Early Opportunities to Read," to improve language development before entering first grade.

8. Utilize the services of an education consultant to assist teachers with writing across the curriculum, to develop curriculum maps that center on themes for each grade level to help children connect learning across the curriculum, to teach the philosophies of mastery learning and learning styles. Strategies from these activities would help teachers adjust their teaching techniques to meet the needs of all students.

9. Utilize grant money to purchase trade books and novels to teach reading and writing skills across the curriculum.

10. Utilize teacher assistants, parent volunteers, and students from nearby universities to work with at-risk students individually or in small groups.

11. Provide daily exposure and practices to concepts, materials, and terminology relevant to End-of-Grade tests.

12. Involve parents in a well-publicized home reading program to improve students' reading interest and reading level. It also provides an opportunity for parents to become more involved with their children's school work. Research shows that when parents are actively involved with students' learning, it increases test scores, graduation rates, and college enrollment.

13. Provide an atmosphere that is nurturing and caring for all.

IMAGINE YOURSELF TAKING OVER AS THE LEADER OF A SCHOOL SYSTEM. DESCRIBE YOUR PHILOSOPHY.

If I were to take over the leadership of the Bellweather School System, I would see myself as a team leader. The progress of children in any school is positive and successful when certain factors and beliefs exist among the team members responsible for improvements in student learning. Our team consists of our teachers, staff, parents, students, and members of our community. Our goals and purposes are the same. We want to inspire our students in such a way that each of them will have a zest for lifelong learning.

We are dedicated to the improvement of children. Therefore, we believe that what is best for children must be our highest priority at all times. Through our partnership and shared vision, we must provide for children a sense of love, hope, fair play, respect for others, and a positive self-image.

The achievements of our children are part of a comprehensive process which does not focus on End-of-Grade tests only, but on the overall improvement of all school components including parental involvement, community involvement, staff development, accountability, positive work climate, and a common belief system. In my current position as principal at Drayton Hall School System, we have focused on the above components to enhance skills in our curriculum. We now have a better sense of sharing, coaching, and mentoring. The knowledge gained from working as a team has enabled us to analyze our progress and map out strategies for future goals and objectives. We realize that true school improvement starts at the school level, but it takes the whole team to make positive outcomes with our children.

I feel privileged that destiny has positioned me as the team leader of this vibrant educational process, and I delight every day in the challenges and opportunities that being a principal offers me as I humbly try to be a positive force in the life of each and every student, teacher, parent, staff person, and community member with whom I come into contact.

IMAGINE YOURSELF TAKING OVER AS THE LEADER OF A SCHOOL SYSTEM. DESCRIBE YOUR PHILOSOPHY.

DESCRIBE YOUR LIFE EXPERIENCES THAT HAVE LED YOU TO SEEK A MASTER'S DEGREE IN SOCIAL WORK.

I came into the world backwards. I was born a breech baby, and my parents welcomed me into the world with open arms. My aunt was there also and every year she reminds me of how I was the only baby in the nursery crying. I may have come into the world backwards, but I have been moving forward ever since.

I am the only child of two great parents. Even though my parents are divorced, they have always shown unwavering love and dedication to me. My family along with God are my main support systems. This not only includes my parents; it also includes my aunts, cousins, and uncles. My family isn't perfect, but I wouldn't trade them for anything. I know they will be there for me when no one else will and I feel truly blessed to be a part of them.

Now that I am older I sometimes feel I missed out by being the only child. I admire some of the special relationships between siblings. I don't have any brothers or sisters, but I have a first cousin with whom I grew up named Jacob. Jacob and I were inseparable from the time we were infants until our college careers separated us. I think of him as a brother at times, and I truly miss not being able to see him as much. When I think about not having any siblings, I think of Jacob and how we are close enough to be considered brother and sister.

One thing I have had to overcome in my immediate family is my parents' divorce. My parents separated when I was 8 years old, and it was a tragic experience for me. For the longest time, I wouldn't tell my peers or other people my parents were divorced, when we talked about our families. I wouldn't say anything because I was embarrassed and ashamed. As I grew older, I realized I had nothing to be ashamed of. I began to understand that sometimes in life things happen and take a different course than the one we would choose. I have learned to deal with my feelings and I have adjusted well. I don't think of my home as "broken." I haven't lacked anything from my parents' divorce. If anything, the situation has made me a stronger person who never gives up.

Waycross, GA, is home for me. I have lived here all of my life, except for the four years I was at college. I've even lived in the same house for 22 years. I have also had the experience of attending several different grade schools in Spring Hill.

I attended the first grade at a Catholic School named St. Joseph's. Even though I was young I still have vivid memories of this school. I thoroughly enjoyed it and thought it was unique to have a nun as a teacher.

The rest of my education was spent at public schools. My elementary education was spent at Waycross Elementary. There were a couple of teachers who influenced my life at this school. One of them was named Mrs. Bingham. I did well in her 6th grade class, and it was a positive experience for me. The best thing I liked about Mrs. Bingham was that she was fair and stern along with being nice. If we got out of line she reprimanded us like our mother. She was a super person and an outstanding teacher in my eyes.

I had many friends in elementary school. My friends were white, black, Asian, and so on. Now that I look back I see why children don't point out color. We were all just kids in each other's eyes.

After elementary school, I attended two junior high schools, Lewis & Clark and Colonial Elementary. In the beginning I didn't adjust well to the 7th grade. Now I had seven different teachers and subjects to keep up with. I missed the one-on-one attention I had before. After a while I adjusted to junior high school, and learned to like it more. I attended the 9th grade at Colonial Elementary because the county changed the school districts. I even made the cheerleading squad, and this really helped to boost my confidence and make me feel proud.

I attended high school at Reed Senior High School. I found myself adjusting again, because all my friends were attending a different high school. As soon as I made new friends it grew on me. Now I had even more friends, and I was also the newspaper editor for my school newspaper during my senior year.

I chose to attend Georgia State, in Atlanta, GA, for my undergraduate study. I chose Georgia State because it had a large population of black students and was known for racial diversity. It also had a great political science program which is what I wanted to study at the time.

After doing more research into political science I realized that it wasn't for me. I wasn't sure about the direction I should take professionally but I did know one thing. Since I was a child, my goal has been to be involved in a helping profession. I thoughtfully and prayerfully considered many alternatives—including psychiatry and psychology. After much consideration I decided and felt that sociology and social work were for me. I feel that this is one of the greatest decisions I have ever made, and I haven't looked back since.

Undergraduate school at Georgia State was one of the biggest learning experiences for me. I have learned and grown tremendously from the time I was a freshman, and even from the time I was a senior almost a year ago. Having completed undergraduate school I can now look back on the whole experience with an unbiased view to see both the positive and negative outcomes.

The positive aspects of my time at Georgia State were: (1) earning my B.A. degree in Sociology; (2) making new friendships; (3) gaining a better rapport with my instructors; (4) learning more about different social situations; (5) being a part of the Student Government Association and the Yearbook Staff; and (6) volunteering for the Atlanta Helpline and an Afterschool Program for children in low-income housing. My experiences have made me a lot more focused as a person. Now I know and understand what I have to do in life to succeed and I am going to do it.

The negative aspects were: (1) not being more focused on my college goals; (2) getting caught up in certain social situations; and (3) not taking advantage of certain opportunities that were open to me, both academically and socially. Even though I've had my share of negative experiences, I don't dwell on them. I look at them as learning experiences. Negative experiences make me more focused for the next obstacle I have to overcome.

DESCRIBE YOUR LIFE EXPERIENCES THAT HAVE LED YOU TO SEEK A MASTER'S DEGREE IN SOCIAL WORK.

Education is a major concern in my life. I see education as the key to succeeding in the future. It is the tool for learning, growing, and broadening the mind. It is a special gift that no one can ever take away from you. With an education one can be more productive in society. Without an education, I feel as though I am at a standstill. That's why it is my goal to further my education by obtaining my master's degree in Social Work.

DESCRIBE YOUR LIFE EXPERIENCES THAT HAVE LED YOU TO SEEK A MASTER'S DEGREE IN SOCIAL WORK.

All of my positive and negative experiences have helped me to become a stronger person. I know I can do anything and overcome anything I set my mind to. I see **no** limitations for myself. There will always be obstacles in life, but with the help of God and my strong will power, I know I can make it, and I intend to. I have had to receive help from others and I have always been grateful for it. Receiving help has made me want to help others even more. I am fortunate and blessed in so many ways, and it is meant for me to return my blessings. I may not be able to save the world, but I can put a dent in it.

I have chosen the Clark University because I feel it best suits my needs. I want to continue my education at a historically black university. Being a black female, I also want to help aid my race and make a difference in my community. I feel comfortable that Clark University can help me do this.

After researching many different universities with MSW programs, I chose Clark University for a number of reasons. The curriculum seems tailored to my needs, which is very important to me. I have also done some research into the faculty and the school as a whole. I have been assured that it is an exceptional school.

I want to gain knowledge from all of these areas of specialization: child and family services, health services, and community services. I feel as though I could benefit and learn from all these areas. Eventually, I would like to work in a hospital setting to help aid patients with their situations and concerns. I am, however, leaving my options open for the possibility of discovering something new in the social work profession that is equally fascinating.

My final thought is that you select me as a student for Clark University's MSW Program. I am a determined and more focused individual who will be successful in all my future endeavors. I will be an asset to the MSW Program, and I am sure that Clark University will be an asset to me.

HOW DO YOU EXPECT YOUR GRADUATE SCHOOL PERFORMANCE TO COMPARE WITH YOUR UNDERGRADUATE EXPERIENCE? EXPLAIN.

In the process of earning my B.A. in Sociology from Buena Vista University, I donated my time extensively in the community through such organizations as the American Red Cross and the Prime Time Afterschool Program for underprivileged children, through which I assisted children with homework and any other problems they were encountering. I also found time to serve my fellow students as a member of the Christian Students Committee. I was also informally a "sounding board" for fellow students who learned of my reputation as a compassionate individual with excellent listening skills and an ability to help those in distress. Indeed, many of my friends referred to me as a "practicing social worker" during my college years. My greatest enthusiasm for life is the enthusiasm I feel when I am in the process of helping others.

While in college, I held down jobs as a waitress/hostess, sales clerk, and cashier in addition to full-time studies in order to finance my college education. Looking back, I feel the necessity to find employment in order to help finance my college education hindered me somewhat from excelling academically throughout college, but that work experience also helped me grow up and become a mature young woman who is now confident about my ability to organize and manage my time for maximum efficiency.

The courses I enjoyed the most in college were the courses which acquainted me with Social Work, including Social Work as a Profession and Human Behavior in the Social Environment. As my transcript reveals, I performed best academically in the last two years of my undergraduate career, and I made the Dean's List.

I feel confident that I can excel in the MSW Program because of my maturity and enthusiasm for social work, and I feel my excellent written and oral communication skills, research and analytical ability, and genuinely caring nature will enable me to be at the top of my class.

EXPLAIN HOW SOCIETAL AND CULTURAL TRENDS/GLOBAL EVENTS AFFECT YOUR THINKING ABOUT A SOCIAL WORK CAREER.

I feel strongly that there are certain segments of the population which need special amounts of "tender loving care" in the future. The segments of the population which particularly interest me professionally are children and elderly people, and I am disturbed by several societal trends affecting both children and the elderly.

I believe there has been a gradual weakening of the family structure with the result that the "home schooling" of children in the area of values and morals are lacking in substance and strength. Children can't raise themselves, but that is exactly what is happening in many homes today, both where children are raised in poverty and in affluence. One article I read recently in a professional journal reported that gangs are increasingly popular with children because gangs offer the structure and security that children used to derive from the family institution. Because children tend to transmit the values and morals they learned to their own children in adulthood,

HOW DO YOU EXPECT YOUR GRADUATE SCHOOL PERFORMANCE TO COMPARE WITH YOUR UNDERGRADUATE EXPERIENCE? EXPLAIN.

EXPLAIN HOW SOCIETAL AND CULTURAL TRENDS/GLOBAL EVENTS AFFECT YOUR THINKING ABOUT A SOCIAL WORK CAREER.

the generation of children coming up may be even more lacking in solid nurturing. While I hope there will be a resurgence of "family values" in our country, I think some of this moral decay will not be stopped, and that is where social workers in the 21st century will need to step in and "make a difference." In some ways, social workers end up becoming "surrogate parents" to both the adults and children of families in distress, and I feel the tender heart and helping instinct which God has given me will enable me to excel in the field of social work. I am eager to embark on a structured program of graduate studies because I feel a tender heart and caring instincts are not sufficient in themselves for helping others; the theories and techniques which I will learn in graduate studies will, I'm sure, help me acquire an inventory of tools and techniques and approaches for use in this helping profession.

Another segment of the population which I feel will be in much need of social assistance in the 21st century will be the elderly and, more long-range, the aging "baby boom" generation, a segment which is 78 million strong! Recent data shows that the first baby boomer hit the age of 50 in 1995, and as this powerful and large segment ages, this will place pressure on many systems and institutions in our country, from health care to social work, and from hospitals to nursing homes. Our society seems to neglect elderly people more than many other cultures, and I feel we should treat elderly people like the "old jewels" of society which I feel they are. I believe caring for the elderly will be a major concern of the 21st century, and I want to be a part of designing and implementing the programs which will be serving this segment.

DESCRIBE HOW EMPLOYMENT, VOLUNTEER, INTERNSHIP, AND/OR LIFE EXPERIENCES DEVELOPED YOUR INTEREST IN SOCIAL WORK AND EXPLAIN HOW YOU WILL BUILD UPON THESE EXPERIENCES THROUGH GRADUATE STUDY.

Since I was a child, my goal has been to be involved eventually in a helping profession. My mother is a single parent and her selfless devotion to me, and thoughtful regard for others, gave me an orientation toward serving my fellow man. For example, my mother made sure that we carefully packed up my outgrown clothes and gave them to other children. My mother taught me, mostly by example, that it is important to be nice to everyone, and I have seen first-hand that nice people do go far in life. Although the stereotype of the only child is that of a clinging and dependent individual, my mother instilled in me the concept that I have an independent destiny to fulfill and that I must discover what my God-given talents are and find ways to utilize them. She raised me to be the very best person I can be, and she taught me to respect differences in others, to value uniqueness, and to help others. As a youth, I "adopted" an elderly woman in my community and acted as her "arms and legs" in taking cans she had collected and trading them for cash. Throughout high school and college, I extensively volunteered my time in crisis centers and in child-tutoring situations in order to reach out to others and nurture the helping instinct that is in inside me.

I have had the experience of growing up as a black female in a town which is adjacent to a large U.S. military base. Therefore, I have had the opportunity to go to school and interact with people from many cultures, ethnic origins, and economic backgrounds. I also feel fortunate that I was brought up to believe in God, so I learned from an early age to value the differences that God instilled in people and to enjoy the diversity of different types of people.

I have been told many times that my greatest talent is that of being a good "listener," and I feel listening is a part of the communication process which is often bypassed and aborted. I have the ability to listen to others with an "open mind" and to be a good sounding board. As an attentive listener, I also have an ability to be objective and to creatively assist the person talking in identifying alternatives for solving the problems he/she faces. I believe my ability to truly listen to others comes from a sincere desire to help them. Listening intently is not the easiest part of the communication process! Talking is easier than listening, but listening is the critical step leading up to the problem-solving stage, and my "listening skills" are refined to a high level.

America is a country of different cultures, and I believe the United States will become even more diversified culturally and ethnically in the 21st century. Already the Hispanic segment of the population is growing very rapidly. I believe we need social workers who truly believe in the basic assumption that all people are valuable and special and who are comfortable dealing with people of varying socioeconomic backgrounds. I have a high degree of comfort dealing with all types of people, and I also offer the ability to communicate effectively with people of diverse backgrounds.

As an undergraduate while earning my degree in sociology, I was not sure about the direction I should take professionally. I have thoughtfully and prayerfully considered many alternatives—including undertaking the study of psychiatry, psychology, and a career in health care administration. After much consideration, I feel certain that my goal should be to earn a Master of Social Work (M.S.W.) degree so that I can refine my helping instincts through the study of theory and techniques which will equip me to even better serve others. The reason I did not undertake graduate study immediately after college is that I wanted to be certain about the direction I take in graduate school. I take my commitments very seriously, and I am committed to a career in social work.

After earning my M.S.W., I would be especially interested in serving as a social worker in a Veterans Hospital, and eventually my long-range goal would be to open a counseling center for children and adults.

Finally, my work experience has helped me develop confidence that I can be a highly effective social worker. Through numerous jobs as a waitress, hostess, and sales clerk, I have learned much about human behavior while refining my public relations, analytical, customer service, and problem-solving skills.

DESCRIBE HOW EMPLOYMENT, VOLUNTEER, INTERNSHIP, AND/OR SOCIAL EXPERIENCES DEVELOPED YOUR INTEREST IN SOCIAL WORK, AND EXPLAIN HOW YOU WILL BUILD UPON THESE EXPERIENCES THROUGH GRADUATE STUDY.

HOW DO YOU SEE YOUR INTERESTS AND CAREER GOALS BEING MET THROUGH THE MSW PROGRAM OFFERED BY BUENA VISTA UNIVERSITY'S SCHOOL OF SOCIAL WORK?

After researching many different schools, I determined that I liked the range of specialization that I could choose from at Buena Vista University, and I also like the way the curriculum seems tailored to my desire to emphasize working with children and the aging, perhaps in conjunction with a health organization or medical service. I have performed some research into the credentials of the faculty, and I feel assured that the faculty is outstanding.

I have prepared myself academically for social work by majoring in sociology as an undergraduate. I have also prepared myself by taking some social work courses. Two of the courses I took were Social Work as a Profession and Human Behavior in the Social Environment.

I believe my extensive volunteer work has also prepared me professionally for the challenges I will face as a Social Worker, and my volunteer activities have taught me that helping others is often a very difficult and stressful undertaking. For example, through an afterschool program for underprivileged children, I assisted students with homework and with any other problems they were encountering. As a social worker in the 21st century, I can foresee myself working to set up voluntary programs within the community so that adult readers can be paired with elementary school nonreaders in order to increase literacy. In another volunteer activity with the American Red Cross, I was trained and then I performed volunteer work as a phone counselor with people calling and seeking help with emotional, mental, and personal problems. That experience gave me insight into the vast network of referral sources and agencies with which the social worker must be acquainted, and those experiences helped me see that I need more formal training—the training that would be provided in a formal Master of Social Work program—in order to provide the maximum assistance to those in distress and need. On numerous other occasions I have also helped with food drives and clothes drives and with projects such as helping needy families at Christmas.

Since I have been a youth, I have demonstrated the kind of "helping instinct" which I believe must be a motivating force for social workers. In college, I undertook sociology as a field of study because I thought it would help me acquire a better understanding of our diversified society and world. I do, in fact, believe that sociology is an excellent foundation for the study of social work at the master's level, and I am very happy I made that decision to make sociology my undergraduate major.

As a matter of philosophy, I believe that people who have had many advantages in life should give back to society. Although I am not rich materially, I feel "rich" in many ways because I have had the support of a loving family that, although I am an only child, encouraged me to spread my wings and soar in pursuit of big dreams and high achievement. I believe the kind of family life I had is the greatest gift a child could ever receive, and I feel I have much to offer the social work field in terms of helping to instill in others the values of self-respect and respect for others which were instilled in me.

WHY DO YOU WANT TO ENTER THE FAMILY AND HUMAN SERVICES DEGREE PROGRAM?

I am the only child of two highly educated parents who have had a happy and stable marriage and with whom I enjoy a warm and loving relationship. I am very proud of my parents! My mother, Lizanne Ballis, is Chairman of the English Department at a public school in Nevada, and she holds a Master's degree in English. She teaches comparative literature and advanced grammar. My father, George Ballis, is a Ph.D. Physicist who specializes in analogical programming for NASA. He has worked at the forefront of technology throughout his career.

WHY DO YOU WANT TO ENTER THE FAMILY AND HUMAN SERVICES DEGREE PROGRAM?

During my childhood, we moved frequently as my dad relocated to be involved in state-of-the-art design and programming activities. I lived in 10 states as a child. Nevada became home for us, however, and my parents live there now. I graduated from Dusty Heights High School, where I took mostly AP courses in my junior and senior years. Active in extracurricular activities, I managed the football and baseball teams. I was also on the school's race relations team, chemistry club, and was a member of the international dance club. In my spare time, I enjoyed riding horses.

I feel that a Master's Degree in Family and Human Services would definitely help me to achieve my goals. My love of children and enjoyment of child care began when I was in middle school. My middle school was unique in that it provided a child care center, and I gravitated toward the child care center after school each day. At first I volunteered in the center, and then I was offered a paid position at a very young age when the little children began getting attached to me and looking forward to interacting with me in the afternoons. I met a little boy at that child care center for whom I later became a live-in baby-sitter when I was a college student.

I completed two years of college at the University of Nevada in Reno, Nevada, and then finished my degree at the Southern Methodist University in Dallas, Texas. I excelled academically at both institutions. My goal upon graduating with my B.S. in Psychology from Southern Methodist University was to become employed in the social services field in a group home environment. During college, I worked up to 40 hours a week at the New Hope Group Home caring for children who had been removed from their homes because of neglect or abuse. Then I began to feel attracted by the challenge of providing child care within a private family environment.

I accepted a position with the family of Dr. Richard D. Smith. I provided child care six days a week, and frequently around the clock for several weeks during the doctor's frequent absences, for one four-year-old girl. Dr. Smith was a renowned cardiac surgeon and traveled worldwide to give lectures at prominent medical schools. I accepted my current position in 1999, and I work for a busy executive who manages a large corporation. Mr. Alexander Stockton was a widow when I joined his family, and I provided support to his two grieving children in the aftermath of their mother's death. I have come to admire the disciplined style of Mr. Stockton as he seeks to provide a structured life for his children.

With experience in private home and group environments, I am confident that I could make significant contributions to the social work field if I were equipped with a degree in Family and Human Services.

DESCRIBE THE COURSE THAT LED YOU TO CONTEMPLATE THE STUDY OF THEOLOGY.

My Christian Pilgrimage started when I accepted Jesus Christ in my life at the age of eight. God blessed me to be a part of a Christian family. My father made sure all of his children attended Sunday School, morning worship, Bible Training Union, evening service, and Wednesday Night Prayer Meeting. I can remember reciting Bible verses after saying grace before meals. Coming from a large family, I was reared by my great-aunt, a strong and God-fearing woman, who also had reared my father.

DESCRIBE THE COURSE
THAT LED YOU TO
CONTEMPLATE THE STUDY
OF THEOLOGY.

I can recall hearing about God at home, in church, and at school. I was surrounded by saints telling me about God, His only begotten Son, and the Holy Spirit. In Sunday School, I can remember singing songs like, "Yes, Jesus Loves Me," and "I Will Make You Fishers of Men." The preacher told me about how God loves me and that God sent His Son to die for me that I may have eternal life.

Before I was baptized, my uncle, who was a deacon at the Ebenezer Baptist Church in Greenville, Kentucky, took me in a back room of the church to question me about my belief and faith in God. After he was satisfied with my response, he prayed with me the sinner's prayer. Then he took me to the assistant pastor to be baptized. The following Sunday, I was given my first communion and the right hand of fellowship. I was assigned by the pastor to be an usher.

After many years as a deacon, my father was called to the preaching ministry. He felt the call to start a church in our home. As the membership grew, the site of the church changed to numerous locations. Although I lived with my great-aunt, I joined my father's church. As I grew in the knowledge of the Lord, I was assigned to work in several positions. I was a choir member, Sunday School teacher, and Vacation Bible School assistant. I was also taught how to be a church trustee and to lead worship services.

As a high school student, I was allowed to take some courses at Gleaton College of the Bible. During my freshman and sophomore college years, I had an opportunity to sing with the Kentucky State University Chorale. During my time with the Navigators in my junior and senior years, I learned about having quiet time for meditation and increased my memorization of scriptures. I also participated in mountain retreats where I took various religious classes. I learned a lot about God and His presence.

In 1976, I joined the U.S. Army. My first tour of duty was at Ft. Dix, NJ. I spent a lot of time at the Serviceman Center, where I learned about doctrinal truths and more about witnessing to the lost. I visited many churches via the Serviceman Center. I enrolled in New Jersey Faith College and took advantage of many correspondence courses which broadened my knowledge in the faith.

I soon was stationed at Fort Benning, Georgia, where I became a member of Duluth Missionary Baptist Church. I served as an usher, Sunday School teacher, and assistant superintendent of the Sunday School. I spent time praying and studying the Holy Scriptures. At the Brixton Baptist Conference, I took Christian education courses and participated in Bible Study. While stationed in numerous countries, I continued to participate in worship services, attend Bible study, and meditated upon God's Word. While in Iraq, our military engineers made roads through the desert in getting ready for the Gulf War. This was a time in which Bible study and prayer became more important to my life. After returning to Ft. Bragg, NC, from the Gulf War, I met my future wife. A native of Mexico, Angela has been a strong supporter of my desire to serve the Lord through the ordained ministry.

My call to the ministry is sure. The initial call was in my youth, but I did not respond positively to it. As I reflect upon my youth, I heard many preachers proclaim the Word of God. However, on one particular night at my father's church, I heard a sermon on the call to the ministry as it related to the Apostles. The minister preached a sound, Biblical message, and I was all ears. After the service, I went home and lay in my bed, trying to go to sleep, but I could not. Consequently, I lay there and noticed that there was complete silence in my room. At that moment, I sensed the presence of the Holy Spirit, and He brought peace to my soul as I realized God was calling me to be a Proclaimer of His Word. After that night, I just pondered over the thought of being a preacher. However, I had my own agenda for life, and being a preacher was not it.

After several years, I graduated from college, and I joined the U.S. Army. I was trying to be all I could be. However, I was struck by a vehicle while walking across the street to pick up my hat. A Toyota Corolla had hit me, causing me to fall and slide several feet. I ended up with a dislocated shoulder and a closed head injury. There I lay lifeless, soaked in my own blood. Many of my friends were crying in disbelief of what had occurred, but there was a friend of mine that believed in the prayer of faith as well as some other saints who had just gotten out of their Sunday night service. They took hold of my hand, and prayed to the Almighty God for my recovery. After they prayed, I regained a state of consciousness. The ambulance soon arrived with medical personnel to take care of me. I was placed in the ambulance and then rushed to a nearby medical center. After I was brought to the center, a team of doctors worked on me until early morning. Then I was placed in the intensive care ward. That morning, I not only heard in my room the sounds of the medical equipment, but I also heard the Spirit of God restating to me the call to be a proclaimer of the Gospel. In my spirit, I realized that there was no getting around my call to preach. I praise God that He allowed me to regain enough health and strength to give Him the glory. I now have no doubts of what God wants me to be and do. More importantly, I realize as the Psalmist says that "The steps of a good man are ordered by the Lord: and he delighteth in his way." (Psa 37:23) I preached my initial sermon on November 11, 1987.

I am committed to preaching and teaching the Word of God. Therefore, I will study His Word so I can become more equipped in spreading the gospel. I am determined to do the will of God in all I say and do. Moreover, I am obligated to praise and glorify His name because He is worthy.

1. I want to be prepared in every aspect of the pastoral ministry. Someday, as a pastor, I would like to be able to communicate effectively with the congregation and community. Therefore, my objective at this point is to earn a Master of Divinity.

2. I would like to confer with and learn from established ministers of the gospel.

3. Finally, I would like to learn about different models of ministry and how I can appropriate those models into my own ministry.

WHAT ARE YOUR CAREER OBJECTIVES?

Since I was a child, my goal has been to helping others. My parents have always stressed the importance of serving my fellow man. Although to some my family didn't have very much, there was always enough to share with those less fortunate than ourselves. My mother grew a garden in which there were always enough vegetables for our table and the neighbor's who had just lost his job or who was ill. As a child, I was known for bringing home stray animals and hungry children. Throughout high school and college, I extensively volunteered my time to the elderly and impoverished so that I could fulfill that drive to help within me.

As an undergraduate while earning my degree in sociology, I was not sure if I wanted to attend graduate school. I was eager to join the workforce and use the knowledge I had gained to help others. I have spent much time considering the best use of my talents. I am now certain that pursuing a Master of Social Work is the direction that I should take. My experience working in the field has only cemented my resolve to help others through the social work profession.

After earning my M.S.W., I would be especially interested in serving as a social worker in the public school system. Eventually I would like to open a counseling center for inner-city families.

HOW WOULD A GRADUATE DEGREE IN SOCIAL WORK RELATE TO YOUR CAREER OBJECTIVES?

There are certain segments of the population that are "falling through the cracks" in our system of government care. I am particularly interested in being a part of that system so that I can catch these missed cases.

I believe there has been a weakening of the American sense of community that at one time supported family structure. As a result, children are spending much less time supervised by an adult who has a vested interest in their upbringing. Many children gravitate to drugs or gangs because they are without direction. A single parent cannot do the job of two parents, especially while trying to make a living. A child that lacks adequate direction and nurturing will become a parent that fails to give direction and nurture.

Children can't raise themselves, but that is what is happening in many homes today, both where children are raised in poverty and in affluence. One article I read recently in a professional journal reported that gangs are increasingly popular with children because gangs offer the structure and security that children used to derive from the family institution. While I hope there will be a resurgence of "family values" in our country, I think some of this moral decay will not be stopped, and that is where social workers in the future will need to step in and "make a difference." In some ways, social workers end up becoming "surrogate parents" to both the adults and children of families in distress, and I feel that God has given me the talents necessary to excel in the field of social work. I am eager to embark on a structured program of graduate studies because I want to help these families and lost children. The theories and techniques which I will learn in graduate studies will, I'm sure, help me acquire an inventory of tools and techniques and approaches for use in this helping profession.

WHAT ARE YOUR CAREER OBJECTIVES?

HOW WOULD A GRADUATE DEGREE IN SOCIAL WORK RELATE TO YOUR CAREER OBJECTIVES?

Another segment of the population which I feel will be in much need of social assistance in the 21st century will be the homeless, a segment which has been largely overlooked in the past. Recent data shows that a rise in mental illness and corporate downsizing has led to a dramatic increase in the homeless population. This segment will place pressure on many systems and institutions in our country, from health care to social work, and from hospitals to nursing homes. Our society seems to neglect the impoverished more than many other cultures, and I feel we should treat all people with respect regardless of where they live. I believe caring for the homeless will be a major concern of the 21st century, and I want to be a part of designing and implementing the programs which will serve this segment.

HOW HAS YOUR ETHNIC, RACIAL, AND RELIGIOUS BACKGROUND AFFECTED YOUR ABILITY TO INTERACT WITH PEOPLE OF DIVERSE SOCIOECONOMIC BACKGROUNDS?

I have had the experience of growing up in a town of exceptional racial diversity. Therefore, I have had the opportunity to go to school and interact with people from many cultures, ethnic origins, and economic backgrounds. Race, religion and social "standing" have never affected my view of others because my environment was so diverse.

I also feel fortunate that I was brought up to believe in God, so I learned from an early age to value the differences that God instilled in people and to enjoy the diversity of different types of people.

My mother taught me, mostly by example, that it is important to be kind to everyone, and I have seen first-hand that kind people do go far in life. My mother instilled in me the concept that I have to stand on my own and follow the plan that God has laid forth for me. It is a horrible sin to not use the talents God has given us, in my mother's eyes. She raised me to be the very best person I can be, and she taught me to respect the differences in others and to value uniqueness.

America is a country of different cultures, and I believe the United States will become even more diversified culturally and ethnically in the future. Already the Asian segment of the population is growing very rapidly. I believe we need social workers who truly believe in the basic assumption that all people are valuable and special and who are comfortable dealing with people of varying socioeconomic backgrounds. I have a high degree of comfort dealing with all types of people, and I also offer the ability to communicate effectively with people of diverse backgrounds.

I believe my basic enthusiasm for life and my sincere appreciation of people of varying cultures, religions, and ethnic backgrounds are well suited for the social work profession.

WHAT FACTORS INFLUENCED YOUR DECISION TO APPLY TO THE SCHOOL OF SOCIAL WORK?

HOW HAS YOUR ETHNIC, RACIAL, AND RELIGIOUS BACKGROUND AFFECTED YOUR ABILITY TO INTERACT WITH PEOPLE OF DIVERSE SOCIOECONOMIC BACKGROUNDS?

WHAT ARE YOUR STRENGTHS AND WEAKNESSES WITH RESPECT TO INTERPERSONAL COMMUNICATION AND COOPERATION?

Because I have a genuine respect for the differences of others, people with whom I am interacting sense my nonbiased and nonprejudiced attitudes, and this becomes a significant strength for me when dealing with others. My oral communication skills are also very polished. I have refined my oral communication skills through several summer and part-time jobs in sales and customer service, and those experiences have given me confidence and poise in speaking with people face-to-face, on the telephone, or in large groups.

I pride myself on my excellent analytical and research skills as well as on my top-notch writing ability, and I believe these strengths are well suited to graduate study in social work. Finally, I am perceived by others as a sentimental and kind-hearted person who cares, and it is true that I face people with problems with a helping instinct and with a desire to solve a problem.

In terms of weaknesses, I do admit to a tendency to become too emotional about the injustices I see in the world. Intellectually, I realize that fairness is not inherent in every situation, but that is exactly how I see social workers making a difference: through their professional contributions, social workers can reduce the unfairness and decrease the suffering and alienation, thereby making the world a kinder and safer place for the less fortunate.

WHAT PREPARATIONS HAVE YOU MADE ACADEMICALLY AND PROFESSIONALLY WITH RESPECT TO YOUR AREA OF STUDY?

I have prepared myself academically for social work by majoring in sociology as an undergraduate. I have also prepared myself by taking some social work courses. Two of the courses I took were Social Work as a Profession and Human Behavior in the Social Environment.

I believe my extensive volunteer work has also prepared me professionally for the challenges I will face as a Social Worker, and my volunteer activities have taught me that helping others is often a very difficult and stressful undertaking. For example, through the Big Brothers/Big Sisters Program, I helped young women with homework and social problems they were encountering. As a social worker, I can foresee myself working to set up voluntary programs within the community so that elderly adults can be paired with students in order to increase a sense of community and to help fill the gap of largely absent extended families. In another volunteer activity with St. Elizabeth's Hospital, I was trained and then I performed volunteer work with hospice patients. I helped address their emotional, mental, and personal needs. That experience gave me insight into the burden placed on our medical professionals and on families dealing with terminal illnesses. These experiences helped me see that I need more formal training—the training that would be provided in a formal Master of Social Work program—in order to provide the maximum assistance to those in distress and need. On numerous other occasions I have also helped with local homeless projects, Habitat for Humanity and am a regular cook at the New Hope Soup Kitchen.

WHY ARE YOU CONVINCED THAT SOCIAL WORK IS THE RIGHT FIELD FOR YOU?

I feel that it is my duty and calling to help others. This is a character trait which I believe must be a motivating force for social workers. In college, I undertook sociology as a field of study because I thought it would help me acquire a better understanding of our diversified society and world. I do, in fact, believe that sociology is an excellent foundation for the study of social work at the master's level, and I am very happy I made that decision to make sociology my undergraduate major.

I have a history of extensive volunteer work which reveals my desire to work professionally in the social work field. My volunteer experiences have also given me a real world view of what professional social work entails. I have also been extensively involved in volunteer programs to aid the impaired and disabled veterans.

WHY ARE YOU CONVINCED THAT SOCIAL WORK IS THE RIGHT FIELD FOR YOU?

As a matter of philosophy, I believe that people who have had many advantages in life should give back to society. Although I am not rich materially, I feel "rich" in many ways because I have had the support of a loving family that encouraged me to spread my wings and soar in pursuit of big dreams and high achievement. I believe the kind of family life I had is the greatest gift a child could ever receive, and I feel I have much to offer the social work field in terms of helping to instill in others the values of self-respect and respect for others which were instilled in me.

WHY DO YOU FEEL YOU CAN EXCEL AT THE GRADUATE LEVEL IN THE FIELD OF SOCIAL WORK?

WHY DO YOU FEEL YOU CAN EXCEL AT THE GRADUATE LEVEL IN THE FIELD OF SOCIAL WORK?

In the process of earning my B.A. in Sociology from Virginia Tech, which I received in May 2000, I donated my time extensively in the community through such organizations as the Reach Out Program and the Mentor-A-Kid Afterschool Program for at-risk children. With the Reach Out Program, I visited senior citizens involving them in local public school activities and community events. The Mentor-A-Kid Afterschool Program allowed me to interact with children who were at risk. I helped teach these children self-reliance and empathy by teaching them life skills as well as involving them with seniors in the community. I also assisted children with homework and any other problems they were encountering. I was also informally a "counselor" for fellow students who learned of my reputation as a compassionate individual with excellent listening skills and an ability to help those in distress, particularly with relationship issues. Indeed, many of my friends referred others to me when they could not provide advice. My greatest enthusiasm for life is the enthusiasm I feel when I am in the process of helping others.

While in college, I held down a very demanding job as a crisis counselor in a women's center in addition to my studies in order to finance my college education. I am glad that I had to find employment in order to finance my college education. The added discipline and perspective provided me by these dual responsibilities taught me much about self-reliance. I do feel that the burden of working so many hours hindered me somewhat from excelling academically throughout college, but that work experience also helped me grow up and become a mature young woman who is now confident about my ability to organize and manage my time for maximum efficiency.

The courses which I enjoyed the most in college were the courses which acquainted me with Social Work, including *Social Work and the Juvenile* and *Research and Social Work.* As my transcript reveals, I performed best academically in courses that directly related to the field of social work.

I feel confident that I can excel in the MSW Program because of my maturity and enthusiasm for social work, and I feel my excellent written and oral communication skills, research and analytical ability, and genuinely empathetic nature will enable me to be at the top of my class.

WHAT SOCIETAL TRENDS AND GLOBAL EVENTS AFFECTED YOUR THINKING ABOUT A CAREER IN SOCIAL WORK?

The rapid increase in domestic violence has definitely shaped affected my thinking about a career in social work. The increase in batterers has a cyclical effect in that children of batterers often become batterers themselves. The ineffectiveness of current law enforcement procedure to disengage the batterer and the battered has reinforced my belief that this is an area where counseling, not law enforcement, would be much more effective.

It is my belief that the biggest obstacle to overcome when dealing with domestic violence is the psychology of the battered. Women and children who have remained in violent relationships for any length of time have been mentally damaged, often more severely than physically. It is the job of the social worker to overcome this obstacle.

WHAT SOCIETAL TRENDS AND GLOBAL EVENTS AFFECTED YOUR THINKING ABOUT A CAREER IN SOCIAL WORK?

Domestic violence has never been a crime of poverty. It is a crime that crosses both socioeconomic and geopolitical lines. It is an area of work in which I feel social workers can actually save lives.

I have volunteered many hours at the June Judkins Women's Shelter and have come to understand how adequate support from a qualified social worker can make the difference to a woman who is deciding whether or not to return to an abusive situation.

Domestic violence is a form of violence that has a clear track of progression. The batterer will first isolate the battered from friends and family, thereby eliminating the normal support network of the individual. Effective counseling can restore these connections and involve the victim's family in an effort to distance the abused from the abuser.

The children of abusive relationships provide another opportunity for social workers. These are children who need intensive assistance and invention. It is my goal to open my own women's shelter someday that provides ongoing support and aid to the victims of domestic violence. A recent study stated that domestic violence was increasing in urban areas at a much faster rate than the rest of the nation. This fits well with my desire to work with inner-city youth.

It is my firm belief that with intervention, the cycle of violence can be broken. Social workers can bridge the gap between law enforcement and volatile domestic violence situations.

While I know that one person or even one career field cannot solve the problem of violence in the home, I truly feel that I could make a significant impact in this area. In some ways, social workers are replacing the huge gap left by extended family in today's relocating workforce. I feel that any effort to restore the sense of family to our society will be a productive one. I am eager to learn from and contribute to a program of graduate studies that will help me to make such an effort. The theories and techniques which I will learn in graduate studies will, I'm sure, help me acquire the tools necessary to help those in need.

WHAT EMPLOYMENT, VOLUNTEER, INTERNSHIP OR LIFE EXPERIENCES HAVE DEVELOPED YOUR INTEREST IN SOCIAL WORK AND HOW WILL YOU BUILD ON THESE THROUGH GRADUATE STUDY?

Since I was a child, my goal has been to help others. My father is a single parent and although he worked many hours to support his children, he always had time to help others. It was impossible to be raised by him and turn away from someone in need. For example, my father was an auto mechanic. Many of the families in my neighborhood had only one car and no one had a new car. Whenever one of their cars broke down, they could count on my dad to help them fix it even after he had worked all day and still had to care for us. My father taught me, mostly by example, that it is important to practice what we believe everyday.

I think that the idea of helping others has been thrown away in our busy society. That is where social workers in the 21st century will need to step in and "make a difference." In some ways, social workers are the only help available to families in distress, and I feel the gifts God has given me will enable me to excel in the field of social work. I am eager to begin advanced study in the field of social work because I feel that it is my calling. I am eager to learn from the experience of the professors who have walked this path before me.

HOW HAVE YOUR EMPLOYMENT, VOLUNTEER, INTERN, OR LIFE EXPERIENCES DEVELOPED YOUR INTEREST IN SOCIAL WORK?

Since I was a child, my goal has been to be involved in a career in which I could help children. As a child of the American foster care system I am eager to work with young children that have been removed from their families of origin. My mother was a single parent and although she tried, she could not care for me adequately. It was at this point in my life that I met a social worker named Penelope D'Alpe. She made the difference in my life. Through her work I was able to come to an understanding of not only my situation, but of my mother's. She managed to guide me through my time in foster care keeping my self esteem intact. Once my mother found work, I was returned to her and she has been the best mother anyone could ask for. She also benefitted from the help of Ms. D'Alpe. Together we realized what a difference a caring and committed social worker could make to a family. It was this experience that developed my interest in the field of social work. My mother taught me never to give up. Ms. D'Alpe taught me to never stop believing in your dreams. Although the stereotype of a foster child is of a troubled youth, I am confident, stable, articulate and have never had trouble academically or professionally. I have always felt that God has given me talents and I must find ways to utilize them.

I have had the experience of growing up as a racially mixed female in a town which is mostly white. I have always been treated fairly and with respect in this small town. It is truly a great place to be from. My race was never made an issue by teachers while I was growing up. I had only one incident of racially motivated strife in my years here. This incident occurred at a football game. I was a cheerleader for our varsity football team at the time. It was common for the opposing team's cheerleaders to meet before the game to work out who would perform first at halftime. At this meeting I overheard one of the girls from the other time whisper that I wasn't "all white." I thought about that comment for a long time and decided that the girl was right. I'm not all white nor am I all black, but I also decided that there wasn't anything wrong with that. I chose to attend undergraduate school at a very racially diverse university. I thought that I would be unprepared to deal with different cultures. In reality I found that the acceptance for who I am that I was shown in my hometown had prepared me to work with people from any race, culture, or background.

Throughout high school and college, I extensively volunteered my time in crisis centers and as a tutor for children for whom English was a second language. This has shown me how much gratification I receive helping others.

HOW HAVE YOUR EMPLOYMENT, VOLUNTEER, INTERN, OR LIFE EXPERIENCES DEVELOPED YOUR INTEREST IN SOCIAL WORK?

I have been told many times that my greatest talent is that of always being ready to help out, and I feel that most of the indifference within society today is basically an unwillingness to be ready at all times to lend a hand. I have the ability to listen to others without being judgmental. As an attentive listener, I have the ability to truly be of assistance rather than merely commiserating with the person talking. I believe my ability to listen springs from my innate desire to help others. Listening intently is not as easy as it seems. Talking is easier than listening, but listening is the critical step leading up to the problem-solving stage, and I feel my "listening skills" are refined to an extraordinarily high level.

America is a country of different cultures, and I believe the United States will become even more diversified culturally and ethnically in the 21st century. I believe we need social workers who truly believe in the equality of people regardless of color or ethnicity. Social work is not a suitable choice for those who are uncomfortable dealing with people of varying socioeconomic backgrounds. I have a high degree of comfort dealing with all types of people, and I also offer the ability to communicate effectively with people of diverse backgrounds.

As an undergraduate while earning my degree in sociology, I knew that I wanted to pursue my Master of Social Work, but I was not prepared to do so immediately upon graduation due to financial circumstances. I am now financially stable and am ready for the challenge of advanced study. I feel certain that my goal should be to earn a Master of Social Work (M.S.W.) degree so that I can refine my skills.

Finally, my work experience has helped me develop confidence that I can be a highly effective social worker. Through numerous jobs as a bank teller, clerk, and receptionist, I have learned much about human behavior while refining my public relations, analytical, customer service, and problem-solving skills.

HOW DO YOU EXPECT YOUR GRADUATE SCHOOL PERFORMANCE TO COMPARE WITH YOUR UNDERGRADUATE EXPERIENCE?

HOW DO YOU EXPECT YOUR GRADUATE SCHOOL PERFORMANCE TO COMPARE WITH YOUR UNDERGRADUATE EXPERIENCE?

In the process of earning my B.A. in Psychology from the University of San Diego, I donated my time extensively in the community through such organizations as the Innocence Project and the San Diego Department of Corrections Intervention Program in which I worked with inmates. My experiences with these men and women confirmed my belief that social work was the profession for me. I also worked with area gang members in negotiating peace talks and community involvement projects. My fellow students thought that trying to negotiate peace with gang members was a waste of time but my personal experiences with these young adults proved that this was untrue. My greatest accomplishments have come from watching kids who had been given up on succeed.

While in college, I held down a full-time job as a nanny for two children in addition to my college studies in order to finance my education. Looking back, I feel the necessity to find employment in order to help finance my college education hindered me somewhat from excelling academically throughout college, but that work experience also helped me grow up and become a mature young woman who is now confident about my ability to organize and manage my time for maximum efficiency.

HOW HAVE SOCIETAL/ CULTURAL TRENDS/ GLOBAL EVENTS AFFECTED YOUR THINKING ABOUT A SOCIAL WORK CAREER?

The courses which I enjoyed the most in college were the courses which acquainted me with Social Work, including Social Work as a Profession and Human Behavior in the Social Environment. As my transcript reveals, I performed best academically in the last two years of my undergraduate career, and I even made the Dean's List. I feel confident that I can excel in the MSW Program because of my maturity and enthusiasm for social work, and I feel my excellent written and oral communication skills, research and analytical ability, and empathetic nature will enable me to be at the top of my class.

HOW HAVE SOCIETAL/CULTURAL TRENDS/GLOBAL EVENTS AFFECTED YOUR THINKING ABOUT A SOCIAL WORK CAREER?

I feel strongly that the cultural diversity of the United States is its greatest asset. In the future, I believe that social workers are going to be needed for extensive statistical research in the future. Sociological research is a rapidly expanding field. In my undergraduate work, I participated in many sociological studies and worked closely with the Chairman of the Sociology Department, Dr. Nathan Hammer.

I believe that effective correlative research will be of incalculable value in developing governmental programs that truly aid the diverse cultural groups within our country and will also dispel myths regarding immigration and migrant populations. I developed and conducted the study, "Do Faculty Evaluations Affect Tenure?" published in the Journal of Sociology. The study, though my first, demonstrates my dedication to the field of statistical research. Many people view the role of social workers in a one-dimensional manner. Even those involved in the field of social work rarely consider pursuing careers in anything other than the usual positions. This has left the field of statistical research sadly understaffed with qualified social workers. Without research, all programs are subject to the commitment of an analytical fallacy. It is my goal to provide research that is the basis for planning based on factual analysis.

WHAT WERE THE FACTORS THAT CONTRIBUTED TO YOUR INTEREST IN SOCIAL WORK?

Since I was a child I have been noted for my exceptional empathy. Raised by my grandmother, I have always been involved with the elderly in my community. My grandmother instilled in me a sense of responsibility for others that survives to this day. My grandmother seldom went any place without her knitting needles and her bible. These represented her basic beliefs that God should go everywhere with you and that there was no excuse for idle hands. She knit blankets and mittens for those who couldn't afford them and taught everyone who would listen the word of God. I believe my grandmother's giving nature is what instilled in me the desire to become a social worker and the desire to help others.

I truly feel my gifts would be best utilized in this field and receiving my Master's Degree would aid me in meeting my goals. I have volunteered my time with troubled children at the Carver School for Girls and the Second Chance Ranch. These experiences gave me a real-world perspective of what a career in social work involved.

It is my goal to continue to volunteer my time helping others while pursuing my M.S.W. I would like someday to be a part of a nonprofit organization that helps professionally inexperienced single parents take advantage of programs available to them for aid, training, and job placement.

I have had the experience of growing up as a white female in a town which is adjacent to the world's largest immigrant population, Miami, Florida. Therefore, I have had the opportunity to go to school and interact with people from many cultures, ethnic origins, and economic backgrounds. I also feel fortunate that I was brought up to believe in equality, so I learned from an early age to value the differences that God instilled in people and to enjoy the diversity of different types of people.

I have been told many times that my greatest talent is that of being a good counselor, and I feel that offering sound, well-reasoned advice is an integral part of a career in social work. I have the ability to listen to others with empathy and to give advice that considers the best interests of that person and all those affected. As an attentive listener, I also have an ability to be objective. I believe my ability to put myself in the place of the speaker comes from my innate desire to help them.

America is a country in transition. With one out of every two marriages ending in divorce, a rapidly increasing portion of the population are becoming single parents. Many of these parents will be young and unskilled. I wish to work with these parents to develop their skills and opportunities so that their children have a fighting chance. I want every child to see that the future is whatever you make of it. I have a high degree of comfort dealing with all types of people, and I also offer the ability to communicate effectively with people of diverse backgrounds.

WHAT WERE THE FACTORS THAT CONTRIBUTED TO YOUR INTEREST IN SOCIAL WORK?

IS YOUR GPA A GOOD INDICATOR OF YOUR INTELLECT AND CAPACITY FOR INTENSE STUDY?

I would respectfully ask that the Admissions Committee look at my GPA and consider the fact that I was coming to terms with my identity and professional goals during my college years. I got off to a good start in college after receiving a $3,000 academic scholarship.

As a freshman, I was elected as a Senator in the Student Government Association. I was also invited to join a prominent sorority on campus. I became very involved in the sorority and my job with the Student Government Association. I also became a member of several committees and the dance line. I found myself committed to many extracurricular activities which taught me excellent time management skills.

These skills were not acquired immediately and as a result, my GPA suffered. I would not trade a higher GPA for the essential lessons this experience taught me.

IS YOUR GPA AN ADEQUATE INDICATOR OF YOUR INTELLECT AND CAPACITY FOR INTENSE STUDY?

I would respectfully ask that the Admissions Committee look at my GPA and consider the fact that I had to overcome overwhelming obstacles during that time frame.

I entered college with an excellent academic record which I maintained through my freshman year.

The following summer I was involved in a near-fatal car accident. The subsequent recovery was extremely difficult for me financially, emotionally and physically. My GPA dropped but I refused to take the advice of friends and family to take a year away from my studies to recover. I refused to let the accident imprison my mind as it had temporarily done to my body. The doctors were unsure if I would ever walk again. The recovery process was slow and took over two years of intensive rehabilitation and physical therapy.

I am happy to say that I can walk and have regained my previous lifestyle. While recovering from the accident was one of the most intellectually as well as physically challenging obstacles I have ever faced, I had to teach myself to think and use the vernacular of a surgeon so that I could understand and fully participate in my care. I had to learn anatomy and physiology so that I could decide which exercises would best return me to my previous strength. I managed all of this while maintaining a full course load.

I hope that my reaction to this trying period of my life clearly demonstrates my ability to overcome obstacles with strength of mind and body.

Part Four: MBA Programs and Business Schools
Essays and Personal Statements

If you want to see strong examples of essays and personal statements for business schools and M.B.A. programs, this section of the book will interest you the most. You will often be asked to communicate your goals and ambitions, and many graduate schools are seeking intensely driven individuals who aspire to the highest levels of achievement.

Professional schools examine your application to determine if your goals and objectives are a "good fit" with the aims of their respective programs. For example, some business schools offer a better selection of entrepreneurial courses than others. Other schools may emphasize international commerce. Read the brochures and catalogs you receive and make sure you have a clear understanding of the particular program to which you are applying. Then make sure your essays and personal statements reflect your understanding of the programs to which you are applying.

ESSAYS AND PERSONAL STATEMENTS FOR MBA PROGRAMS AND BUSINESS SCHOOLS

Date

The American Graduate School
Of International Management
15249 N. 59th Ave.
Glendale, Arizona 85306-6003

**LETTER OF APPLICATION
TO GRADUATE SCHOOL IN
PURSUIT OF A MASTER'S
DEGREE**
You may want to send your
application with a
transmittal letter, such as
this one.

Dear Sir or Madam:

With the enclosed application and supporting documentation, I am expressing my sincere interest in being accepted into the Master of International Management graduate program at The American Graduate School Of International Management.

I am extremely well equipped for graduate studies in international business, and I feel certain I could one day become a distinguished alumnus of your fine institution. As you will see from my resume, I already hold a B.S. degree in Business and Marketing and I read, write, and speak Spanish fluently. My Spanish language skills were refined as an intelligence professional and Spanish linguist in the U.S. Army, and I traveled extensively throughout Latin and Central America working on projects related to making our country safer from illegal drugs and weapons.

In addition to my experience as a military professional and Spanish linguist, I believe my extensive work experience will also help to make me a valuable part of the MIM program. While working in summer and part-time jobs to finance my college education, I excelled in positions as an assistant retail manager, sales representative, and merchandiser and I have also worked in the construction, hospitality, and transportation industries.

As you will see when you read my essay, my goal is to become the chief executive officer of a company doing business in Latin America, and I feel my background thus far, combined with the program of graduate studies offered by the American Graduate School of International Business, will help me achieve that aim. I am committed to helping my community, and I offer an extensive "track record" of volunteer service which is summarized on my resume. I feel I would be a credit to the business community because of my strong conviction that the economic necessity to make a profit must be balanced by concern for customers and respect for employees.

I can assure you in advance that I would be a credit to the next entering class and as a graduate. Thank you for your consideration of my application.

Sincerely yours,

Patrick Knowlton, Jr.

WHY SHOULD THE SELECTION COMMITTEE CHOOSE YOU FOR OUR PROGRAM?

My work experience can clearly demonstrate that I am an extremely hard worker. I have worked since I was 15 years old in the business that my family owns. In that business called Natural Organics, Inc., I applied my entrepreneurial instincts as my family and I contracted with local grocery stores to supply non-chemically treated vegetables for their produce department. I grew, cultivated, and monitored our small crop while expanding our harvest through innovative techniques. My efforts led to an $8,000 profit increase. From that experience I learned valuable lessons about what it takes to balance success and research expense. During the summers and college breaks, I also held jobs as a cook and as a nurse's aid in a hospital.

Through those jobs I learned that the productivity of every person in an organization is important; for example, it was my work as a cook which was often the general public's most tangible impression of the facility, and a bad meal would have discredited even the finest medical care. My favorite jobs, however, and those which most related to my professional interests, were those in which I cultivated a love for the outdoors and a reverence for nature. One summer I was a senior organizer for the Special Olympics and, since graduating from college, I have worked as a volunteer firefighter, a job which has required extensive training in areas related to medical emergency care and other areas.

WHY SHOULD THE SELECTION COMMITTEE CHOOSE YOU FOR OUR PROGRAM?

DESCRIBE A SITUATION IN WHICH YOUR INITIATIVE HAD A POSITIVE EFFECT ON OTHERS.

A situation in which my initiative had an effect on others was through a sales experience. I took the initiative to present to a customer a smarter and more advantageous way to borrow money. Through extensive conversations and product understanding, I was able to illustrate to a customer how he could best utilize not only the equity in his home, but the possible tax advantages with using real estate as collateral.

DESCRIBE A SITUATION IN WHICH YOUR INITIATIVE HAD A POSITIVE EFFECT ON OTHERS.

However, the full benefits of my initiative did not come into fruition until weeks later when this client referred a friend to me who was in immediate crisis. This man's wife had been unexpectedly hospitalized and required an expensive operation. After conversation and some research I discovered that he, too, could use equity from his home to access the desperately needed funds to cover medical costs for his wife's surgery.

This event, although seemingly routine, demonstrates the tremendous impact which strong initiative can make. In dealing with my first customer, I arduously discussed financing options with an effective customer service demeanor. In doing so, my initiative was relayed to another customer. Fortunately, I was able to provide this new customer with sound financial advice.

HOW DID YOU BECOME INTERESTED IN WHARTON BUSINESS SCHOOL?

HOW DID YOU BECOME INTERESTED IN WHARTON BUSINESS SCHOOL?

I first became interested in Wharton Business School after discussing the top MBA schools with an Economics professor. My professor's strong recommendation, coupled with information I read from your annual catalog about the school, solidified my decision to apply. Finally, I spoke with some fellow alumni about your program. All the informational avenues I sought regarding Wharton echoed the same thing: quality, uniqueness, and opportunity. Understanding the doors that become opened from graduates from your fine institution, I could not help but be attracted to your school. My own track record of outstanding results academically and in work situations give me the impetus to "aim for the best," which is what Wharton is.

WHAT ARE THE MOST IMPORTANT THINGS IN YOUR LIFE AND WHY?

WHAT ARE THE MOST IMPORTANT THINGS IN YOUR LIFE AND WHY?

Two things in my life are more important to me than any others. My Eagle Scout award came to me through much hard work and perseverance. It ranks as the most meaningful source of pride for me. The Eagle award recipients constitute less than one percent of all young men who enroll in the Boy Scouts. It requires confidence, hard work, and common sense, but above all the Eagle badge is a mark of leadership. No one can become an Eagle without carrying out an Eagle Project, which directly measures how well one plans and gives leadership. Therefore, the Eagle Scout award received in high school is a great source of pride for me because of what it symbolizes.

A second thing which is very important to me is cycling. I own two racing bikes and I use them to get around just about everywhere. I love cycling and racing so much, in fact, that I have secured an employment at a local bicycle shop while in college. Here I gain more knowledge daily as I see new models of bikes being released daily. This 30-hours-per-week job also gives me an opportunity to "feed my habit," as I am able to purchase bicycle parts at a discounted rate. I plan to make cycling a part of my life for some time to come.

IF YOU HAD A DINNER PARTY AND COULD INVITE ANY THREE PEOPLE WHO EVER LIVED, WHO WOULD YOU INVITE? WHY?

IF YOU HAD A DINNER PARTY AND COULD INVITE ANY THREE PEOPLE WHO EVER LIVED, WHO WOULD YOU INVITE? WHY?

If I were having a dinner party and could invite any three people who ever lived, my guests and I would tread a span of time and ideology for a revealing evening. On my left would sit the philosophical mind of Jonathan Edwards; on my right the sensibility of Abraham Lincoln; and in front of me would sit the pioneering Christopher Columbus.

As the exaltation from my initial greetings dissolved, I would begin my interrogation. Starting with Christopher Columbus, the objective for his attendance would be two-fold. Namely, due to the controversy of his intentions to discover new lands, I would require a full explanation of his personal motives and expectations in setting sail for virgin lands. When Columbus stumbled over the resources and opportunities of the new world, did his religious beliefs or his human passions dominate? Did God have preeminence over all these wonders, or did Columbus and his supporting cast fall into thoughts of covetousness, disregarding the God in whose name they traveled? Second,

I would request of Mr. Columbus that he reenact the scene prior to the voyage. I have always longed to know the authentic emotion of facing the absolute unknown.

Next, I would address Mr. Lincoln. Finding, or even defining, a great leader is difficult today. Since Mr. Lincoln epitomized leadership in the most turbulent years in American history, I would request a view through his paradigm regarding an effective leader. Coupled with this perspective, I would ask him to parallel a person today whom he felt matched the criteria. Lastly, I would ask Mr. Lincoln why he at one point attempted to have African-American people deported back to Africa, and yet was the main factor in the abolishment of slavery? Did he genuinely confess that all people were equal and could successfully be integrated, or did he believe black and white had their respective places apart from one another?

Finally, I would converse with Jonathan Edwards, the prototype of the thinker. The reason I would request his presence at my dinner would be two-fold. First, I could have him explain concisely his beliefs about the Christian doctrine of predestination. This is one of the most debated principles in Christianity, and a thought-provoked explanation would be cherished. Secondly, I would ask Mr. Edwards to defend himself against the rampant creed perpetuated today that he was a hell-and-brimstone preacher. Did he retrospectively perceive himself to be condemning or loving when it came to confronting a "lost person?" Or was he so lovingly concerned with the salvation of souls that he came across as stern?

The evening would unquestionably be memorable. Questions which have confounded me at times would finally be resolved. The only problem, however, is that my cast of guests would inherently contain the propensity to unleash questions of one another. Abraham Lincoln might ask Jonathan Edwards why he could not reach a compromise with the doctrine of predestination; Jonathan Edwards might ask Christopher Columbus how exactly he tried to Christianize the Indians; and Christopher Columbus probably would want to know why America did not have a King and Queen.

AS A BUSINESS LEADER, EXPLAIN THE CORRELATION BETWEEN THE DEMANDS PLACED ON WORKING PARENTS AND ABSENTEEISM. WHAT WOULD YOU DO ABOUT IT?

AS A FUTURE BUSINESS LEADER, EXPLAIN THE CORRELATION BETWEEN THE DEMANDS PLACED ON WORKING PARENTS AND ABSENTEEISM. WHAT YOU WOULD DO ABOUT IT?

It is not necessary to go into a long explanation about the correlation between absenteeism and the demands placed on working parents. As the president of this large company in a suburban/industrial research park, I would take the following steps to try to create an environment in which the company could respond to the pressures of working parents with the twin goals of maximizing employee morale and reducing employee absenteeism.

1. First, I would make it a matter of corporate philosophy that the company seeks to assist parents in every practical way possible to satisfy the demands placed on them because of their family responsibilities. I would wholeheartedly support the Family Leave Act passed by Congress and I would go further than the act requires **because I feel that this would be in the best economic interests of the company and its shareholders.** I would have it known throughout the company that the top management believes that family should be the first commitment of every individual with the commitment to

the company being second. With this bold corporate philosophy stated and made a reality of corporate life, I believe the company would reap much favorable public relations just by virtue of having such a policy which recognizes the importance of family life.

2. I would create an advisory committee of employees—both working moms and dads and perhaps with some single individuals on the committee so that they do not feel their feelings are ignored—which would be empowered to make recommendations to the president on all matters related to family issues. This advisory committee would understand that the company is first and foremost an economic unit designed to make a profit but that the company has "soul" and wishes to be responsive to the desire of parents to raise loved and well adjusted children. In my view, there is no greater contribution one can make to society than to raise happy and well-adjusted children who wish to make a contribution to society, and I believe a strong corporate philosophy which articulates this point of view would ultimately be very beneficial in terms of both employee relations and customer relations.

3. Based on recommendations of the advisory committee which would have to be approved by the president, the company would experiment with varied methods of responding to parental pressures. Possible approaches which could be examined by the committee would be as follows:

• Certain employees might work in environments which would allow for the working moms and dads of children under 1 year old to set up a playpen in the office. This would not work for all employees but could be permitted if practical.

• The committee might wish to discuss the possibility of creating a calendar of "necessary leave" which would allow employees to use a designated number of hours per year to address certain family needs (i.e., sick child, sporting event, etc.). These hours would be separate from regular vacation or sick leave time. This would allow parents to leave work a little early or come in a little late if necessary.

• The committee could actually have a small budget which it could administer which would go toward supporting youth activities. For example, it may be that the company could buy uniforms for two or three youth sports teams each year. Uniforms would clearly have the corporate name emblazoned on the shirt so that the company would reap public relations advantages from its corporate "good turn."

• The committee could encourage parents to be involved in their children's activities and would encourage the company to be responsive, as is practical, to such needs. For example, fathers who wish to leave at 5 P.M. promptly in order to coach a youth team sport could be allowed to do so if they were not, for example, traveling on company business.

• If the company had the physical space, the advisory committee might wish to recommend that the company accept solicitations from day-care vendors and allow on-premises day care to be provided by qualified providers. The employee would pay for the day care service, but an on-site option might allow working moms and dads to visit the child during the day on breaks.

• A possible recommendation of such an advisory committee might be that working parents could be offered part-time positions, and possibly two full-time employees might become involved in job sharing. This would give some employees an option other than "full time job" or "no work."

• Where appropriate, employees with newborns (after the appropriate maternity leave had expired) could be provided with laptops or home computers in order to work from home.

In summary, I do not feel that a company president could be aware enough of the wide range of needs to be able to individually create a package of options and opportunities which would address the needs of working parents. I would create an advisory committee of employees and I would work with them at a specified monthly meeting to address the concerns of working parents and listen to their recommendations. A company newsletter could make known the names of employees on this advisory committee so that employees could make their specific suggestions and needs known to those individuals.

Finally, I wish to stress that a company philosophy that stresses the importance of family life and seeks to be responsive to the needs of working parents would be good for business, good for employees, good for children and families, and good for society. I believe a company has a responsibility to be a good citizen in society.

AS A BUSINESS LEADER, EXPLAIN THE CORRELATION BETWEEN THE DEMANDS PLACED ON WORKING PARENTS AND ABSENTEEISM. WHAT WOULD YOU DO ABOUT IT?

DESCRIBE YOUR MOST CHALLENGING TEAM EXPERIENCE.

My most challenging team experience is the work environment I am in presently. I am on an elite, precise, high-performance Honor Guard for the Joint Readiness Training Center of Fort Polk, Louisiana.

The role is unique because the small select group of soldiers are all required to maintain exceptionally high physical and moral standards. In addition, we perform under close scrutiny for many high profile situations and dignitaries, including the post's Commanding Generals, honored retirees, and visiting VIPs.

My specific role is the honored responsibility of holding the only the female position on the ten-soldier team. To be able to assimilate into a male-dominated squad was itself a challenge. I was required to learn leadership skills from a disadvantaged position. I outranked all but two members of the team and on many occasions I would have to take charge in procuring equipment, arranging practices and appointments with dignitaries, and delivering orders to subordinates. In addition to this challenge, I also had to expertly and graciously handle the particulars of military drill and ceremony, including precision movements, attention to detail, and performance under stress by supervisors.

The group became very close while dealing with these issues. We weren't plagued with any of the sexual harassment that has been abundant in other areas of the Army. In great part due to my ability to place each soldier at ease, and by not using the fact that I was a female as leverage, we learned to interact with each other using respect and dignity. We became friends aside from being co-workers, which is unique in the military. This performance squad was selected by our General and our Sergeant Major so there was no favoritism in being selected and that method ensured none of us had worked together before. We each came from entirely different jobs, backgrounds, and goals. All factors meshed to make a team that functioned as one top-quality entity.

Being selected for this job had a major benefit in that we were, for the most part, exempt from field duty. Due to the many ceremonies we performed and the traveling that was required, the field became a secondary responsibility. I took full advantage of this situation and took eighteen to twenty-one hours of college classes a semester. My goal was to graduate from college immediately after my time in service expired. I am going to meet that goal by leaving the Army in February 2001 and graduating from Louisiana State University in May of 2001. I have excelled academically in spite of my intensely demanding schedule and have a 3.5 GPA. Even though my team was exempt from field duty, we had many after-hour and weekend events to participate in, so relentless time management was of the utmost importance. I took every opportunity to study. I carried my books with me every time we traveled and the other soldiers in my squad would help me learn by quizzing me on formulas or facts I needed to know. This process brought us even closer. As a matter of fact, two other soldiers have been encouraged to start their college careers after witnessing me balance the demands of our team, a college course load, and a part-time weekend job.

My membership in the Honor Guard will make me a better leader of others in the future as I strive to manage by the principle of "leadership by example."

DESCRIBE YOUR PROFESSIONAL EXPERIENCES.

My diverse professional experiences have included military and civilian organizations, unionized and non-unionized work forces, as well as manufacturing, production operation, and job shop environments. My goals have evolved as I have found myself tested in those diverse settings, and my goal now is to obtain my MBA from the Turpin School of Business and then to join a consumer products company where I can distinguish myself in the area of marketing with the eventual goal of becoming Chief Executive Officer.

My path toward my current goal has not been a straight one, but my personal and professional goals have always been high. Born the oldest of four daughters to a proud, Christian family in Arizona, I graduated from a public school and for ten years participated in 4-H, which afforded me numerous opportunities to refine my public speaking skills. My parents strongly believed in instilling in us values of self-reliance and independence, and they felt that their daughters should shoulder 100% of their college educations. My younger sisters enrolled in college immediately after high school graduation and financed their education with student loans and part-time jobs; they obtained their bachelor's degrees when they were 22—one became a computer programmer and the other majored in communications and now works as a sales representative for a food company. I took a different route. I decided to wed my twin passions for computers and architecture by embarking on an Architectural Technology Degree program at a community college. Two years and sixty credits later, I was impatient to use my skills in a real-world environment, so I decided to work full-time as a Computer Operator and continue my studies part-time, with a view to one day becoming a programmer. While excelling in my full-time job, I enrolled for one semester at the University of Arizona at a time in my life when my career goals were shifting from programming to business management. By that time, I had been exposed to the worlds of construction, manufacturing, and retailing, and I had discovered the thrill of working with others on creative teams dedicated to achieving the customer's goals in the most cost effective fashion. While working as a Computer Operator for McKinney Operations, I was promoted to coordinate the communication process among the company's account specialists, the personnel in our shop responsible for product construction, and the client's project manager. I was excelling in business, and I loved it, and that work experience was transforming my career goals from computers to business management.

Once I realized that my goal was to obtain a bachelor's degree in Business Administration, I had to figure out how to find the money to achieve that goal. Although I enjoyed my job at McKinney Operations, this 500-person, unionized company was not extremely supportive of employees attending college because the company had lost several employees once they earned their degrees. Therefore, I obtained similar employment at a smaller company which valued my expertise and which encouraged me to pursue my educational goals. Although I thoroughly enjoyed working at McKinney Operations, the production schedule combined with my ineligibility for in-state tuition and financial aid prevented me from attending college. I did not give up, however.

One day as I renewed my driver's license at the Arizona Army National Guard Armory, I saw a poster that was a person's face shown as half camouflaged soldier

DESCRIBE YOUR PROFESSIONAL EXPERIENCES.

and half college graduate complete with mortar board. The caption beneath read, "We will give you the time <u>and</u> the money for college." Needless to say, my interest was piqued. So I took a pamphlet, filled out a business reply card, and dropped it in the box. Several weeks later, an Army Recruiter contacted me and after some initial screening, I was offered a good Military Occupational Specialty with an enticing educational package.

DESCRIBE YOUR PROFESSIONAL EXPERIENCES.

I enlisted in the Army and entered Basic Training in October of that same year. During my time in the military, I was afforded the opportunity to travel throughout the South, Southeast, and Midwest regions of the United States. The military provided me with the opportunity to work with many different types of people, including ethnic, background, and religious differences plus gender integration. The military atmosphere has enhanced my discipline and taught me attention to detail and leadership skills that I utilize daily. I was trained in two Military Occupational Specialties: communications specialist and parachute rigger. The communications job required me to know how to transmit and receive properly on several different types of communication equipment and maintain records for the equipment. I was awarded a Secret level security clearance for this job. In addition to the primary tasks of communication, I handled personnel and administrative work for 275 personnel records.

After a while, I transferred to active duty army and the job of parachute rigger. This job required me to pack and maintain personnel parachutes and to rig air delivery cargo. This particular job required an extreme sense of attention to detail because parachute and air delivery carry hundreds of thousands of dollars of equipment safely to the ground. More importantly, however, the chutes my team and I packed and repaired were used during airborne operations by paratroopers. Daily, we had soldiers' lives in our hands and that mission was taken very seriously. Incorporated with mission and to ensure quality control, my entire job field is required to be airborne qualified and participate regularly in airborne operations Only 10% of the Army is airborne qualified and only 1% of those are female paratroopers due to the high physical fitness required. It is an elite status.

Upon signing in and completing my inprocessing into Fort Polk, Louisiana, I immediately enrolled in college and began to fulfill my goal of graduating with a Bachelor's Degree. After the first year of attendance at Louisiana College, I chose to transfer to Louisiana State University because it offered a better availability of classes. In addition, I preferred the atmosphere at LSU. I found an equally stimulating atmosphere when I visited your university and am especially pleased with the feedback from the students currently enrolled.

The path toward earning my bachelor's degree has not been an easy one. Because I am a highly motivated individual who is known for absolute reliability and integrity, I have always been selected ahead of my peers for supervisory roles, even though I have been vigorously and rigorously involved in earning my college degree in the hours when I am not working full-time. Indeed, I was selected for my current job as member of an elite Honor Guard, and I am proud that I am the only woman on this 10-person team. I am also proud that I have earned a reputation with my colleagues as someone known for the highest moral, personal, and professional standards.

My weekly schedule is rigorous and I believe it is a testament to my passion for education, my absolute determination to achieve a goal once I decide to do so, and my ability to excel in academic environments.

I believe I could make major contributions to the learning environment at the Turpin School of Business. I am by nature a highly motivated young professional who understands the value of education and who is dedicated to improving myself throughout my lifetime by continuing education. I am confident that I could enrich the classroom through my hands-on experience in civilian and military environments, my experience in both unionized and non-unionized companies, and my interaction with numerous major segments of our economy including retail, construction, and manufacturing. My professional experiences thus far have enabled me to gain much confidence in my ability to set very high professional goals because I know that I will maintain the personal dedication and hard work necessary to achieving ambitious goals. I feel certain that, just as the Turpin School of Business could offer me many opportunities for knowledge and insight, I could become a rich source of learning and support for other students, and I would welcome all such opportunities to promote the personal growth and professional competence of my fellow students.

DESCRIBE YOUR PROFESSIONAL EXPERIENCES.

WHAT ARE THE FOUR MOST IMPORTANT REASONS THAT YOU FEEL YOU WOULD BENEFIT THE PROGRAM AT OUR INSTITUTION?

1. **I am a strong Christian.** With an attitude of respect for all other religions, I do believe that my strong religious beliefs will enable me to become known as a businessman of the highest principles and ethics. I set no less lofty a goal than that for myself. I have already seen in my banking experience that there are many temptations to succumb to greed. The savings and loan fiasco which our country is still paying for is evidence of that. I am committed to the highest moral and ethical principles.

WHAT ARE THE FOUR MOST IMPORTANT REASONS YOU FEEL YOU WOULD BENEFIT THE PROGRAM AT OUR INSTITUTION?

2. **I am a competitor and a winner.** As a star basketball athlete in high school, I have enjoyed the thrill of competition and victory, and I believe my strong competitive instincts are well suited for a career at top management levels.

3. **I am a goal setter who works relentlessly until I achieve my goals.** I set a goal to graduate from college in three years, and I did it. I decided not just to meet but to exceed all corporate performance goals while in my current position, and I have done that; in fact, I was a major reason why two different operations centers where I worked achieved record sales results. I thrive on the challenge of doing something better than anyone else has ever done it while simultaneously working in a cooperative and harmonious relationship with my colleagues.

4. **I have unusually strong communication skills.** With top-notch public speaking and writing skills, I believe my communication skills are well suited to a career in management.

WHAT ARE YOUR GREATEST ASSETS?

**WHAT ARE YOUR
GREATEST ASSETS?**

I am a strong public speaker with excellent communication skills which I began to refine as a youth and especially during the 10 years when I participated in 4-H. During those years, I won several awards for state, district, and national competitions. 4-H also taught me strong values, patriotism, and responsibility for civic duties.

Strong Religious Values and Moral Principles

I am a strong Christian and am in the process of transferring my membership to the First Baptist Church from my home church in Arizona. I try to dedicate as much time as possible to the activities in my church and plan to join several committees after graduation.

Outstanding Time Management Skills

Combining a demanding full-time job with a challenging college course load has been an activity which has helped me acquire excellent time-management skills. With the eventual goal of becoming a Chief Executive Officer, I am intensely dedicated to the path I have to travel in order to achieve my goals.

Taking GMAT again in January 2002

On my first attempt at taking the GMAT, I scored 580 and performed in an outstanding fashion on the quantitative section as well as the two verbal sections. I was somewhat disappointed with my score on the Data Sufficiency Section, and I am "prepping" to take the GMAT again in order to improve my score on the Data Sufficiency Section.

DESCRIBE YOUR WORK EXPERIENCE AND WHY YOU FEEL THAT BUSINESS IS YOUR CALLING.

My work experience since graduating from college has confirmed my feeling that I belong in the business world. A highly competitive individual who thrived as a youth on the thrill of sports competition, I have progressed at an unusually rapid rate with Bank of San Francisco from Consumer Banker I, to Consumer Banker II, and then to Consumer Banker III. I have exceeded all performance goals and am thriving on the challenge of helping Bank of San Francisco reposition itself as a full-service financial institution that can provide all financial management and investment services. Despite my youth and inexperience, I have become respected by senior industry executives and am routinely sought out for my advice related to portfolio management as well savings, investments, and protection and credit products. My sales and consulting skills have been tested in a sophisticated business arena, and I have demonstrated executive abilities.

While I am excelling in the sales, marketing, and consulting aspects of my job and have been told that I have a bright future in management with the bank, I am eager to gain the knowledge that I will need in order to help me become an outstanding general manager.

I am attracted by Wharton's emphasis on instilling a generalist perspective in its MBA students, and I am also attracted by the program's emphasis on teamwork and on its inclusion of a field study project. From my experience in the banking industry, I have become acutely aware of the fact that international facts and figures are background factors in even local lending decisions. We are a global economy; I am seeking a graduate school that emphasizes the international nature of business.

I am a very focused and highly motivated individual who does not take goal setting lightly. Throughout my life, I have exhibited the ability to make strategic decisions about my future and implement them with aggression and efficiency.

The only disadvantage that I can see to resigning my position in order to obtain an MBA is that I would have to get off the "fast track" I am now on and which I find exhilarating. This past year, I received the distinction of having the highest number of securities sales referrals, and I also exceeded the sales performance of my companion consumer banker who is ranked 2nd in the state and whom I respect tremendously.

Although I will miss the corporate rewards that result from outstanding accomplishment, I feel I would equally thrive in an environment of highly competitive MBAs who have high personal goals and top-notch skills.

DESCRIBE YOUR WORK EXPERIENCE AND WHY YOU FEEL THAT BUSINESS IS YOUR CALLING.

DISCUSS YOUR GOALS AND PLANS AFTER GRADUATION.

DISCUSS YOUR GOALS AND PLANS AFTER GRADUATION.

My goal is to become the chief executive officer of an international company doing business in Latin America. While recently serving my country in the U.S. Army, I achieved rapid fluency in Spanish and utilized my language skills as a "Special Forces" Intelligence Professional/Spanish Linguist conducting projects with military professionals from El Salvador, Venezuela, Ecuador, and other countries related to stopping the flow of illegal drugs and weapons. While working with high-ranking foreign officials and with numerous government agencies including DEA, Customs, and the U.S. Marshals Service, I took pride in the role I played in obtaining information used to prosecute drug traffickers and weapons dealers, which has led me to the realization that the company I work for must be marketing goods and services I can feel proud of.

Since NAFTA, new markets "across the border" are developing and, as an international executive, I would be able to apply my undergraduate degree in Business and Marketing as well as my understanding of Hispanic cultures in order to determine the company's proper marketing mix, optimize its market share, and create a strategic plan to ensure long-term growth and profitability in a highly competitive multinational environment.

You will see from my resume that I have a "track record" of extensive voluntary community leadership. For example, in college I joined a fraternity known for its social conscience, and I spearheaded our fraternal response to Hurricane Hugo victims. I also chaired a subcommittee which helped elderly people find affordable housing, and I have volunteered my time to projects including Adopt-a-Highway, Special Olympics, the Waccamaw Boys Home, and in Rotary Club service activities. My extensive community involvement in college was on top of a rigorous B.S. program in Business and Marketing as well as challenging part-time jobs which I held to finance my college education. I truly believe that business executives should be committed to making the world a better place, and it is my goal to be a leader known for honest dealings.

From the nonmilitary experience shown on my resume, you will see that I have proved my ability to excel in sales and management, and I have been promoted rapidly into management in nearly every job I have held within profit-making companies. For example, in one job as a bartender, on my own initiative I implemented highly effective new promotional strategies while also securing the services of a local taxi company in providing free transportation to customers in no condition to drive. In another job as a waiter, I was promoted to schedule the wait staff and supervise the kitchen.

I have excelled in jobs selling cars and newspaper advertising. Those "building blocks" in my career taught me the importance of attention to detail, and I came to believe that honesty and professionalism are two of the best ways to gain and keep customer respect. Known for my extremely strong work ethic, diligence in accomplishing all tasks, and highly determined nature, I believe that persistence is the key to success in most ventures. I am convinced that, as an executive in the 21st century, I can create an intelligent and supportive management structure which is open to new ideas and which is capable of leading, mentoring, and developing employees to their fullest human potential. I am excited about the management challenges and opportunities that lie ahead in the 21st century, and I want to provide visionary business leadership. My "track record" of extensive service in numerous elected leadership positions demonstrates my proven leadership ability and strong desire to serve my community.

GIVE A CANDID EVALUATION OF YOURSELF, DISCUSSING THOSE CHARACTERISTICS YOU FEEL ARE YOUR STRENGTHS AND WEAKNESSES.

My three main strengths are my diligence/persistence, my deeply ingrained work ethic, and my reputation for integrity and rock-solid principles. I believe all these qualities have been responsible for my high degree of success so far in my military career, civilian jobs, and volunteer activities.

My diligent attitude has given me the strength on many occasions to persist in numerous simultaneous activities, even when I felt "maxed out" and at my physical and mental limits. For example, in college I carried a full load in a rigorous Business/Marketing program while also working up to 20 hours per week in demanding jobs as well as shouldering extensive leadership responsibilities in the community.

GIVE A CANDID EVALUATION OF YOURSELF, DISCUSSING THOSE CHARACTERISTICS YOU FEEL ARE YOUR STRENGTHS AND WEAKNESSES.

Although I know how to relax and have many hobbies that I enjoy, I have been accused of being a "workaholic" because of my determination to follow through aggressively on all my commitments.

Finally, I am proud of my reputation for integrity, and I have learned that honesty and high moral principles are essential to the relationship with customers and co-workers.

In terms of weaknesses, I admit to a tendency to say "yes" to too many volunteer leadership activities because of my conviction that true leaders are known for their unselfish service. Nevertheless, I am continually refining my ability to prioritize demands placed on my time so that I do not spread myself too thin.

WHAT DO YOU FEEL YOU HAVE TO OFFER THE GRADUATE PROGRAM TO WHICH YOU HAVE APPLIED?

WHAT DO YOU FEEL YOU HAVE TO OFFER THE GRADUATE PROGRAM TO WHICH YOU HAVE APPLIED?

My fluency in Spanish, along with my "real-world" experience in traveling and working in Mexico, Panama, Honduras, El Salvador, and Guatemala, will be assets to the graduate program.

Since many cultural differences obviously exist between Central/Latin America and the United States, I consider it an advantage for me career-wise, as well as an advantage for the graduate program, that I have come to appreciate and understand the cultural underpinnings of our mostly Catholic neighbors "across the border." As a military professional, I interacted with a wide range of people, from top-level foreign officials to the working class, in my efforts as an Intelligence Professional/Spanish Linguist involved in capturing information related to drug traffickers and illegal weapons dealers. My hands-on knowledge of Hispanic cultures should be of great advantage in the classroom.

Furthermore, I also bring to the graduate program a wealth of experience in the civilian world, I have worked since I was 16 years old, and worked throughout college to finance my education. While working for both large and small companies, I have learned the importance of teamwork and have gained insight into what makes some managers more successful than others.

WHY DID YOU SELECT YOUR PARTICULAR LANGUAGE? (SOMETIMES IT IS NOT POSSIBLE FOR ALL CANDIDATES TO BE ACCEPTED INTO THE LANGUAGE TRACK OF THEIR FIRST PREFERENCE. THEREFORE, PLEASE INDICATE A SECOND AND THIRD CHOICE.)

WHY DID YOU SELECT YOUR PARTICULAR LANGUAGE?

For the past three years, I have been working as a Spanish Linguist for NATO. I was selected to attend the prestigious Defense Language Institute in Monterey, CA, and I was asked to choose among these languages: Arabic, Korean, Mandarin Chinese, Russian, and Spanish. I chose Spanish because (1) Spanish is the second-largest spoken language in the U.S., (2) there is a need for future businesses to target products and services towards the Hispanic population, both in Latin America and in America, (3) there has been a dramatic increase in the number of firms operating south of the border, and (4) I felt my study of Latin in high school would help me rapidly master Spanish, which it did.

As a international linguist and translator for NATO, I had an opportunity to work in numerous Hispanic countries, and I am positive that the Spanish track is where I belong and where I can make my greatest contribution to the graduate program. Due to the similarity of the Portuguese language to Spanish, I would consider the Portuguese track as my second choice.

DESCRIBE YOUR MOST SIGNIFICANT WORK/LIVING EXPERIENCE.

DESCRIBE YOUR MOST SIGNIFICANT WORK/ LIVING EXPERIENCE.

As an Intelligence Professional/Spanish Linguist with the famed "Special Forces," I was involved in numerous projects in Spanish-speaking countries. I refined my ability to think, analyze, and solve problems in two languages simultaneously while "debriefing" Special Forces teams returning from special missions, and I supported government agencies including DEA, Customs, U.S. Marshals Service, and the Bureau of Alcohol, Tobacco, and Firearms.

On one special project, I worked in the U.S. Embassy in Mexico, and I created and implemented databases for the U.S. war on drugs. I analyzed intelligence reports, translated seized documents, and briefed the attache from the U.S. Drug Enforcement Administration on narco-organizations, drug traffickers, and other matters while also creating a unique organizational link diagram used to aid DEA. On a special project in El Paso, I was Translator/Team Leader of a translation cell which translated documents and performed classified activities supporting the Department of Justice in prosecuting international drug traffickers and weapons dealers. In another special project, I trained Special Forces units from Venezuela, El Salvador, and Ecuador in interrogation techniques and acted as a translator for foreign executives and military officers. I have also traveled in Mexico, Panama, Honduras, and Guatemala.

DESCRIBE YOUR LEADERSHIP ROLES IN EXTRACURRICULAR COLLEGIATE, COMMUNITY, OR PROFESSIONAL ACTIVITIES.

Throughout college, even while working in various jobs to finance my college education, I was a leader in numerous organizations and in the community. I was elected vice president of my freshman class, president of my club football team, vice president of my fraternity, and secretary of the American Marketing Association (AMA).

I also donated my time extensively while in college to volunteer activities. In fact, I chose to join a fraternity which is known for its social conscience and community involvement. During Hurricane Hugo, I led the fraternity's efforts in organizing and managing a Relief Donation point for victims in Florida; I contacted radio stations to create public awareness, personally went door-to-door in the community, and challenged other fraternities to help in achieving a canned goods goal of 5,000 cans. I also chaired a fraternity subcommittee which helped relocate elderly people into affordable housing. I promoted a Turkey Run each November which raised over $5,000 in two years for the Shriners Crippled Children's Fund.

Finally, I have volunteered my time to other projects such as Adopt-A-Highway, Special Olympics, the Wikima Boys Home, and in several service projects sponsored by the Rotary Club. I truly believe business leaders have a responsibility to provide their leadership skills to help the communities in which they live, and I sincerely derive great satisfaction from helping the less fortunate.

DESCRIBE YOUR LEADERSHIP ROLES IN EXTRACURRICULAR COLLEGIATE, COMMUNITY, OR PROFESSIONAL ACTIVITIES.

LIST ADDITIONAL COURSES YOU WILL COMPLETE BEFORE ENTERING THE SCHOOL OF BUSINESS ADMINISTRATION.

Before entering the School of Business Administration, I will have completed a typing course and a one-month intermediate Spanish Language class, possibly in Guatemala or Costa Rica.

During my last two years I have been enrolled in several MBA courses with Xavier University and in an International Relations program with Norfolk University, which, due to military obligations, I was unable to complete. I am an avid reader and regularly consume numerous business publications and trade journals, including the Salvadorian newspaper "La Prensa Graphica," and the quarterly journal, "Economic Industry Unit (EIU)," to stay abreast of happenings in Central America.

LIST ADDITIONAL COURSES YOU WILL COMPLETE BEFORE ENTERING THE SCHOOL OF BUSINESS ADMINISTRATION.

DESCRIBE THE FACTORS THAT MOTIVATED YOU TO CONSIDER A CAREER IN BUSINESS.

DESCRIBE THE FACTORS THAT MOTIVATED YOU TO CONSIDER A CAREER IN BUSINESS.

In selecting a career I have always been told to figure out what you like to do and then make a career out of it. Eight years ago, armed with this bit of philosophy, I set out to find out what I like. In college I came to the realization that my interests lie in business.

My courses in business were the ones I always looked forward to, and my business projects and presentations were the most challenging and rewarding of all my undergraduate course work. Upon graduating, I interviewed with, and was offered several enviable positions with well-known consumer product firms in Charlotte, NC, and Atlanta, GA. I forewent these offers and decided to join the military not only to serve my country but also to learn a language and earn money for my pursuit of a graduate degree in International Business sometime in my future.

Through my international exposure in the military as well as my business background, I have actively placed myself in a position to take full advantage of and excel in an International Business program such as that of Wharton.

Other reasons I offer for my decision to pursue an International career are: 1) my passion for travel, 2) my sincere desire to be exposed to and understand other cultures, philosophies, and beliefs of other people, and 3) the ability to have a favorable impact on their lives by improving the flow of goods and services.

In the military I have been afforded many opportunities to travel, learn the Spanish language, work in a U.S. Embassy in Central America, and interact with many Latin Americans in both professional and recreational environments. It is very rewarding to me and I receive tremendous personal satisfaction in expanding my own personal horizons and sharpening my ability to think and reason on a global level.

Obtaining an advanced degree has always been a personal goal of mine which I will obtain within the next three years. I have actively pursued a graduate education while in the military, in the form of MBA courses and International Relations courses through nearby universities.

As a highly dedicated student at Wharton I will be able to utilize my travel abroad, fluency in Spanish, and real-life work experiences abroad to contribute intellectually to the internationally focused classroom environment. Furthermore, I offer a different outlook that will foster discussion and provoke intelligent discourse.

Part Five: Colleges and Undergraduate Schools including the Ivy League and military academies Essays and Personal Statements

In this section you will find examples of essays and personal statements used in application for college and undergraduate school. This section contains essays used to apply to private colleges, public universities, Ivy League institutions, and military academies. By looking at sample essays, you will be better prepared to write your own essays.

The Ivy League: Many people have been dreaming since youth of applying to the Ivy League, that select group of eight universities often considered to be among the nation's most elite institutions. If you are planning on applying to those eight institutions (Harvard, Yale, Brown, Columbia, Dartmouth, University of Pennsylvania, Princeton, and Cornell), you can do it in one of two ways. 1) You can write or call each school to request an application and you can fill out each institution's separate application or 2) you can download the "Common Application" from a common website (www.commonapp.org) or from the individual school's site. For example, you can download the Common Application by logging on to Harvard's site at www.harvard.edu. At this writing, 209 institutions accept the Common Application. Applying to the Ivy League is a relatively complex process, and you will have to write essays and/or personal statements as part of the application process. Just for fun, we thought we'd compare the essay questions and personal statements on the Common Application filled out by the class of 2001 and the class of 2004. You will notice that the questions remained remarkably similar!

Personal Statements requested of the class of 2001:
1) Evaluate a significant experience or achievement that has special meaning for you.
2) Discuss some issue of personal, local, national, or international concern and its importance to you.
3) Indicate a person who has had a significant influence on you, and describe that influence.

Personal Statements requested of the class of 2004:
1) Evaluate a significant experience, achievement, or risk that you have taken and its impact on you.
2) Discuss some issue of personal, local, national, or international concern and its importance to you.
3) Indicate a person who has had a significant influence on you, and describe that influence.
4) Describe a character in fiction, an historical figure, or a creative work (as in art, music, science, etc.) that had an influence on you, and explain that influence.
On pages 118-120 you will find some of the essay questions asked by Ivy League and other institutions on their freshman applications for 2001.

The U.S. Military Academies: In this section you will see essays used to gain admittance to a U. S. military academy. The addresses of the five academies are provided for those who wish to write for information. On page 150 you will find an essay written to obtain a scholarship to a private military academy. Senators and congressmen often request an essay such as the one on page 150 when they are determining their choices for nominations to the academies; this type of essay would be an appropriate response to a senator's request for an essay in the process of requesting a nomination.

WHY ARE YOU INTERESTED IN BROWN UNIVERSITY?
WHAT ARE TWO IMPORTANT PASSIONS IN YOUR LIFE?

WHY ARE YOU INTERESTED IN BROWN UNIVERSITY? WHAT ARE TWO IMPORTANT PASSIONS IN YOUR LIFE?

One area of academia which interests me a great deal is computer science. I am interested in computer operation and programming and will consider pursuing a career in this field. Physics also interests me, as I always enjoy having knowledge about how things and how natural laws affect everyday events. Mathematics and computers go hand in hand; therefore, a curriculum encompassing both would be desirable.

My reasons for applying to Brown university are simple. I desire to attend a college in the Northeast whose reputation stands above many other colleges in the international marketplace. Brown is a center of learning which combines prestige with a curriculum I find appealing; therefore I have decided to apply. I have developed an interest for Brown university after seeing the brochure which arrived in the mail. It is a university which offers excellent programs coupled with lots of culture.

I believe that two passions in my life are more important to me than others. My passion for scouting led to an accomplishment of which I am proud because my Eagle Scout award came to me through much hard work and perseverance. It ranks as the most meaningful source of pride for me. Eagle award recipients constitute less than one percent of all young men who enroll in the Boy Scouts. It requires confidence, hard work, and common sense, but above all the Eagle badge is a mark of leadership. No one can become an Eagle without carrying out an Eagle Project, which directly measures how well one plans and gives leadership. Therefore, the Eagle Scout award is a great source of pride for me because of what it symbolizes.

A second passion which is important to me is cycling. I own two racing bikes, and I use them to get around just about everywhere. I love cycling and racing so much, in fact, that I have secured an employment at a local bicycle shop. Here I gain more knowledge daily as I see new models of bikes being released daily. This 18-hours-per-week job also gives me an opportunity to "feed my habit," as I am able to purchase bicycle parts at a discounted rate. I plan to make cycling a part of my life forever.

GIVE AN EXAMPLE OF YOUR LEADERSHIP ABILITY.

I have been called upon for leadership many times in the past. However, no single situation is as prominent in my memory as the leadership I provided in carrying out my Eagle Scout project. Through the successes and headaches present throughout the process, I learned much about what motivates people to work.

The first difficulty I encountered in the beginning was getting workers to the site. I had heard many "horror stories" about Eagle candidates who worked on their projects along with only one or two helpers. Of course, the purpose of an Eagle project is to test one's leadership and organizational skills, so I was determined to put mine to the test. On the first of two days, sixteen people besides myself showed up to work. I am used to leading large groups of young people from my Boy Scout troop experience, so the first day was a breeze. Everything went smoothly, and all planned work was finished. The next day, however, proved to be somewhat more "interesting." At first, only six people showed up, and I prepared for a long, hard day of work. However, about noontime, sixteen *other* people showed up. These people had not warned me ahead of time that they would be there, so needless to say I got a lot of exercise scrambling for more tools.

In the end, though, everything came out for the best. At the end of a long, hard second day, I was able to sit back and say to myself, "man, people are lazy unless you yell at them." I had a dickens of a time keeping everyone busy, and I came close to tearing my hair out for frustration as I realized that I had only half as many tools as I did people. All of this taught me the value of prior planning and communication between workers and supervisors, which is a lesson I won't forget.

GIVE AN EXAMPLE OF YOUR LEADERSHIP ABILITY.

**CHOOSE ONE OF THE FOLLOWING QUOTATIONS.
DISCUSS WHY YOU AGREE OR DISAGREE.
HOW MIGHT IT BE RELEVANT TO YOUR FUTURE?**

1) **"The highest ethical life consists at all times in the breaking of rules which have grown too narrow for the actual case."**
-- **William James**
2) **"Contrary to what some people would have you believe, there is no difference between values and economics. They are one and the same."**
--**Malcolm Stevenson Forbes**

William James once said, "The highest ethical life consists at all times in the breaking of rules which have grown too narrow for the actual case." This is particularly true in today's world, where many people are concerned with doing only what they are obligated to do, as opposed to doing what is right.

In many situations, one is forced to choose between following established rules and precedent and attempting to take the right course of action. When the dust settles, all that is left in any situation is the consequences suffered and one's conscience. Therefore, you must take care to analyze every situation carefully in an attempt to make a decision that is the correct one. Just as my Drafting instructor emphasizes every day, every situation demands a careful inspection of facts and a decision which you can live with.

Therefore, when faced with a situation which has two possible solutions, one legal and one dubious but more correct, the one to go with should be the right one. In today's world, all the arguments tend to say, "Follow the letter of the law." I would argue that the spirit, not the letter, is more important.

I can think of several examples of situations in which the breaking of rules would be preferred, even if those "rules" are social conventions or traditional expectations of others. One situation is that of a politician who must "break the rules" and make decisions counter to the expectations of his major contributors. Another situation is when a "whistle blower" in a company is driven by conscience to "break the rule" of the company's code of secrecy if he/she believes that an internal activity *may* be wrong. In short, a life lived according to conscience is to be preferred to the life lived in obedience to the rules.

DESCRIBE YOUR FEELINGS ABOUT YOUR EDUCATIONAL EXPERIENCES AND GOALS DURING HIGH SCHOOL. PLEASE MENTION ANY SPECIAL CIRCUMSTANCES OR FACTORS WHICH HAVE INFLUENCED YOUR EDUCATION.

I feel that my educational experience thus far has been exceedingly diverse. Not only have I been exposed to high levels of math and English language studies, but I also have studied two foreign languages: Spanish and German.

My goal has been to learn as much as possible, as good grades are only meaningful if they are won by learning as opposed to merely memorization. Although memorization is an important part of many studies, especially mathematics, it is no substitute for comprehension. In order to profit from educational experiences, one must comprehend, retain, and be able to creatively make application of the material presented.

I deliberately accelerated my Spanish language studies by taking a Spanish course one summer at UCLA which permitted me to "skip" Spanish III and go straight into Spanish IV in my sophomore year and then into AP Spanish in my junior year while also embarking on German. I am planning on learning to speak several languages. The science courses I have taken also reflect the diversity of my courses, and I learned much from chemistry. However, my favorite courses in high school have been my history courses, which I believe is a credit to my extraordinarily gifted teacher Mr. David Lillies. He has made AP US History and AP European history come to life for me!

WHICH BOOK DID YOU FIND MOST INTERESTING? WHY?
(50-word limit)

The book which interested me most recently was "Pavlov's Trout," because it is written from a fresh perspective. It appeals to my love of fishing, and it is philosophical in approach without being excessively moralizing as it draws a parallel between many real-life situations and fishing situations.

DESCRIBE YOUR FEELINGS ABOUT YOUR EDUCATIONAL EXPERIENCES AND GOALS DURING HIGH SCHOOL. PLEASE MENTION ANY SPECIAL CIRCUMSTANCES OR FACTORS WHICH HAVE INFLUENCED YOUR EDUCATION.

WHICH BOOK DID YOU FIND MOST INTERESTING? WHY?

IN A PARAGRAPH EACH, ANSWER EACH OF THE FOLLOWING STATEMENTS IN SUCH A WAY THAT THE ADMISSIONS COMMITTEE CAN GET TO KNOW YOU.

"I am..."
"I like..."
"I believe.."
"I do not care for..."
"I am tired of..."
"I hope..."

I AM..., I LIKE..., I BELIEVE..., I DO NOT CARE FOR..., I AM TIRED OF..., and I HOPE..."

I am a soccer player, a cross-country runner, a track runner, and a straight-A student. However, I am more than the sum total of my interests and accomplishments. I am a person who loves animals, and I persisted relentlessly in badgering my father until he relented to let me adopt my beloved basset hound, Bud. If I had no parental restrictions on my animal family, I would immediately seek out pets including an indoor cat, an elephant, a giraffe, and at least 10 monkeys. I am an adventurer and if I were allowed to take six months off from school and pursue activities with unlimited funds, I would buy a yacht, a submarine, an airplane, and an island full of monkeys, and I would go on my submarine everyday, looking for the lost city of Atlantis. On a regular day, however, and in my regular life, I am happy to be alive, excited about the future, and grateful for my blessings.

I like playing soccer in the rain and in the sunshine. I like spending the night at my friends' houses, and I like having my friends spend the night at my house. I like going swimming in the ocean and in pools. I like the rain. I like the snow. I like the thrill of having just run a three-and-a-half mile race and having just played and won a soccer game. I like cooking, and my favorite things to cook are brownies, fudge, macaroni, and chocolate chip cookies. I also like eating all of the aforementioned. I like playing pool, and I really like beating my opponent when I play pool. I like sleeping in after staying up until an obscenely late hour. I like getting out of high school.

I believe in God and that He created the world and that He created me. I believe that life is the most beautiful and most meaningful when each of us is using our special talents and abilities. I believe that life is not fair; how is it fair that one child gets a dedicated parent, while another gets a negligent parent? I believe that what happens to me in life is largely dependent on the choices I make—whom I choose as friends, whom I marry, and what kind of work I choose. I believe life is an adventure and should be appreciated and enjoyed to the fullest. I believe that the lost city of Atlantis does exist. I believe that the Loch Ness Monster does also exist. I believe that I will be a multimillionaire by my late twenties. I believe that I will one day be the richest human ever to live.

I do not care for dishonest people or hypocrites. I do not care for adults who treat teens like criminals in search of the next opportunity to plunder or deceive, even when they have done nothing wrong. I do not care for people who are arrogant and self-absorbed and who think they are better than others. I do not care for individuals who use their free time to vandalize or steal. I do not care for boring books or movies lacking in plot. I do not care for olives, mayonnaise, or mints.

I am tired of school. I am tired of repetitive exercises which do not promote learning or inspire thought. I am tired of asking my dad for permission to cut my own hair. I am tired of only seeing reruns of Law and Order. I am tired of books and movies lacking in interesting story lines and characters. I am tired of finding misspelled words and incorrect grammar usage in books. I am tired of cleaning up my room. I am tired of dogs that bark in the middle of the night and burglar alarms in my neighborhood that constantly go off, especially when I'm trying to sleep. I am tired of ordering a chicken sandwich with NO MAYONNAISE from Wendy's and discovering, upon my arrival at home, the dreaded mayo. I am tired of ordering "fast food" and wondering where the "fast" went. I am tired of news media who take an issue and beat it to death.

I hope I will have a long and happy life. I hope I will get all A's on my next report card. I hope it will snow again this year. I hope I get a car this summer. I hope I will find and buy lots of new clothes. I hope that I go to a good college. I hope my basset hound, Budweiser, does not get lost again. I hope television will not be full of reruns this summer. I hope I will finish my Girl Scout Gold Project this summer. I hope I will increase my skill and running speed in track and cross-country. I hope I will learn to be a good cook. I hope I will be a credit to my family, school, and community. I hope I will one day own a dark green Jeep Wrangler or a silver Mercedes convertible with a black top and gray leather interior. I hope I will one day own a very large house on the beach of a tropical island.

"I AM TIRED..., I HOPE..."

GETTING INTO THE U.S. MILITARY ACADEMIES

Many young people dream of getting into one of the U.S. military academies. If you want to write for information about the academies, here are their addresses:

Candidate Guidance Office
United States Naval Academy
Annapolis, Maryland 21402-5018

Admissions Office
United States Merchant Marine Academy
Kings Point, New York 11024-1699

Director of Admissions
United States Military Academy
606 Thayer Road
West Point, New York 10996-9902

HQ USAFA/RRSS
United States Air Force Academy
USAF Academy, Colorado 80840-9901

Director of Admissions
United States Coast Guard Academy
New London, Connecticut 06320-4195

You should also send a brief letter to your state senators and the congressional representative from your district asking them to send you the paperwork required in order to apply for a nomination to the service academies. Some of the senators and congressmen will ask you to write an essay, too, usually explaining why you want to attend an academy.

A critical factor in applying to the military academies is to begin the process at the end of your junior year, if possible, or early in the summer between your junior and senior year. For many senators and congressmen, the deadline for receiving your application, SAT scores, essay, high school transcript, and letters of recommendation is October 31 of your senior year, so that your name may be "placed in the hat" along with other seniors applying for a nomination to the U.S academies. This is a separate process from completing the individual academy's application. Just begin as early as possible requesting the application materials and forms you need.

On the facing page, you will see actual essays written by a successful applicant for admission to the U.S. Military Academy at West Point. The West Point application asked that the essay responses be handwritten and not typed or word processed. When you are in such a situation, you should make numerous copies of the original form so that you can draft and redraft your replies, refining them numerous times before handwriting them in final in black ink.

WHICH OF YOUR CURRENT ACADEMIC COURSES INTEREST YOU THE MOST? EXPLAIN.

The course which interests me the most is my Architectural Drafting class. One reason for my interest is the fact that I love to see a finished product which I have created with my mind and body, such as a house plan or landscaping layout. I also like and respect my instructor, who is one of the most dynamic and appealing teachers I have ever had the pleasure of learning from. In addition to teaching our class many key drafting skills, he has also persisted in convincing the administration to buy computers for the drafting department which are powerful enough to run CAD/CAM programs. This has enabled students such as myself to learn programs used by many large corporations and construction companies.

DISCUSS THAT WHICH YOU COUNT AS YOUR GREATEST SUCCESS DURING THE LAST TWO YEARS.

I consider earning my Eagle Scout rank to be my greatest recent achievement. In the present-day world, when few people are who they seem, the Eagle is still recognized to be one who has worked hard to achieve this mark of excellence. I have never met an Eagle Scout whom I did not immediately classify as being a moral and honest person. Therefore, I myself strive to represent those ideals. Perhaps the most important thing I learned on the trail to Eagle is the value of a job well done. If a job is done correctly the first time, there should be no further need to redo it later. For instance, an hour spent carefully pitching a tent is much more efficient than a five-minute job, as a poorly pitched tent will wake you up in the middle of the night as it collapses, leaving you two hours of work in the dark sorting out all the poles.

POSE A QUESTION THAT YOU WOULD LIKE TO ASK AND ANSWER IT.

Why do you strive for perfection in running?

When I am running, I push myself to the limit in order to achieve the best time, the longest distance, and the fastest sprints. This is because I plan to compete in the Olympics at some point, and also just so that I can see a tangible result of hard work. A shorter time is something I can point to and say, "Yes, I did that."

DISCUSS THE SOCIAL ISSUE IN YOUR COMMUNITY THAT MOST CONCERNS YOU.

The most disturbing issue for me in my local community is the incompetence of the school board. Composed mostly of old rich people and bureaucrats, the school board continually ignores the pleas of the community and its own employees, our teaching professionals, who are underpaid and ill-equipped to educate the children of our community. Our local government does not, in my opinion, place enough emphasis on schools. For instance, while $2.2 million was cut from our country's school budget this year, the City Council plans to build a new multimillion-dollar recreation area downtown. While teachers must stand in line to receive small rations of paper, $64,000 has been set aside for "administrative raises" within the school's management staff. How our government can prioritize new office buildings ahead of replacing 75-year-old school buildings remains a mystery to me.

ACTUAL ESSAYS USED IN THE PROCESS OF GAINING ADMISSION TO THE U.S. MILITARY ACADEMY AT WEST POINT

In the year these essays were written, the applicant was asked to handwrite his responses to these essay questions and was instructed not to use a word processing program or type writer. In such a situation, you are advised to make several copies of the actual application so that you can "play" with drafting your essay questions and then check your spelling and grammar before putting your essays in final form on the real document using a black pen.

PLEASE DESCRIBE HOW YOU USE YOUR LEISURE TIME.

PLEASE DESCRIBE HOW YOU USE YOUR LEISURE TIME.

I do not have an abundance of leisure time since I work after school every day from 4-7 and on Saturday from 10-5 as a Bike Mechanic, but in my spare time I enjoy cycling. I am an amateur racer in my community, and I enjoy maintaining a high level of fitness. This is my main sport this year. All my other free time is spent on my computer doing various types of research, creating new games and programs, and exploring the Internet. I take Autocad and Autocam at school in my Drafting III course and I am a self-professed "computer nut."

WHAT ARE YOUR CAREER OBJECTIVES, INTENDED COLLEGE MAJOR, ETC. WHY HAVE YOU MADE THOSE CHOICES?

WHAT ARE YOUR CAREER OBJECTIVES, INTENDED COLLEGE MAJOR, ETC. WHY HAVE YOU MADE THOSE CHOICES?

I am as yet undecided about my intended career, but I am considering Economics and Linguistics as major areas of study. It is possible that I might enter into the business world as a linguist and interpreter since it is certainly my goal to speak several languages. I believe I have a gift for learning languages and have excelled academically in these courses in high school. I have also excelled in my AP History courses and have thoroughly enjoyed them, so substantial course work in history is a possibility. I do wish my college curriculum to be diverse, as has been my high school curriculum, so I would be attracted to courses in Applied Science especially in the computer science area. I feel I could benefit from a strong education in Economics, hence that choice as a possible major.

DESCRIBE AN ACTIVITY OR HOBBY AND ITS MEANING TO YOU.

DESCRIBE AN ACTIVITY OR HOBBY AND ITS MEANING TO YOU.

Everyone needs a pressure outlet of some sort. In each person's lifetime, he or she is placed under pressure which, at its most intense, could crack one's sanity. Whether it comes in the form of a calculus final exam, a history paper, or a demanding job, this pressure must be drained from mind and body before it reaches overflow.

One stress-relieving method which I find to be effective is riding a bicycle. This happens to be my favorite hobby. But cycling to me is more than riding a bike; I am at my best when I am at peace within, so before each ride I like to sprint on the bicycle for 15 minutes or so, followed by a period of deep breathing before embarking on a ride. This has been very helpful in relieving pressure due to school, especially before history tests. History is one of my favorite subjects, but tests nevertheless give me a nervous feeling. So after a long night of studying, I like an early-morning ride to calm down.

Bicycling is excellent for keeping you peaceful inside. When you ride through the woods on a beautiful, sunny day, everything seems to be at peace. All of nature functions in harmony around you, and the sun shines overhead, sifting through fluffy white clouds much as soothing music can filter through the air towards you.

WHAT IS THE SINGLE MOST SATISFYING (OR REWARDING) EXPERIENCE YOU'VE HAD IN HIGH SCHOOL TO DATE? BRIEFLY DESCRIBE AND EXPLAIN.

My single most satisfying experience has been earning my Eagle rank. There is an old Spanish saying which I like a lot which says, "Your family falls out of the trees like monkeys; your friends you pick." What that implies is that much can be known about us, in terms of our character and values, by the friends we choose and the company we keep. Looking back over my years as a youth, I am extremely happy that I chose to be in the company of Scouts. The Boy Scouts of America is a unifying force for today's youth, and the B.S.A. provides our nation with moral, responsible members of society who often prove to be competent leaders. In my opinion, the B.S.A. is absolutely the best way to prepare a boy for manhood. Not only does exposure to boys of the same age hone social skills, but also camp-outs can boost a boy's self-esteem by giving him a sense of accomplishment. Camping can also develop real-life problem-solving skills.

WHAT KIND OF PERSON WOULD YOU HOPE TO HAVE AS A ROOMMATE FOR YOUR FRESHMAN YEAR IN COLLEGE?

A roommate should be clean and honest. I hope to be placed with an intelligent and interesting person with whom I can discuss political issues. Anyone who cleans up after himself would be an absolute joy to live with. Aside from the neatness issue, I hope for a roommate who does not use drugs because I find drugs to be society's greatest corrupting force and a pernicious tool in the spread of disease.

WHAT WOULD YOU LIKE TO SEE IN A ROOMMATE?

A roommate must be honest and clean to be tolerable. I hope to be placed with an intelligent and interesting person with whom I can discuss political issues; however, anyone who cleans up after himself would be an absolute joy to live with.

Aside from the neatness issue, I refuse to tolerate anyone who uses any type of illegal drugs, and I will report any such trash to the authorities in half of a heartbeat. Drugs, in my opinion, are society's greatest corrupting force, not to mention the fact that they are remarkably efficient ways of spreading AIDS (IV drugs) and especially that drugs are an excellent way to go into debt. Alcohol is out, too, because it causes a person to do things that he or she would normally not do.

WHAT IS THE SINGLE MOST SATISFYING (OR REWARDING) EXPERIENCE YOU'VE HAD IN HIGH SCHOOL TO DATE? BRIEFLY DESCRIBE AND EXPLAIN.

WHAT KIND OF PERSON WOULD YOU HOPE TO HAVE AS A ROOMMATE FOR YOUR FRESHMAN YEAR IN COLLEGE?

WHAT WOULD YOU LIKE TO SEE IN A ROOMMATE?

OF ALL THE THINGS YOU HOPE OR EXPECT TO GAIN FROM YOUR COLLEGE EXPERIENCE (OTHER THAN A DEGREE!), WHICH TWO OR THREE WOULD YOU PLACE AT THE TOP OF THE LIST IF YOU HAD TO MAKE UP SUCH A LIST TODAY? (BE AS SPECIFIC OR AS GENERAL AS YOU LIKE.)

OF ALL THE THINGS YOU HOPE OR EXPECT TO GAIN FROM YOUR COLLEGE EXPERIENCE (OTHER THAN A DEGREE!), WHICH TWO OR THREE WOULD YOU PLACE AT THE TOP OF THE LIST IF YOU HAD TO MAKE UP SUCH A LIST TODAY? (BE AS SPECIFIC OR AS GENERAL AS YOU LIKE.)

New friends and acquaintances are the most important things I could gain from my college experience, in my opinion. College should be a way to meet new people and connect with different points of view while learning and studying in an atmosphere of intense concentration. After living in a relatively small town for all of my life, I hope to see a change of scenery, such as a large metropolitan area with lots of culture. Also, being from a conservative section of the Bible Belt, I hope to expose myself to new ideas and experiences (within the limits of the law and common sense, of course.)

I would also hope that I meet up with people who share my passion for cycling. Everyone needs a pressure outlet of some sort. At some sort in each person's lifetime, he or she is placed under pressure which, at its most intense, could crack one's sanity. One stress-relieving method which I find to be effective is riding a bicycle. This happens to be my favorite hobby. But cycling to me is more than riding a bike; I am at my best when I am at peace within, so before each ride I like to sprint on the bicycle for 15 minutes or so, followed by a period of deep breathing before embarking on a ride. This has been very helpful in ventilating pressure, and bicycling is excellent for keeping you peaceful inside and making you feel in harmony with nature.

DISCUSS A BOOK YOU HAVE READ LATELY AND ITS MAJOR THEMES AND RELEVANCE TO YOUR LIFE.

Two of the most important themes in *A Separate Peace* by John Faulkner are the importance of friendship and the destructiveness of jealousy. The importance of friendship is a significant theme in this book because it is incorporated throughout the course of the book and is the basis of the entire plot. The destructiveness of jealousy is also illustrated throughout the book. It is the basis for the plot and one of the most important morals to be learned in this novel.

Gene is philosophic and unrealistic. He is intelligent but has poor judgment many times. Gene's motivation for pushing his best friend, Finny, out of the tree is his jealousy over Finny's great sport-related accomplishments and his ability to get away with anything by talking his way out of difficult situations with adults by charming them and appealing to their appreciation for youth.

Finny is oblivious, naïve, and, like his best friend, somewhat unrealistic. While he is good at sports, he is not very interested or involved in his studies. Finny proves just how naïve, unrealistic, and oblivious to what is happening around him he is when he refuses to accept that Gene pushed him from the tree, despite the obvious, and the fact that Gene tries to tell him many times.

Gene and Finny were two best friends. Gene was a wonderful student, and Finny was a wonderful athlete. They decided to have a club where the initiation and basis of the club was a dangerous stunt of jumping out of a tree into a river.

One day, Gene's envy of Finny's great accomplishments in sports got the best of him, and he subconsciously pushed Finny out of the tree. Finny broke his leg in this fall and was expected to never walk again. He surpassed the odds, though, and learned to walk again. He tried to train Gene for the 1944 Olympics but Gene did not make it.

During the time in which they had been training for the Olympics, Leper Lepellier had joined the army. Gene was asked to come and see him because he had escaped from the army. Gene visited him and, while mentally ill, Leper accused Gene of pushing Finny out of the tree; this was the first time anyone had really made Gene mad by accusing him of the truth.

Gene went back to Devon School and, after a little while, the war (World War II) became more real to Gene and Finny than it had previously been. Later, Brinker accused Gene of pushing Finny out of the tree. Enraged, Finny left the mock trial and fell down the stairs, breaking his leg a second time. Because of this fracture, a piece of bone marrow got into the bloodstream and this is what killed Finny. Soon, Gene realized that he had killed his demons at school and his war had ended before he ever even put on a uniform.

The book illustrates the pervasiveness of envy in our most important relationships and equips the reader with new insights into human relationship and into the power of jealousy. It also illustrates that there is the most potential for betrayal in our deepest and most intense relationships.

DISCUSS A BOOK YOU HAVE READ LATELY AND ITS MAJOR THEMES AND RELEVANCE TO YOUR LIFE.

DISCUSS A BOOK YOU HAVE READ LATELY AND ITS MAJOR THEMES AND RELEVANCE TO YOUR LIFE.

The author, Charles Dickens, was born near Portsmouth, England. At the age of twelve, he was taken from school and put to work briefly in a blacking warehouse by his parents. He had a sense of being abandoned which eventually caused him to fill his fiction with abused or neglected children. His work, ***The Pickwick Papers,*** serialized in 1836 and 1837, was a huge success. His next work was ***Oliver Twist,*** which showed the darker side of his genius. It also seemed to confirm his reputation as England's leading young novelist. Dickens appealed to Victorian readers largely due to his sentimentality and emotionalism. Sentimentality seemed to play a smaller role in his 1850s works; these were dominated by bitter social satire. Starting in 1850, Dickens worked full-time as a newspaper editor and a novelist, and, at the same time, lecturing in both England and America. Dickens had ten children.

The book, ***Great Expectations,*** used vivid imagery. Charles Dickens described every detail of everything in the book and the book would have been lacking if he had not done so. He also used the first person point of view. This was definitely the correct choice for point of view in this book. In order to get the full extent of the emotions this book has to offer, it must be in first person point of view. Dickens also used symbolism throughout this book which certainly added to the reader's enjoyment.

Two of the most important themes in this book are the importance of loyalty and the destructiveness of money. The importance of loyalty is significant in this book because it is incorporated all throughout the book. This book also teaches a wonderful lesson about money. It shows that money is not only destructive to those who possess it, but also to those around them and those that they love, along with just about anyone else they encounter.

Pip is an orphan who is raised by his sister and her husband until he comes into a large sum of money from an unknown benefactor. He wastes all of his money. His money ends up damaging many of his relationships, which he later tries to fix. Joe is a kind, shy, and nervous man. He is always very sincere. He is ignorant but hardworking. He always tries his hardest at everything he does. He is a forgiving man. He seems to attract love and pity from the reader. He is funny to the reader. Estella is mean, cruel, rude, and proud, both as a young lady and a woman, however somewhat less as a woman. Pip is in love with her, despite how mean she is to him. Unlike Joe, Estella does not attract the reader's pity as much as she attracts the reader's hatred.

The book roused my deepest emotions of sympathy, hatred, despair, and hope as Dickens portrayed characters who became as real as the real people I see daily. I believe I gained important insight into human relationships and into the power of money to sully the most precious things in life.

DO YOU THINK YOUTH UNDER THE AGE OF 18 SHOULD BE ALLOWED TO VOTE? WHY OR WHY NOT?
(Limit your response to 300 words or less.)

I believe that youth under the age of eighteen should be allowed to vote in elections. There are three main reasons I would advance to support my view.

1. Voting is the most important right of citizenship and young people should not be denied that right just because they are young.

2. Youth pay sales and other taxes to the government and, because of the fact that they are youth, and therefore denied voting rights, have no say in government, which is not only discrimination, but also taxation without representation.

3. Because of the fact that government greatly affects all youth in many ways, having no voice in political matters can drastically change and possibly shorten a youth's life.

Teens in my generation could be responsible, or even involved in, a change that could possibly lower voting age requirements from the current age of eighteen. I would vigorously support such a movement.

DO YOU THINK YOUTH UNDER THE AGE OF 18 SHOULD BE ALLOWED TO VOTE? WHY OR WHY NOT?

WHAT IS THE BEST SHOW YOU HAVE SEEN ON TELEVISION?

WHAT IS THE BEST SHOW YOU HAVE SEEN ON TELEVISION?

The best show I have ever seen on television is "The Nanny." At first, I was not expecting to like the show, but after watching it a few times, I was pleasantly surprised. The actors and actresses are all very good at what they do. It does not have the type of plot that a typical show would, and that is one reason I like it. It features Fran Drescher as the main character in the series. Because of her voice, I normally don't like to watch shows or movies featuring Fran Drescher. This show changed my mind. The show lasts thirty minutes and I spend most of it laughing. The show is a comedy, and it is one of the few comedies that I truly regard as amusing and find myself laughing out loud at.

WHAT IS THE WORST SHOW YOU HAVE SEEN ON TELEVISION?

WHAT IS THE WORST SHOW YOU HAVE SEEN ON TELEVISION?

The worst show I have ever seen on television is "Dawson's Creek." I consider this the worst show on television because it is so predictable. The actors and actresses do not do quite the job that I think they could and should. I don't like to see dramas where the stars do not seem to be working to their fullest potential. Every single episode of "Dawson's Creek" seems to me as though it has the same plot as the previous ones. I can always predict what is going to happen next in the show. Another thing that I don't like about the show is that it is never the least bit funny. If the show is going to be as predictable as it is, it should at least be made less dull by including some humor.

DISCUSS YOUR CONCEPT OF THE PERFECT FAMILY.

DISCUSS YOUR CONCEPT OF THE PERFECT FAMILY.

My concept of the perfect family is one with two parents. The two parents have never been divorced. There is at least one child, but probably no more than five. There could be more than five children, but only if the father makes enough money to support his entire family, without his wife having to work. The mother should never have to work. Her family's finances should be adequate without her having to work outside the home. Every child should have his own pet. Every child should make straight A's on his report card, so, just like his parents, he goes to the Ivy League school of his choice, and he goes on to be very successful in whatever profession he chooses.

WHAT BOTHERS YOU MOST ABOUT THE WORLD?

WHAT BOTHERS YOU MOST ABOUT THE WORLD?

What bothers me about this world is that whenever students or children under the age of eighteen commit a crime, either their parents, the media, or modern entertainers are blamed for it. I don't think that is fair to any of these three parties, because it is nobody's fault but the child's. Marilyn Manson is one of the "modern entertainers" I am speaking of who seems to get blamed for nearly every crime that can be pinned upon him, for one reason or another. The truth is, though, that Marilyn Manson has done nothing except try to make a living, which he does through his song lyrics. If children want to blame their parents, Marilyn Manson, or the media for the crimes they have committed, they can, but the truth is that they have committed the crimes all by themselves and it is unfair to place the blame on others. It is unprincipled to try to shift the blame to others when someone commits a crime all by himself.

WHAT DO YOU LIKE ABOUT THIS WORLD?

What I like about this world is that there is not just a nation of opportunities, here in the United States of America, but there is a world of opportunities, here in our world, where we live. No matter who you are, or where in this world you live, if you work hard enough and try hard enough, you can succeed in whatever you would like to do. If you work hard enough, you can get into whatever college you want, get any job you want, move to any other country in the world that you want to, or get yourself or your family a better life, despite where you live in this world. That is definitely the greatest thing that there is and ever will be about this world. In truth, opportunities to advance may be greater in the U.S. than in many other countries, but an individual always has the freedom to make something of himself and his life.

WHAT DOES BEING INDEPENDENT MEAN TO YOU?

To be truly independent would be to be at least eighteen and to be living here in the United States of America, where you are guaranteed to be free and independent the rest of your life, just as long as you abide by the rules of our nation, and do not violate the rights and freedoms that belong to everyone else here in America. One reason why I chose the age of eighteen for the minimum age to be free is because that is the age at which American citizens are considered adults and are permitted to vote in elections. The right to vote is one right that makes a person more independent. Another thing that would make a person truly independent is financial independence. This means that a person depends on no one besides himself for money, which is a big part of being independent. In the United States, there are many more rights and freedoms that make people truly independent, such as freedom of speech, freedom of press, and many more.

IF YOU COULD RUN ANYWHERE, WHERE WOULD IT BE?

If I could run anywhere, it would be to New York. I would run to New York, especially in the winter, because I would like to go there again to see all of the snow that I only got to see and play around in for a few hours the last time I was there. I also want to go to New York to visit my brother who is going through college at West Point, because I haven't seen him for a while. I would like to see the Statue of Liberty because I haven't ever seen it up close. I would like to go shopping in New York City, because that is something that I have never done and would like to do. The main reason, however, that I would like to run to New York is because I would like to get some good exercise, and if I could run all the way to New York, I know I could run just about anywhere else.

DISCUSS THE STATUS OF RACE RELATIONS IN THIS COUNTRY.

The status of race relations in this country is not good, yet not too bad. What I mean is that while it could obviously stand to be much better, it is still not as bad as it could be. We have come a long way since the days of Martin Luther King, Jr., Rosa Parks, Malcolm X, and the other great African-American leaders, but we haven't quite realized the dream that Dr. Martin Luther King, Jr. had hoped we would. I believe that with each decade, we will get closer and closer to reaching the goal that Dr. King had in mind for us years ago. With each decade, African-Americans and Caucasians will become more tolerant of each other, and once we have fully learned to tolerate each other, we will learn to appreciate one another, until it gets to the point where the races don't notice any differences whatsoever in each other.

WHAT DO YOU LIKE ABOUT THIS WORLD?

WHAT DOES BEING INDEPENDENT MEAN TO YOU?

IF YOU COULD RUN ANYWHERE, WHERE WOULD IT BE?

DISCUSS THE STATUS OF RACE RELATIONS IN THIS COUNTRY.

DESCRIBE HOW YOU SPENT A RECENT DAY.

DESCRIBE HOW YOU SPENT A RECENT DAY.

Today I began the day by rising at 6:30 a.m. and running 3.1 miles in my best time this year. I was accompanied by other members of the Cross Country Team of Terry Sanford Senior High School. I came home and was "home alone" since my brothers were in a tennis tournament at Fort Bragg. Their absence allowed me to work in peace and quiet on my Journal assignments for a few hours. After a few hours I'd had enough peace and quiet, and I decided to go see a movie entitled "Notting Hill," a comic drama which I enjoyed. As soon as I returned, I worked on my journal for an additional couple of hours until I received a telephone invitation from a friend to go see another movie! We saw "The Sixth Sense" starring Bruce Willis, which is a thriller that features a bizarre surprise ending. I came home and went to sleep about midnight, and I fell fast asleep after an action-packed day that was full of physical exertion and mental stimulation.

WHAT IS A BEST FRIEND?

WHAT IS A BEST FRIEND?

A best friend should be someone who respects my privacy, knows how to keep a secret, is a good listener, and is both smart and fun-loving. A best friend should be someone who adds joy to my life, not someone who consumes my energy and intellect by having me continuously solve her problems. A best friend can have ideas which are different from mine, but in general a best friend will share my moral and ethical values and will set high goals for herself, as I do for myself. A best friend should be someone I can be around every minute but who doesn't cling to me every minute because he/she is jealous of my spending time with others. A best friend would be protective but not possessive.

WHO IS THE PERSON YOU CONSIDER A HERO?

WHO IS THE PERSON YOU CONSIDER A HERO?

The person I would consider a hero is my mother because she makes a living for my family and is always there to help me solve my problems. She always knows the right thing to say, no matter how I'm feeling. She's smart and is a great writer, and I admire the fact that she has graduated from both the University of North Carolina at Chapel Hill and from the Harvard Business School. She has written about 10 books and is a great author. I also admire the fact that she started her own business nearly 20 years ago, not knowing if it would flourish or fail. She is a very creative person and a very resourceful problem solver.

WHAT ARE TWO ESSENTIAL SKILLS YOU MUST HAVE FOR SUCCESS?

WHAT ARE TWO ESSENTIAL SKILLS YOU MUST HAVE FOR SUCCESS?

I am learning that two essential skills that I must have for success in life are time management and organization. Time management is essentially planning ahead and scheduling tasks appropriately so that I do not have everything to accomplish at "the last minute." Especially since I enjoy numerous activities, including Girl Scouts, cross country, soccer, and softball, I must manage my time effectively in order to keep myself from being stressed out. Furthermore, since nearly all of my classes are Honors classes, I must use excellent time-management skills in order to achieve outstanding grades across the board. Organization is a "cousin" of time management, and it is also an essential skill which I am trying to master. By staying well organized, I can use my time for maximum productivity.

DESCRIBE A DREAM YOU HAD RECENTLY.

I had a dream that my mother was pregnant with another child. Maybe this was a wish appearing to me as a dream, because I had often told my mother that I wanted to have a sister, since I had two older brothers and one younger brother. The strange thing about this was that when my mother finally had her child, she had twins. Not only were they twins, but they were not of the human race; they were a dog and cat, and they were my mother's "peace offering" to me to appease my strong wish for a little baby sister who would join forces with me against my pesky brothers. After I woke up from this strange dream, which kept reoccurring as my subliminal desires kept expressing themselves, I heard the sound of a dog barking and a cat meowing, and I raced downstairs to become not a big sister but a mother to my new canine and feline family members.

WHAT HAVE YOU LEARNED BY LIVING IN YOUR HOMETOWN?

Living in Gardner Grove has made me realize that I am fortunate that I do not have to live in a major metropolitan area with a high crime rate. Furthermore, living in Gardner Grove has made me realize that I am a Southerner and have unique cultural differences from people in the northeast, west, or midwest. Living in Gardner Grove has made me realize that there are advantages to being born and raised in a medium-sized town compared to a small rural area or a huge, densely populated city. Living in Gardner Grove has made me realize that I enjoy living in a house rather than an apartment or condominium, because I enjoy the pleasures of having a dog and cat that live in my backyard and front yard.

WHAT WAS YOUR MOST EMBARRASSING MOMENT?

My most embarrassing moment was when I baby-sat for the two Smith children. About ten minutes into the job, the younger child claimed to need to go to the bathroom. I believed her and took her to the bathroom. It turned out that she had only wanted to play with her mother's makeup. After I realized this, we spent about ten minutes getting her cleaned up, so the entire problem took about twenty minutes to take care of. Jenny, the older sister, had decided that her younger sister had fallen into the toilet. Instead of asking what had happened to her little sister, Jenny went ahead and called 911. I had not realized that this had happened until I heard sirens blaring outside. The doorbell rang, and when I answered it, I was very surprised to find myself face-to-face with both a local fireman and the local Chief of Police. After they had realized that there was no real emergency, they gave both Jenny and myself a harsh warning about the effects of calling 911 about false emergencies. Every time this family needs a baby-sitter now, I now coincidentally (and mercifully) have other plans.

FINISH THIS SENTENCE: "I've never been able to master..."

I've never been able to master the art of cleaning up my room in a way that totally satisfies my mom. The piles of clothes which look orderly to me seem cluttered to her. The dust on my sports trophies doesn't bother me at all, but drives her crazy. She doesn't seem to understand that I like to save up my dirty towels so that I have a really nice pile to put into the washer at one time. The "lived-in" look which I find charming about my bedroom makes my mom roll her eyes in disbelief and despair. The music which is frequently blaring from my room seems to have the opposite effect on her as it does on me; it soothes me and confuses her. Finally, my mother doesn't seem to understand that the one item in my room which I must be able to locate at all times is my telephone—a teenage girl's best friend.

FINISH THIS SENTENCE: "Something I'm really good at is..."

FINISH THIS SENTENCE: "Something I'm really good at is..."

Something I'm really good at is organizing my time. This is a very important skill which permits me to be involved in many extracurricular activities while maintaining high standards of academic excellence. I have been adept at organizing my time all my life, because I have always been involved in so many activities that it was necessary for me to learn at a young age how to budget and allocate my time. This skill is becoming even more important as I move on to higher grade levels and new challenges, because the challenges and activities I am involved in require me to be able to focus quickly and intently on complex tasks. Since I am aware of how important organizational skills are to my quality of life, I am always seeking to find new ways to refine my techniques in this area. I believe my extensive homework requirements will provide me with new opportunities to use this skill!

FINISH THIS SENTENCE: "Something I like about school is..."

FINISH THIS SENTENCE: "Something I like about school is..."

Something I like about school is the fact that it allows me to be in many school-related extracurricular activities that I would not even be aware of were it not for my school. For example, I am a member of the Girls' Cross Country Team at Terry Sanford High School, and I am enjoying this affiliation and opportunity to test my physical endurance and abilities. I believe that a strong mind is enhanced by a strong body. I am excited that college provides many opportunities for extracurricular involvement, and I want to become involved in the forensics club, Spanish Club, debate team, Highland Dancers, the soccer team, the cross country team, and other activities.

FINISH THIS SENTENCE: "My parents think I'm special because..."

FINISH THIS SENTENCE: "My parents think I'm special because..."

My parents think that I am special because I am their only daughter. They also think I am special because I am very hard-working and I have performed in an excellent fashion in my school work. My parents think that I am very responsible in taking care of my school work, and they know they can count on me to accomplish my requirements before the due date. My parents think I am honest, and they know that they can trust me and count on what I say. My parents think I have the potential to excel in anything I take on, and they encourage me very much to set my goals high. My parents think I should work harder to maintain a clean and orderly room that could pass parental inspection, but my parents do not realistically think my room will ever win an award for Most Tidy Bedroom.

FINISH THIS SENTENCE: "My favorite color is...because..."

FINISH THIS SENTENCE: "My favorite color is...because..."

My favorite color is green because I visit Jamaica every year, and the wonderful, tropical climate there makes me "think green." Even the tropical Caribbean sea is as much green as it is blue, and everywhere one looks in Jamaica, there is green. Jamaica is called "the land of wood and water" and the "wood" refers to the dense and mountainous forests on the island as well as the many green and flowering trees which decorate the landscape. My eyes used to be green before they evolved into a hazel color, and I liked my green eye color. Green is a color which reminds me of new growth and a healthy environment, and green is my favorite color because it reminds me of the wonders and richness of nature.

DO YOU BELIEVE YOUR STATE SHOULD HAVE A LOTTERY?

I believe that we should have a lottery because by playing the lottery, North Carolinians are already helping fund smaller classes and other educational improvements. This is how Attorney General and candidate for Governor Mike Easley feels. He is a Democrat.

I do not believe that the lottery is a "voluntary tax on poor people." A "voluntary tax on poor people" sounds as though the poor are being punished by playing the lottery, but the truth is that the lottery is "voluntary." The lottery is mostly played by poor people because they are the ones in need of enhancing their fortunes.

The North Carolina lottery is helping to fund education, but it is actually helping to fund education in other states. A very significant problem is the reduction of class size, which would result in increased individualized instruction and improved discipline.

Official statistics will tell you that the average North Carolina school has 16 kids for every teacher. However, almost 40% of children are in classes of 26 or more. Schools can even have maximum class sizes ranging from 26 to 32 kids per class, or go as far as to get waivers to make classes even larger.

Smaller classes should not just be a perk for the underprivileged, and with the help of the money from the North Carolina lottery, smaller classes resulting in increased individualized instruction and improved discipline could become a reality.

WRITE A SHORT POEM ABOUT YOURSELF.

Sally

Intelligent, talented, creative, and caring.
Daughter of Marcia and David; sister of Joe, Jim, and John.
Lover of cats, dogs, and ice cream.
Who feels on top of the world after winning, ashamed after losing,
    and tired after running the mile.
Who needs water on a hot day, love from my parents, and attention
    from my parents.
Who gives headaches, friendship, and attention to my friends.
Who fears cockroaches, big dogs (besides my own), and bees.
Who would like to see London, Paris, and Australia.
Resident of Philadelphia.

McDonald

WRITE A POEM ENTITLED "What Should I Be Today?"

I sit at home and contemplate
What I'd like to be by 28.

Some days I think it would be fun
To be a policeman with a gun.

On other days I'd like to be
A writer of philosophy.

But if I were a softball queen,
A national title would be my dream.

Or I could be a dancing girl,
And go on stage and twirl and twirl.

If law school were to be my aim,
The legal field would be my game.

To play a symphony in Carnegie Hall,
I'd have to dedicate totally all.

If I were to become a vet,
Much school training I'd need to get.

I hope one day to be a nurse,
Though it's not a life filled with mirth.

So much thinking, so much brainwork,
All this imagining makes my head hurt!

I'm really glad I'm still so young,
Now I'll go play and have some fun!

**WRITE A POEM ENTITLED
"What Should I Be Today?"**

DESCRIBE A SITUATION WHICH DEMONSTRATES YOUR ABILITY AND WILLINGNESS TO ACCEPT RESPONSIBILITY AND MAKE DECISIONS.

DESCRIBE A SITUATION WHICH DEMONSTRATES YOUR ABILITY AND WILLINGNESS TO ACCEPT RESPONSIBILITY AND MAKE DECISIONS.

It is my style to make decisions carefully, after extensive analysis and thorough investigation. As I approached the summer between my junior and senior year of high school, I decided after careful analysis that I would put in some long hours looking for a job in which I could begin to develop some professional skills, not just a "lifeguard" or "waitress" job, which I have held previously as summer jobs. I carefully embarked upon the process of deciding which company I wanted to work for. After extensive analysis, I decided that IBM was the best employer in Mayfield and I performed the networking which led to my employment in the summer as an Analyst. Because of my excellent performance during the summer and my willingness to accept responsibility, I have been asked to work part-time during my senior year of high school, and I work Monday-Friday from 5-9 pm.

Throughout my summer at IBM, I became known for my eager acceptance of additional responsibilities and I consistently volunteered for involvement in as many projects as I could. Although I enjoy the "textbook training" I receive in high school, I feel there is no better teacher than hands-on experience, and I have valued my ability to increase my knowledge through hands-on problem solving experience which I have gained because I have volunteered for additional projects and responsibilities during one of the busiest times in the company's history. In my current position, I shoulder a large amount of responsibility and yet work with little to no supervision. I am proud of the fact that I was recognized for "Exceptional Customer Service" in IBM Technology's Customer Integration Center, and this recognition was due in part to my ability and willingness to accept responsibility and make decisions.

A situation which illustrates my willingness to accept responsibility as well as my ability to make decisions was a summer project for which I volunteered which involved the responsibility for automating incidental billing for IBM's Eastern Region. This was a high-profile assignment with vast implications and, if executed well, the bottom line would save IBM considerable operating expenses and produce increased revenue.

As a key implementer of this project for the Eastern Region, I became the customer's "go-to guy" for any issues that arose, and I was frequently in a position in which I had to make logical and common-sense decisions which balanced customer needs with company requirements. Although I was a very junior employee, I was entrusted with complete decision-making authority and was essentially in a policymaking role since so many of my decisions pertained to issues which were in "uncharted territory." An example of such an issue concerned a large customer. This customer was the recipient of poor service. This was causing the customer to switch more and more of its business to a competitor. On my own initiative, I investigated the reason for the declining service and discovered a forecasting issue which the customer was not aware of. After analysis, I alerted the customer to the procedures it needed to follow, and the result was an increase in the customer's business and a restoration of business to IBM by this major account. I was commended for my solid judgment and ability to make prudent decisions after careful and thorough analysis.

DESCRIBE A SITUATION WHICH DEMONSTRATES YOUR ABILITY TO PRESENT IDEAS ORALLY AND YOUR SKILL IN ORAL EXPRESSION.

During my junior and senior years in high school, I sought to refine my oral communication skills as I attended a week-long Bernard Haldane class in New York City which is utilized by many top executives to refine their abilities in this area. I plan on becoming a part of the Forensics Club in college, so that I can continue refining my skills in this area.

My skill in oral communication was a major factor in my success in my summer position as a Systems Analyst for Brandigan Manufacturing Company, since the majority of my workday was spent communicating on the telephone. High school students are normally not hired as Systems Analysts, but the company was experiencing a serious shortage of personnel in a full-employment job market.

Without excellent oral communications, including the ability to choose the right words and to communicate them in an appropriately expressive manner, I could not achieve positive results for the company and for its customers. In my job, oral communication was the tool for solving most of the problems I encountered and oral communication was the tool for implementing most of the solutions. While on the telephone, I was normally involved either in training or in providing technical support to Brandigan's valued customers, and I worked with a diverse range of people ranging from warehouse workers to company presidents. My skills in communication were the major reason why I received an award of recognition for providing "All Star Customer Service."

Ongoing oral communication with my supervisor was an area in which I excelled, as I kept my immediate supervisor aware of the current status of any ongoing projects in which I was involved. As projects progressed, I orally briefed coworkers who had a "need to know" and I accomplished those briefings in a tactful, efficient, and easily understood manner. I have learned that oral expression—how the words are said, not just what words are said—is vital in the success of the communication process, and I make a concerted effort to clearly articulate and express myself.

A situation which illustrates my ability in this area concerns an e-mail that I received from upper management. The issue concerned poor bill of lading data that a customer was submitting. Not being a subject matter expert in this area, I was confused as to what the immediate issue was and what exactly I was looking for. The written communication was confusing and lacking in specifics. My first step was to seek out a known expert in this area. Upon receiving clarification, I was able to see the underlying concern. I was then able to recommend and implement changes in this customer's bill of lading patterns. Upon apprising the customer of the situation, he understood that his bills of lading needed to be generated using my suggested format, and I took the time to train the customer in the proper paperwork procedures so that written communication would be clear and obtain the desirable results in a timely fashion. All future bills were successfully interfaced in Brandigan's computer systems. As a result, the proper billing has provided for a more timely and efficient movement of this customer's products and the company and customer enjoy a superior relationship. I was commended on my strong oral communication skills which produced outstanding bottom-line results for both my employer and the customer.

DESCRIBE A SITUATION WHICH DEMONSTRATES YOUR ABILITY TO PRESENT IDEAS ORALLY AND YOUR SKILL IN ORAL EXPRESSION.

DESCRIBE A RECENT MEANINGFUL SUMMER EXPERIENCE.

The full name of the YMCA is the Young Men's Christian Association. This organization has a broad range of purposes, including providing programs which encourage the development of body, mind, and spirit. The YMCA has been in operation for more than 150 years. It was founded in 1844 by George Williams, a young London clerk, and a group of his friends. Their purpose was to spread Christianity among young men. The YMCA quickly became international, with the biggest membership surges in the U.S. and Canada. By 1855, when the first YMCA World Conference was held in Paris, the YMCA had grown to 30,360 members who belonged to 370 associations in seven countries. Until 1869, no YMCA had ever held all its activities in the same place. In 1874, the San Francisco YMCA admitted the association's first women members. During World War II, the YMCA established more than 450 clubs for the Allied armed forces and raised in excess of $12 million to aid the six million war prisoners of all nations. In the early 1970s there were 5,400,000 members in 85 countries. By 1980, over 1800 YMCAs had approximately three million members in the U.S., including people of all religions such as Protestants, Roman Catholics, Eastern Orthodox adherents, and non-Christians. Today there are more than 36 million members in over 90 countries.

As a summer volunteer at the YMCA, I worked with the third grade summertime daycare class and their supervisors/teachers. As a volunteer, I had many responsibilities varying day to day. These included assisting in watching children at the pool, helping the children to find tables at which to sit during lunch, and even helping the kids to play baseball. Something I learned from my volunteer experiences is that there is much more time and work involved in child care than I had ever thought. One important skill I learned during my volunteer experience is how to be creative and resourceful "on a moment's notice," as you will read about in my story.

My job was originally supposed to be helping with the basketball camp at the YMCA during the week of August 2nd-6th. We confirmed my appointment and my schedule during the last week of July, and we were assured by YMCA staff personnel that my services would be needed at basketball camp.

I showed up for my first day of work at 8:30 a.m. and I reported to the assistant director's office. To my surprise, I learned that the basketball camp had been rescheduled for the previous week! Apparently there had been a lack of internal communication within the YMCA, and I realized that the YMCA is, indeed, a large organization with many programs operating independently of each other.

Luckily, there was an opening in the daycare school, and I was assigned to the third grade class as a helper. When the door opened to the class which would be my work home for the week, I saw the smiling faces of 20 children who quickly called me "teacher."

I believe my job contributed to the goals of the organization through the way in which I cared for the children and nurtured them in body, mind, and spirit. The staff supervising me gave me much freedom to implement activities which would stimulate the children intellectually and creatively. For example, I helped the children with numerous crafts through which I discovered how much young children enjoy hands-on learning activities and "making things."

What impressed me the most about the organization is how many simultaneous activities and programs take place. It takes a large staff with people specializing in many different areas to make a YMCA work. What impressed me the least about this particular YMCA is that it appeared somewhat disorganized. For example, the head of the basketball program was just down the hall from the assistant director's office, and yet the two had not communicated or coordinated regarding the rescheduling of the basketball camp to which I had been assigned.

I would like now to relate an anecdote from my experience at the YMCA as a volunteer, which my friend and I often refer to as "Crafty Craft Makers." On my fourth day of work at "the Y," I showed up for work at 9:00 a.m. as usual and the children and I made crafts; after that we went to the gym to play basketball. We then found out that we would be on "rainy day schedule," which means that we would be going back to the craft room for a second time in the morning. My supervisors had not anticipated this, and they were, therefore, unprepared.

My friend Kris and I had to think of something! We were facing 20 restless children, cooped up in a room with nothing to do for an hour except, perhaps, braid my hair and perform beautician services on Kris. Kris and I returned to the craft room anticipating the discovery of many materials and art supplies which could be used to entertain the children. To our dismay, all the cupboards which contained such supplies were locked, which meant that we had to work with the limited materials on the counter. Our imaginations went to work. On the counter were the following supplies: hot dog containers, napkins, crayons, tissue paper, and pipe cleaners. As a joke, I made a "cockroach" out of a hot dog container and pipe cleaners. Kris saw potential in this concept and she colored it, which transformed it into a caterpillar. As soon as she was finished, the children walked into the room which meant that we were forced to make this craft or face the consequences. We showed the children our "crafty craft" and they thought the caterpillar was a cockroach! We convinced them it was, indeed, a caterpillar, and they proceeded to color their hot dog containers in preparation for making caterpillars. The boys all colored theirs brown so that theirs would be cockroaches, and the girls chose "pretty colors" so that they could make caterpillars. After we discovered that we had too few pipe cleaners, most of which were black and brown, we proceeded to cut every pipe cleaner into thirds so that all the children would have equal portions. After everyone had made his caterpillars, we looked on the other side of the craft room and found three more bags of pipe cleaners in all colors! Because we still had ten minutes left before lunch, we decided to make pipe cleaner children, which the children really enjoyed.

From this experience, Kris and I learned that one must often improvise and be resourceful in work situations.

ESSAY QUESTIONS POSED ON THE APPLICATIONS FOR THE CLASS OF 2005:

As part of this section on undergraduate essays and personal statements, we thought we would show you some of the questions posed in applications for the entering class of 2005:

Please write an original essay on one of the following topics:

1. "The house of the soul," "a musical instrument," and "machine" are three examples of the many metaphors that are often employed to describe the human body. Write an essay in which you examine how the use of metaphors affects the ways in which we study human life, see our bodies, take care of ourselves and others, or define health. Be sure to include and explain your own metaphor for the human body.

2. At our university, a political science professor uses contemporary fiction by African authors to teach about the politics of southern Africa. If you were to design a course around the music, art, film or literature that you like, what would the course be about? What would you hope to teach your student? Please include a listening/viewing/reading list with your essay.

3. Using a piece of wire, an egg carton, and any inexpensive hardware-store item, create something that would solve a problem. Tell us about your creation, but don't worry: we won't require proof that it works!

4. Choose a person or event that has been important in your life and describe in detail what makes the person or event significant to you.

Along with this application, please submit an essay of 150-300 words, in the form of a personal statement. The personal statement should provide the Admissions Committee with a sense of you as an individual so that we may have the opportunity to get to know you better through your writing.

On a separate sheet of paper, please answer both questions below (maximum of 250 words for each answer.) Be sure to include your name and U.S. Social Security number, and staple the page to the application.

1. Describe your intellectual interests, their evolution, and what makes them exciting to your.

2. Tell us what appeals to your about the school/college you indicated above. How will you utilize its academic programs to further explore your intended major or field of interest (or general academic interests if you're undecided).

Pick one of the following topics, and write a one-page essay on a separate sheet of paper. We're interested in which topic you choose, how you develop your idea, and how well you express yourself.

1. Think about something you never did in high school but wish you had done. Now imagine your time at college. Propose taking up something daring and new, and describe how it might affect your life.

2. "A stone, a leaf, an unfound door." *Look Homeward, Angel,* Thomas Wolfe. Write about three objects that would give the admissions selection committee insight into who you are.

3. On rereading his personal journals in the last few years of his life, E.B. White, author and journalist wrote: "Where I would like to discover facts, I find fancy. Where I would like to learn what I did, I learn only what I was thinking. They are loaded with opinion, moral thoughts, quick evaluations, youthful hopes and cares and sorrows. Occasionally, they manage to report something in exquisite honesty and accuracy. That is why I have refrained from burning them."

Please write an essay from your own life journal that reports something "in exquisite honesty and accuracy."

Since we do not have the opportunity to meet all applicants personally, you can help us get to know you better through this required personal essay. Please read the topics carefully. Choose one topic from below that will allow you to best represent your creativity and who you are. Your essay should be one page or less and should fit in the space provided on this page.

TOPIC 1: Drawing on your family's experiences and your personal circumstances, tell us what you would like us to know about you that you have not already been able to tell us.

TOPIC 2: Provide a creative writing sample that is in some way autobiographical.

Here are the essay questions for Stanford University's application for 2001:

Here are three short essay questions which need to be answered in approximately 250 words:

1. Of the activities, interests, and experiences (you) listed on the previous page, which is the most meaningful to you and why?

2. Sharing intellectual interests is an important aspect of university life. Describe an experience or idea that you find intellectually exciting and explain why.

3. Jot a note to your future college roommate relating a personal experience that reveals something about you.

Then Stanford asks applicants to write a longer essay, fitting on one page, on one of two topics, either a) or b):

a) Attach a small photograph (3.5 X 5 inches or smaller) of something important to you and explain its significance.

b) If, for a period of time, you could live the life of any individual (fictional or non-fictional), who would you choose? How does this choice reflect who you are?

Here are the essay questions posed by Dartmouth College on its 2001 application:

1. What was the highlight of your summer?

2. Which of your pursuits, in or out of school, do you find most fulfilling? Why?

3. The character of the College is a mosaic formed by the life experiences of its students. Share with us aspects of your background that you believe would add to the Dartmouth community.

4. What else should we know? Tell us more about yourself, explain an interest, describe a talent, or raise an issue of concern. Anything goes!

On its Application for Undergraduate Admissions, 2000-2001, the University of Pennsylvania asks applicants to answer the following questions.

5a. What characteristics of Penn, and yourself, make the University a particularly good match for you? Briefly describe how you envision your first year in college. How will your presence be known on campus?

Your intellectual abilities, your sense of imagination and your creativity are important to us. With this in mind, please respond to one of the following three requests. You may use the space provided or enclose an additional sheet of paper. Your essay should not exceed one page.

6a. Your have just completed your 300-page autobiography. Please submit page 217.

6b. First experiences can be defining. Cite a first experience that you have had and explain its impact on you.

6c. Recall an occasion when you took a risk that you now know was the right thing to do.

The 2001 application to Brown College poses this essay question to applicants:

In reading your application we want to get to know you as well as we can. We ask that you use this opportunity to tell us something more about yourself that would help us toward a sense of who you are, how you think, and what issues and ideas interest you most. Your statement should be done *in your own handwriting.* Be sure to sign at the bottom of page 4 certifying that this statement is entirely your own original work and that all information included is accurate to the best of your knowledge.

Cornell University asks these questions in its 2001 Personal Application:

Describe your intellectual interests, their evolution, and what makes them exciting to you.

Tell us what appeals to you about the the school/college you indicated above. How will you utilize its academic programs to further explore your intended major or field of interest (or general academic interests if you're undecided.)

Take a look at your activities and work experiences. Please tell us about the one you value most and why.

Here's the essay portion of the freshman application to Yale College for entrance in September 2001:

1. There are limitations to what grades, scores, and recommendations can tell us about any applicant. We ask you to write a personal essay that will help us to know you better. In the past, candidates have written about their families, intellectual and extracurricular interests, ethnicity or culture, school and community events to which they have had strong reactions, people who have influenced them, significant experiences, personal aspirations, or topics that spring entirely from their imagination. There is no "correct" way to respond to our request. Write about what matters to you, and you are are bound to convey a strong sense of who you are. (Observe a one-page limit.)

2. Now write the essay you would have written if you were not trying so hard to say just the right thing to the Yale Admissions Committee. Perhaps you felt torn, wondering which of two topics to discuss. Regain your equanimity by writing about the one you didn't choose. (Observe a one-page limit.)

Part Six: Medical School, Physician's Assistant Program, Dental School, Veterinary Program, and Residency Program Essays and Personal Statements

This section contains essays and personal statements used in application for medical school, dental school, physician's assistant programs, veterinary programs, and residency programs.

.

TO: Selection Committee, Medical School of Stanford University
FROM: Devlin Murphy
DATE:
RE: Application for Admission to the Stanford Medical School

My goal to become a medical doctor is a logical extension of my lifelong interest in saving lives, helping people, rescuing others, and excelling personally and professionally in all I do. My interest in medicine began when I was a child as I watched my Austrian grandfather devote himself as a physician to his patients in a rural setting. My interest in medicine intensified as I watched my sister, born with numerous birth defects, visit doctor after doctor and clinic after clinic in country after country throughout Europe. Throughout my childhood, I grew up overhearing medical theories and medical explanations and yearning for medical solutions which, in my sister's case, never came true. I look back upon my childhood and feel that I grew up in a medical laboratory of sorts.

A Passion for Helping Others is Evident in Everything I Have Done.

If my helping instincts were genetically determined and then environmentally encouraged, on my own initiative I have made life choices as an adult which reveal my genuine passion for rescuing, helping, and saving others. I have worked as a Veterinary Assistant for Krepp Veterinary Clinic, a job which places me in situations daily where I am trying to save the lives of our animal friends. In this job I have earned widespread praise for my excellent decision-making skills in emergency situations, and I have discovered that I have the ability to keep a cool head and think strategically in a crisis. In another job as a volunteer in a homeless shelter, I have gained great satisfaction from helping people find safety and solace in an emergency shelter, and I have discovered that the health problems of family members was often what led to the financial ruin and subsequent homelessness of many of those individuals.

My Volunteer Activities Demonstrate My Dedication to Saving Lives, Molding Character, and Contributing to Social Justice.

Even as a youth, I volunteered my time in medical environments, as I worked as a Volunteer at the University Hospital in Los Angeles and as a volunteer at a nursing home. More recently, as a volunteer Police Officer with the San Diego Police Department, I organized the first police officer exchange between Austrian and American officers while helping citizens to arrange neighborhood watches, teaching children about safety issues using puppet plays and a police robot, and patrolling neighborhoods. As a volunteer EMT/Firefighter with the San Diego City Fire Department, I was constantly involved in saving people's lives while fighting fires and searching houses for victims. In 1999 I received the city's Outstanding EMT Award. My communication, listening, and counseling skills were refined in that firefighting job as I gave fire demonstrations at schools and child care centers. As a volunteer with Habitat For Humanity, I have derived much satisfaction from helping others, and that involvement has cemented my passionate belief that everyone has a right to (1) receive an education, (2) have adequate shelter, and (3) obtain medical care. As a Volunteer Rescue Scuba Diver with the San Diego Fire Department, I have searched for drowning victims and rescued survivors. I passionately believe that society's leaders must be involved in socially responsible ways in the community. I have worked tirelessly as a Cub Scout den leader with Boy Scouts of America helping boys aged seven and eight grow in self confidence and self discipline.

My Academic Achievements Reveal My Highly Motivated Personality as well as My Ability to Excel in Rigorous Academic Studies.

I have excelled in every training program in which I have participated, including EMT training, Police Academy Training, and Firefighting Training. In college, too, I have excelled and have a 4.06 average at the current time at San Diego State College where I am triple majoring in biology, chemistry, and sociology while earning my B.S. degree. I received the Chi Psi Award given to the top 3% of seniors and juniors, and I was named to *Who's Who in American Colleges*. I also received the Chemistry Award of the Year. My scholastic achievements have resulted in my induction into Alpha Chi Honorary as well as the honorary Psychology club, the honorary Biology club, and the honorary Sociology club. I always approach my studies in such a way that I try to maximize my learning experience, because I believe that our best educated scholar-doctors may one day be able to unlock the doors to some of our deepest medical mysteries. I am a highly motivated individual who always aspires to be at the top of my class and to be a leader in all I do.

I Offer a Character That Would Be a Credit to the Medical Profession.

I believe my character is well expressed in the types of activities and involvements I have chosen as an adult, which I have described briefly above. Principles of honor, integrity, and human kindness guide me in all my life decisions and human interactions, and I am very confident that I could one day be a medical doctor who would be a credit to the profession, a blessing to the communities I serve, an inspiration to medical staff and hospital employees with whom I would be working, and a source of pride to the institution from which I graduate.

Yours sincerely,

Devlin Murphy

Felicia D'Allesandro

SSN: 000-00-0000

Application for Physician's Assistant Program

Valuable role models and influences

My desire to become a contributing part of the medical profession was aroused in me as a child, as I watched my mother, a Registered Nurse, serve her patients with selfless dedication. The many cards, letters, and gifts my mother continues to receive from her patients have indicated that her compassion and professional skills are appreciated. I have also watched as my mother and her colleagues spent many unnoticed hours after work discussing patient care and sharing their thoughts for improvements in the quality of nursing services. Another important role model for me was our family friend and our family doctor, Dr. Matthews. He donated his time unselfishly by traveling overseas to provide medical services to the poor, and I observed as a youth that Dr. Matthews seemed motivated by concern for humanity and treated medicine as his calling in life.

My decision to become a Surgical Technologist

I tested my desire to become involved in the medical profession when I volunteered at age 14 as a member of my church youth group at the Veterans Administration Hospital. Even as a youth, I was commended for my ability to work with patients in a professional manner that was unusual for a teenager. By the time I went to college, I knew that I wanted to become a medical professional.

Excellent academic performance in earning my A.S. Degree/Surgical Technologist Diploma

I graduated at the top of my class with a 4.0 GPA in all my surgical technologist classes while earning my A.S. degree from Wormley Technical College in Decatur, GA. With excellent academic credentials and a reputation for excellent communication and human relations skills, I was one of only two students selected to work as a Surgical Technologist at Richland Memorial Hospital in Decatur, GA, prior to actually graduating from the program. This early work experience gave me valuable opportunities to assist surgeons, and it was at that point that I began to formulate my professional plan to one day become a Physician's Assistant. Working as a surgical Physician's Assistant is one of my goals within the PA field, but I am versatile and would enjoy rotating to other specialties including family practice.

Excellent reputation within my field

After graduating from Wormley Technical College, my husband and I moved to Kentucky, and I have been working as a Certified Surgical Technologist at McDonnell Regional Hospital in Dixon, KY. I am highly regarded by all surgeons with whom I work because of my excellent technical knowledge, my absolute reliability, as well as my cheerful nature. I am currently specializing in cardiovascular surgery. I am specifically requested by many of the surgeons at the hospital.

Why I want to be a Physician's Assistant

Although I am excelling as a Surgical Technologist, I desire more contact with patients than I currently have, and becoming a Physician's Assistant would give me an opportunity to work with patients. On my own time, I am learning Spanish and I plan to be bilingual in Spanish by the end of the Physician's Assistant program. Being able to speak Spanish will be of great value as I attempt to communicate with and help patients as a Physician's Assistant. I am constantly seeking to upgrade my knowledge and skills, and that is why I have availed myself of twice the required number of continuing education hours at McDonnell Regional Hospital. I am a current member of the Beta Beta Beta Biological Honor Society, and I am a member of the Association of Surgical Technologists.

Although enrolling in a Physician's Assistant program requires a financial sacrifice for me since I will have to resign my full-time job as a Surgical Technologist, I am ready to make that sacrifice. I am confident that I can become a credit to the medical profession as a Physician's Assistant as I have been as a Surgical Technologist.

Yours sincerely,

Felicia D'Allesandro

APPLICATION FOR MEDICAL SCHOOL

Kathryn Anne Davenport

APPLICATION FOR MEDICAL SCHOOL

I know a gentleman who suffers from cancer. Physically, he is a mere shadow of the man he once was. Mentally and emotionally, he is a giant. Because of the luminous qualities of his character, I can see through the cancer that weakens but does not rule him. Despite what the disease has taken, it has left in place his resilience and perseverance. When I look beyond his physical frailty, I see his strength of character. Perhaps defying science, he is determined to overcome great odds as he continues his fight. Therefore, what consumes my attention most is not the cancer but the qualities of his character which sustain him.

For years the mind and the body were treated as separate entities. I understand the patient's physical loss of control and the psychological ramifications, yet I fail to understand the disease itself. The body and spirit are inseparable and the study of one is incomplete without the study of the other. In essence, I began my journey toward medical school by initially earning a B.A. in Psychology. Now I am compelled to study the body so that I may offer to future patients a holistic evaluation of their physical health.

Many believe we are a product of our experiences. Having had nine years of extensive involvement in geriatrics and with the severely infirm, I have encountered everything from diabetes to AIDS. As an employee/volunteer at Medical Village, I provided care to the Alzheimers and AIDS patients, diabetics, quadriplegics, and paraplegics that comprised the 159-bed facility. I was trained in both the Restorative Feeding and Restorative Walking programs. Sensory stimulation as well as hand-eye coordination were integral parts of my patient contact. Through those experiences, I learned how to approach, communicate with, and care for patients suffering from Alzheimers and dementia. With the brain-stem injured, I performed range-of-motion exercises to prevent contraction of muscles and promote circulation. Evaluating and documenting patients' abilities and progress also comprised my duties.

For four years I volunteered at the Ronald McDonald House where I lent emotional support for critically ill children and their families. I continued my involvement with the infirm at Texas State Hospital and Dallas Medical Center. During that time, I was trained in the assessment of auditory deficiencies of premature infants. Outside of these medically related experiences, I acted as a soccer coach for Special Olympians and counselor for underprivileged children at a Christian camp.

At the age of 23, I look back over my brief life and see the faces I have encountered. I have responded to their physical needs with the compassion necessary to sustain their emotional health as well. However, the care I provided is minuscule compared to the wealth of knowledge I received from those patients. They have taught me that life is not simply a series of unrelated events. Rather, we are defined by our experiences and also by our choices. I made a choice in my youth to become involved in caring for the diseased and elderly, and that choice has shaped my aspirations. Involvement with the infirm has accelerated my maturity. Dedication to "my patients" has cemented a sense of responsibility toward my fellow man. I understand that our time here is crucial. I feel compelled to be productive and my experiences have convinced me that I belong in the medical field. When a patient needs care, no task is beneath me and no challenge is too great.

My decision to choose a medical career was made with intense consideration. The reality of facing grueling hours of clinical duties combined with taxing studies does not dampen my enthusiasm or lessen my desire. I can perceive of no other endeavor that would allow me to contribute so unselfishly to mankind. Physically, emotionally, and spiritually I would find any other profession less fulfilling and challenging.

As I embark upon a career in medicine, I am reminded of the cancer patient who captivated my attention. Long after he is gone, I will remember the part of his soul he allowed me to see. He exposed his fighting spirit and tenacious character and, in doing so, he helped me recognize and appreciate those same qualities in myself. That cancer patient is my grandfather. As for now, he continues to fight his battle. I desperately want to help win the war.

APPLICATION FOR MEDICAL SCHOOL

PLEASE IDENTIFY AREAS OF MEDICINE WHICH MAY BE OF PARTICULAR INTEREST TO YOU AND YOUR REASONS FOR THEIR SELECTION.

At this point in my life I believe that my focus will be family practice because of my wish to be a general practitioner in a rural area where I will be able to work with families and watch my patients grow and be a part of their lives. I want to be practicing in a setting where there will be a high level of interaction.

I am not leaning toward a speciality area where I may see a patient only for a particular problem or situation and not have the opportunity to follow through with their care on a regular basis. I want to be a part of my patients' lives.

WHAT FACTORS ARE MOST IMPORTANT IN YOUR CHOICE OF A MEDICAL SCHOOL?

Because of my strong wish to be a rural area family practitioner, I am interested in attending a medical school which will prepare me to be a well-rounded physician and where the emphasis of the program is to allow medical students to be knowledgeable of all the many aspects of medicine: that is, to be generalists rather than specialists.

DESCRIBE HOW YOU SELECTED YOUR UNDERGRADUATE SCHOOL AND CURRENT MAJOR AREA OF STUDY.

I originally came to the Chicago area because of my husband's job and researched several of the area's respected colleges. One of my main reasons for choosing your institution was because it is a small, private school with a reputation for being very good in the sciences and where the faculty-to-student ratio is better than at the larger state universities.

I have excelled in my triple major in cellular biology, chemistry, and sociology as well as in additional major course work in psychology. I am also proud that I have excelled in a rigorous academic curriculum while distinguishing myself at home and in my job: I am the proud mother of three beautiful children, I am the wife of a respected civil servant, and I am a valued and respected employee of the company for which I work. I am known for my ability to juggle simultaneous responsibilities and excel at them all.

WHERE DO YOU SEE YOURSELF AT THE MIDPOINT OF YOUR MEDICAL CAREER? WHAT PERSONAL TRAITS AND CHARACTERISTICS WILL YOU BRING TO MEDICINE?

As a very family-oriented person, I want a career in medicine in a rural area where I can practice as a family physician with extensive patient contact. My orientation has always been to focus on the patient and to do everything I can to be an important part of my patients' lives. I want to see my patients grow up and be a part of the community where I can be counted on to provide very personalized care and where, at the midpoint of my career, I will be an integral part of people's lives and of the fabric of the community.

Since I was a young girl growing up in Pennsylvania, I have been certain that medicine is to be my life work. Successful as an international In-Flight Service Coordinator for Fly The World Air Lines, I earned widespread praise for my excellent decision-making skills in emergency situations, During an in-flight emergency I reacted quickly and helped save the lives of 178 people and received a special award for heroism which cited my decisiveness.

International flight can often seem like a "flying emergency room" where anything can happen. I have resuscitated passengers who have suffered heart attacks and utilize my expert skills in CPR and first aid on a daily basis. I am often responsible for making decisions which could mean the difference between life or death and am a humanitarian who can contribute quick thinking and fast response time in emergencies as well as personal principles of honor, integrity, and unselfish human kindness which guide me in everything I attempt.

WHERE DO YOU SEE YOURSELF AT THE MID-POINT OF YOUR MEDICAL CAREER? WHAT PERSONAL TRAITS AND CHARACTERISTICS WILL YOU BRING TO MEDICINE?

BRIEFLY DESCRIBE YOUR MOST REWARDING EXPERIENCE OR SOME ACHIEVEMENT OF WHICH YOU ARE PROUD.

BRIEFLY DESCRIBE YOUR MOST REWARDING EXPERIENCE OR SOME ACHIEVEMENT OF WHICH YOU ARE PARTICULARLY PROUD.

One of the greatest accomplishments of my life was an incident when I saved a four-year-old girl and her five-year-old brother from being kidnapped by their father and taken from the U.S. to Portugal illegally. The mother was a personal friend and when I saw the father had one-way tickets to Portugal and I knew the mother had legal custody, I realized what was happening. Normal procedures would not allow an international flight to be turned around but the pilot knew me and trusted my judgment. The mother was at least 45 minutes from the airport so I called the police and had the plane held. The father was arrested and convicted of kidnapping. It was discovered that the father had filed for custody in his native country and could have taken the children permanently away from the mother if I had not reacted quickly.

PLEASE IDENTIFY AREAS OF MEDICINE OF PARTICULAR INTEREST TO YOU AND YOUR REASONS FOR THEIR SELECTION.

PLEASE IDENTIFY AREAS OF MEDICINE WHICH MAY BE OF PARTICULAR INTEREST TO YOU AND YOUR REASONS FOR THEIR SELECTION.

At this point in my life I believe that my focus will be family practice because of my wish to be a general practitioner in a rural area where I will be able to work with families and watch my patients grow and be a part of their lives. I want to be practicing in a setting where there will be a high level of interaction. I am not leaning toward a specialty area where I may see a patient only for a particular problem or situation and not have the opportunity to follow through with their care on a regular basis. I want to be a part of my patients' lives.

IS THERE ANYTHING THE ADMISSIONS COMMITTEE SHOULD KNOW ABOUT YOUR ACADEMIC CAREER THAT WOULD NOT BE EVIDENT FROM YOUR TRANSCRIPT?

IS THERE ANYTHING THE ADMISSIONS COMMITTEE SHOULD KNOW ABOUT YOUR ACADEMIC CAREER THAT WOULD NOT BE EVIDENT FROM YOUR TRANSCRIPT?

I do not believe my undergraduate GPA is a good indicator of my intellect and capacity for intense study. I would respectfully ask that the Admissions Committee look at my GPA and consider the fact that my undergraduate studies were greatly affected by unavoidable circumstances that made it difficult for me to concentrate solely on academic achievement.

During my freshman year of college, I became the sole guardian of my younger brother, Dionne. Although I didn't balk at the responsibility, it was a tremendous adjustment for me as a teenager to suddenly become a father to a five-year-old boy. I remained in school but was required to move out of campus housing and into an apartment. The added costs of childcare and housing meant that I had to get a second job which affected the amount of time I could spend studying. I also had to invest time in rearing a young child.

Today Dionne is a handsome, intelligent, and articulate young man that any father or brother would be proud to have. He is twelve and excelling in his studies. I am a settled family man with a wife and two other children. I am not afraid of responsibility as witnessed by the dedication and care given my younger brother and feel these are qualities that would reflect admirably on our institution should you accept my application. I currently work as a nurse in the emergency room of St. Mary's Hospital. I have seen parents who work full-time bring their children to the emergency room at night because there is no alternative care for them. I have also seen these cases result in serious medical conditions for the children who have had to wait for care. This is the reason I am interested in family practice.

It is my intention once I attain my medical license to open a clinic for these children where they can receive quality care at a price and time that are accessible to their families. I intend to provide immunizations and nutritional counseling as well as gang intervention advice for troubled youth.

As you can see, I am an individual dedicated to the greater good of the community and society as a whole and while the kind of practice I envision is not as financially well-recognized as some other medical specialties, I feel that my reputation will someday be a boon to your program.

IS THERE ANYTHING THE ADMISSIONS COMMITTEE SHOULD KNOW ABOUT YOUR ACADEMIC CAREER THAT WOULD NOT BE EVIDENT FROM YOUR TRANSCRIPT?

Essay in Application for Dental School
by David Martin

To explain concisely why I am interested in the dental profession, I must begin with my childhood. From the time I was about ten years old, I spent most of my summers visiting with grandparents in Kansas where my grandfather is a small-town family dentist. This gave me a great opportunity to see first hand what a rural practice can be like by observing procedures as well as the business aspects of running a small practice. I was given a rare opportunity to observe and participate in lab work and sculpting and discovered that I possess a raw artistic talent as it relates to dentistry. This also gave me a chance to become moderately well versed in oral anatomy and oral procedures at a young age and to absorb and appreciate my grandfather's talent for making his patients feel comfortable. I became aware at a young age that I wanted to be a dentist and that, in my grandfather, I had a wonderful role model. I also know that I have the drive, intelligence, and natural qualities that would be needed.

Presently I am volunteering in the office of Dr. Dixon Delbert's family dentistry practice in Wichita. Dr. Delbert has arranged for me to freely observe throughout his sophisticated practice which offers services related to endodontics, oral surgery, and periodontics. This has given me a chance to talk with professionals in varying dental specialties and to observe the contrast between a small practice like the one my grandfather runs and a large, modern facility.

I believe my academic pursuits have prepared me well to enter the dental profession. I earned a B.S. degree in Marketing with a 3.34 GPA in my major at Georgia State University, and my undergraduate marketing degree equipped me with valuable insights into interpersonal relations. I feel my well-rounded personality would also be of value in the customer-and-employee relations aspect of dentistry, and I credit my involvements in high school as contributing measurably to my ability to interact socially with others in a gracious manner. In high school, in addition to being named to the National Honor Society and winning the Freshman English Student of the Year award, I was elected Sports Editor of the yearbook staff, was co-captain of the football and soccer teams, was captain of the golf and tennis teams, was selected for inclusion in *Who's Who Among American High School Students*, and was active in community service activities.

As soon as I arrived at college, I became perceived as a campus leader and organizer; I was active in a philanthropic event that benefitted orphans and I held nine separate elected positions within my fraternity. In those elected positions I expressed not only my leadership ability but also my natural creativity; for example, I created several T-shirt designs which captured the spirit of certain events.

My interpersonal skills have also been refined through jobs as a sales representative in a men's clothing store, phone representative for a marketing research firm, door-to-door salesman of educational books, and salesperson in a golf pro shop. I look back on my job with Southwestern Company as a major tool in refining my management skills; after a one-week training session, I was sent to a small town in Ohio and had to find a place to live while functioning as an entrepreneur selling educational books door-to-door. It was like getting thrown into deep water and being told to "sink or swim," and I believe I changed from a boy into a man that summer.

Just three weeks after graduating from Georgia State University, I enrolled at Kansas City College in the program pursuant to a B.S. in Biological Sciences and have excelled in completing nine hours a semester while working 20 hours a week. At Kansas City College I have earned a 3.925 GPA and have been inducted into Beta Beta Beta, a national collegiate biology honor society in which invitations to become a member are based on grades, interest in the field, and faculty sponsorship. I have also joined the American Student Dental Association so that I can receive their publications and keep up with changes and new procedures in the dental profession. This semester I also completed Organic Chemistry I and Human Anatomy & Physiology courses at the University of Kansas with a 3.5 GPA.

One reason I feel I would be a credit to the profession of dentistry is that I believe I offer a rock-solid character. As a matter of personal philosophy, I try to live according to Christian values. I am known for my high ethical and moral principles, and I perceive of dentistry as a profession in which one can be of service to mankind and to the community.

In conclusion, I must emphasize that I was exposed to the dental profession at an early age and became fascinated with the possibilities of what I could accomplish with my artistic aptitude, intellectual abilities, and desire to enhance the quality of people's lives by providing quality dental care.

Yours sincerely,

David Martin

DEMONSTRATE YOUR ABILITY TO COMMIT TO LONG-TERM GOALS.

ESSAY AS PART OF AN
APPLICATION TO
VETERINARY SCHOOL:
DEMONSTRATE YOUR
ABILITY TO COMMIT TO
LONG-TERM GOALS.

My twelfth birthday was my most memorable. After many years of riding lessons and summer riding camps, I had become the proud owner of a beautiful Hackney pony mare. I was finally free of the constraints of ranch-owned horses and generic riding trails; I was free to ride everyday after school and could not wait until summer. Twenty years later, my love for horses continues; that same beautiful Hackney pony mare is still with me. And although we don't explore any new trails or fields anymore, she is still a huge part of my life. I also now have the pleasure of owning a Quarter Horse gelding that has been with me for eight years. My love for animals has always been strong, and my relationships with them demonstrate my ability to make commitments and remain loyal to those commitments.

My work life, too, demonstrates my orientation toward sustaining long-term commitments. I have been with UPS for nearly 13 years. I began employment with UPS in Miami and am now employed by UPS in Gilston because of my outstanding work performance.

With a current GPA of 3.78 as a senior and Biology major, I possess a commitment to lifelong learning and academic excellence which was not revealed in my initial college adventure more than 10 years ago. When I first embarked on college studies, my priorities were out of balance and I lacked the maturity, dedication, and patience to persist in achieving long-term goals. After my first halfhearted attempt at college studies, I decided to drop out of college and go to work. That is when I became employed with UPS, and I have grown up through the rigors of achieving high standards of service while functioning as part of a dedicated team.

Six years after obtaining employment with UPS, I realized in a more mature way that my true desire was to be in a helping profession related to animals and I made the commitment to do whatever it takes to achieve my goal of applying to veterinary school. I started with a small but significant step as I realized that my math skills needed strengthening; I enrolled in continuing education classes at a local community college and mastered the basics, then moved on to algebra, calculus, and the "hard" sciences. My success in those foundation courses gave me new knowledge and confidence which empowered me to proceed further.

I finally saw a way to make my dream a reality, and I began to methodically plan my college courses so that I would have the prerequisites needed to apply to veterinary school.

Shortly after I started college for the second time, I became involved in a new adventure which strengthened my resolve to enroll in veterinary school and which helped me acquire knowledge and skills which I am certain will be valuable throughout my career. I met a woman named Nellie Norton (please see letter of recommendation), who is a dynamic woman committed to the rescue, rehabilitation, and eventual release of injured and orphaned wildlife. She was involved in starting an organization called Second Chance Wildlife Rescue, and I was attracted to her cause and zeal. Through her, I learned much about wildlife and the vital role public education plays in the survival of our natural species. She also taught me how the prosperity of our wildlife is a reflection of the environmental "health" of our communities. I gained experience in rehabilitating wild species including hawks, owls, songbirds, foxes, squirrels, opossums, bats, and raccoons and, in addition to performing triage and the full spectrum of rehabilitation techniques, I have trained other rehabilitators, handled media interviews, raised funds, and then became co-president of this sizable wildlife rescue organization. I am grateful to this organization for the practical skills I have gained in examining animals, diagnosing disease/injury, setting broken bones, handling wound care, and many other areas. I have also become a sub permittee on a federal wildlife rehabilitation permit.

In more orthodox veterinary settings, I have also gained valuable experience related to my hoped-for career in veterinary medicine. Through my jobs in emergency and general practice experience, I have become skilled in many aspects of treating domestic animals. While excelling in my full-time job at UPS **and** excelling in college, I became employed as a kennel attendant and quickly moved up through the ranks to assist the veterinarians and perform technical duties. At the present time, I am employed at an emergency animal hospital and have received the highest evaluations of my performance in all areas (please see letter of recommendation).

My long-term goals after veterinary school now include qualifying for a surgical residency and eventually working as a surgeon for a specialty practice. I hope to become a productive member of the veterinary community and will always be committed to significant volunteer roles in wildlife rescue and rehabilitation throughout my lifetime.

ESSAY AS PART OF AN APPLICATION FOR VETERINARY SCHOOL

APPLICATION TO VETERINARY SCHOOL

As a child, I grew up in a military family with a mother, three older sisters, and the family dog. My father had died and left my mother to raise the family. My sisters were much older than I and they married when I was small; I was raised almost as an only child. I was fortunate to have had a mother who was raised on a farm and who liked animals, especially birds. Bird watching and identification was our favorite hobby together.

Losses in life drew me close to my animal friends. Besides the death of my father, I experienced the loss of several of my closest friends. My pets became a mechanism for coping with my grief over the loss of my human loved ones. By the time of high school, my home had grown accustomed to an assortment of animals–dogs, cats, skunks, rabbits, livestock, horses, birds, wildlife, and reptiles. I was involved in showing horses and was skilled in all aspects of the sport of rodeo. My original intention when I left for college was to achieve one of two goals: to become a veterinarian or psychologist. I believed that I could relate well enough to people to help them with problems through counseling. I also loved animals and wanted to help improve their quality of life. I chose a school that offered both degree programs as well as an intercollegiate rodeo team. I was offered scholarships from the Rodeo Teams at both Texas A&M and University of Texas, and I decided to attend Texas A&M.

What became clear to me early in my college career is that I had neither the emotional maturity nor commitment that it would take to aggressively tackle the science curriculum needed for pre-veterinary studies. Because of my youth and inexperience, I did not understand the importance of mastering scientific theory so that one can prudently and creatively apply those theories and concepts in practice. I decided to pursue a degree in psychology with the intention of returning to graduate school to earn a Ph.D.

After graduation from college, I grew emotionally through a diverse variety of jobs which included waitress, scuba diving clerk, mental health counselor, lifeguard, and nursing assistant. My "second-choice" career goal became a reality without the necessity of graduate school. The Department of the Army hired me as a "psychologist" and trained me as a Substance Abuse Counselor. This career opportunity enriched me and enabled me to cultivate many mature qualities which included patience, understanding, ethical awareness, emotional maturity, as well as tolerance of and appreciation of the difference in others. During those years, I continued to enhance my education in the sciences. At the same time I was refining my knowledge of wildlife and environmental issues. At that point in my life I made the decision to focus my efforts on obtaining a Ph.D. in Animal Behavior. That degree program has prerequisites which are very similar to pre-veterinary studies.

In the fall of 1994 I became actively involved with a wildlife rehabilitation organization that would forever change my life and goals. The president of that organization was moving and needed to find someone who would take over her job. An acquaintance who has since become a very good friend and I decided to act as co-presidents since neither of us had the time to devote to the position by ourselves. (Both of us were working full-time while pursuing rigorous academic studies.) It was through my involvement with this wildlife rehabilitation organization called Second Chance Wildlife Rescue, as well as through the encouragement of my co-president Anne Brown, that I became attuned to the fact that my true career goal is to pursue veterinary medicine with a secondary interest in earning a Ph.D. in Animal Behavior. As co-president of Second Chance Wildlife Rescue, I realized that no one in the organization had much interest in birds. Since I already had a background in bird identification and behavior, I became the natural leader for the club's bird rehabilitation efforts. I have received the necessary state and federal permits to allow my involvement in wildlife rehabilitation of mammals and birds, but my knowledge and experience are concentrated in the rehabilitation of birds. As co-president I was also involved in public education and fund-raising as well as rehabilitation.

While excelling in my full-time job, I continued wildlife rehabilitation activities and have simultaneously pursued necessary prerequisites at night school in order to qualify myself academically for admission to veterinary school. I am the owner of a Border collie and have become skilled in training him for obedience, sheep herding, and competitive events. During the past year, I was also employed on a part-time basis at an animal emergency clinic, and I have volunteered on a part-time basis at a primary care veterinary practice.

My main professional goal is to be admitted to veterinary school with a long-term goal of obtaining my Ph.D. in Animal Behavior. I would like to specialize in avian and exotic medicine and will continue my activities in wildlife rehabilitation and rescue.

APPLICATION FOR ADMISSION TO VETERINARY SCHOOL

RESIDENCY PROGRAM FOR ANESTHESIOLOGY
APPLICATION FOR RESIDENCY
Personal Statement

In this personal statement, I would like to describe 10 reasons why I believe I would be an extraordinarily valuable asset if accepted for a residency in anesthesiology.

1. I offer extensive expertise related to anesthesiology. My background includes extensive "hands-on" expertise as an anesthesiologist in Guatemala from 1992-1999. During that time, I worked closely with doctors in all types of medical and surgical specialties including OB-GYN, neurosurgery, cardiovascular and thoracic surgery, plastic surgery, urology, orthopedics, pediatrics, othorynolaryngology, and others. I also worked with patients in all kinds of medical condition when they were brought into the emergency room or operating room.

2. I also offer proven teaching skills as an anesthesiologist. At the Central Military Hospital in Guatemala, I was an instructor at the Internship and Residency Program of Anesthesia, and I supervised and trained residents. During that time I earned a reputation as a skilled communicator who excelled in teaching difficult and complex concepts. Furthermore, I have developed extensive skills related to communicating with and "teaching" the general public. For example, when I was in charge of a Program of Attention Mother-Infant (PAMI) described later in this personal statement, I planned and delivered at least 14 educational lectures for the community in the preventative medicine area, and I directed public information and public relations related to two huge vaccination campaigns.

3. My reputation for scholarship is established, and I have a deep desire to continue to contribute to the advancement of knowledge in the area of anesthesiology. I offer a demonstrated ability to excel in academic production and to perform in the academic area, including preparing and delivering professional papers. For example, I lectured in November 1987 at the Central American Congress of Anesthesia on "Experience with Vecuronium (Norcuron R) in Anesthesia for Cardiovascular Surgery." I am eager to contribute to the academic community through professional papers, conferences, and a true interest in clinical research.

4. I offer a proven capacity for hard work and long hours. For example, I worked three jobs from 1995-99, averaging more than 80 hours per week, while maintaining the highest quality in every aspect of my work.

5. Because of my expertise in anesthesiology, I have been the recipient of several honors and distinctions. I was selected as the primary anesthesiologist in the first two successful heart transplants in Peru, which took place at the El Cajon Clinic in 1997. This was a special honor bestowed on me after considerable hard work and after a rigorous selection process. From 1995-98, I had been selected for special training for cardiovascular anesthesia and organ transplants. After that intensive training, I became an anesthesiologist member of the cardiovascular and organ transplant teams which eventually performed those two successful heart transplants in Peru. Because of my outstanding credentials as an anesthesiologist, I was registered at the Health Ministry as one of the very few anesthesiologists permitted to participate in organ transplant surgery in Peru. I have a long-standing interest in cardiology; indeed,

I was nominated for post-degree training in Anesthesia for Cardiovascular Surgery at the Premier Hospital, Paris, France.

6. As an anesthesiologist, I have received extensive exposure to emergencies. As an anesthesiologist, I have participated in, and therefore gained exposure to, nearly every type of medical and surgical emergency, and I believe my background has refined my ability to make wise decisions in situations where "split seconds" mean the difference between life and death. For example, at the Central Hospital of Guatemala, I was in daily contact with medical surgical emergencies resulting from terrorist fighting in Peru. I gave anesthesia for emergency war surgery and participated in the treatment decisions of patients in ICU.

7. Creativity and skill in program development are two additional professional attributes. From 1991 to 1992, I was a General Medical Doctor at the San Jose Health Center in Guatemala. In that capacity I was in charge of the Infant-Maternal Program (PAMI), and I totally reorganized this program which covered approximately 1,000 very low-income families.

8. I offer experience as a general physician. I gained experience as a general physician during my externship, internship, and civil service from 1989-91. Furthermore, I routinely functioned as a "general physician" even as an anesthesiologist from 1992-93 because the largelyw rural population I served thought of me simply as "a doctor" and sought my knowledge/training in internal medicine.

9. My knowledge of foreign languages could be an asset. With the population becoming increasingly Hispanic, I feel that my language skills could be valuable. I speak Spanish fluently, since it is my native tongue, and I speak Italian and French.

10. I have a stable and supportive family and can provide outstanding personal and professional references. Finally, I believe that my stable family life and excellent moral character would be assets to the medical profession and to the communities I would be serving. Happily married with one child, I have spent the last two years getting reestablished in the United States after getting married in 1998. My husband is totally supportive of my career, and he has a mature understanding of the sacrifices he will need to make in order for me to pursue my career in anesthesiology.

In conclusion I simply want to add that, upon your request, I will provide outstanding personal and professional references which will offer further illustrations of the expertise in anesthesiology, scholarship, teaching skills, personal integrity, and other qualifications and qualities I would bring to your fine institution. I have made the decision to submit this application to your fine institution only after careful consideration of the opinions of colleagues as well as my analysis of the information contained in brochures and other literature discussing your mission and needs. I feel certain that I could be an asset to you, but I also feel that your institution would provide numerous advantages to me. I would welcome the opportunity to participate in teaching and clinical research while working in a position whereby I could keep myself continually updated and receive special training. The "mother city" of your institution is one that I feel my family and I would enjoy living in very much, and we would welcome the opportunity to contribute to community activities. I hope you will favorably consider my application for a residency in anesthesiology.

FAMILY MEDICINE RESIDENCY PROGRAM

APPLICATION FOR RESIDENCY

In what specific areas do you think you can contribute to this program?

FAMILY MEDICINE
RESIDENCY PROGRAM

Knowledge of all specialties: In my experience both as a general physician during my externship, internship, and civil service and as an anesthesiologist in Guatemala, I worked closely with doctors and patients in every type of medical and surgical specialty including OB-GYN, neurosurgery, cardiovascular and thoracic surgery, plastic surgery, urology, orthopedics, pediatrics, orthorynolaryngology, and others. I also worked with patients in all kinds of medical condition when they were brought into the operating or emergency room.

IN WHAT SPECIFIC
AREAS DO YOU THINK
YOU CAN
CONTRIBUTE TO THIS
PROGRAM?

Creativity and skill in program development: From 1991 to 1992, I was a General Medical Doctor at the El Hermanos Clinic in Guatemala. In that capacity I was in charge of the Infant/Maternal Program (PAMI), and I totally reorganized this program which covered approximately 1,000 very low-income families.

Proven teaching skills: From 1995 to 1997 at the Central Army Hospital in Guatemala, I was an instructor at the Internship and Residency Program of Anesthesia, and I supervised and trained residents. During that time I earned a reputation as a skilled communicator who excelled in teaching difficult and complex concepts. I have also had considerable experience in communicating with the general public; for example, when I was in charge of the Infant/Maternal Program (PAMI), I planned and delivered at least 14 educational lectures for the community in the preventive medicine area, and I directed public information and public relations related to two huge vaccination campaigns.

Demonstrated ability to excel in academic production: I offer a proven ability to perform in the academic arena, including preparing and delivering professional papers. For example, I lectured in November 1987 at the Central American Congress of Anesthesia on "Experience with Vecuronium (Norcuron R) in Anesthesia for Cardiovascular Surgery," and I am eager to contribute to the academic community through professional papers, conferences, and a true interest in clinical research.

Exposure to emergencies: As an anesthesiologist, I have participated in, and therefore gained exposure to, nearly every type of medical and surgical emergency, and I believe my background has refined my ability to make wise decisions in situations where "split seconds" mean the difference between life or death. For example, at the Central Hospital of Mexico from 1991-93, I was in daily contact with medical and surgical emergencies resulting from the terrorist fighting. I gave anesthesia for emergency war surgery and participated in the treatment decisions of patients in ICU.

Proven ability to excel in professional practice: I was the primary anesthesiologist in the first two successful heart transplants in Peru, which took place at the San Bernadine Clinic in 1995. This was a special honor bestowed on me after considerable hard work and after a rigorous selection process. From 1995-98, I was selected for special training for cardiovascular anesthesia and organ transplants. After that intense training, I became an anesthesiologist member of the cardiovascular and organ transplant teams which performed those first two successful heart transplants in Peru. I was registered at the Health Ministry as one of very few anesthesiologists permitted to participate in organ transplant surgery in Peru. I have a long-standing interest in cardiology, and indeed was nominated for post-degree training in Anesthesia for Cardiovascular Surgery at the Emperor's Hospital, Paris, France.

Knowledge of foreign languages: With the population becoming increasingly Hispanic, I feel that my language skills could be valuable. I speak Spanish fluently, since it is my native tongue, and I speak Italian and French on a basic level.

IN WHAT SPECIFIC AREAS DO YOU THINK YOU CAN CONTRIBUTE TO THIS PROGRAM?

PERSONAL STATEMENT OF JANE SULLIVAN
for ALABAMA STATE HOSPITAL

DISCUSS YOUR OBJECTIVE, GOALS, AND ACHIEVEMENTS

Objective: a residency in internal medicine

I would like to be considered for a residency in internal medicine, and I believe I have much to offer a medical center which is also a teaching hospital. As you will see in this statement, I combine proven teaching ability and extensive teaching experience with nine years of experience as an anesthesiologist in Mexico. I am keenly interested in participating in clinical research.

Long-range professional goals

My experience as an anesthesiologist in Mexico has led me to discover that I want to ultimately establish a practice in internal medicine in southeastern Alabama and eventually I would envision becoming a skilled cardiologist. Although my apparent specialty is anesthesiology, I wish to point out that, in Mexico, any medical specialist is more or less a "country doctor," and it was because of my knowledge of and education in internal medicine that Mexico came to me for help. Now married to an American citizen, I wish to make my professional contributions in the U.S. and I have pinpointed southeastern Alabama as a location where I could be of benefit.

Highlights of professional achievements

There are numerous achievements in my background which indicate my potential to be a skilled doctor of internal medicine and cardiologist.

Heart transplant experience: I was the primary anesthesiologist in the first two successful heart transplants in Mexico, which took place at the Mortedeus Clinic in 1991. This was a special honor bestowed on me after considerable hard work and after a rigorous selection process. In the 1990s, I was selected for special training for cardiovascular anesthesia and organ transplants. After that intense training, I became an anesthesiologist member of the cardiovascular and organ transplant teams which performed those first two successful heart transplants in Mexico. I believe this achievement illustrates that my interest in cardiology is a long-standing one.

Exposure to emergencies: As an anesthesiologist, I have participated in, and therefore gained exposure to, nearly every type of medical and surgical emergency, and I believe my background has refined my ability to make wise decisions in situations where "split seconds" mean the difference between life or death. For example, at the Central Hospital of Mexico from 1993-95, I was in daily contact with medical and surgical emergencies resulting from the terrorist fighting in Mexico. I gave anesthesia for emergency war surgery and participated in the treatment decisions of patients in ICU.

Knowledge of all specialties: As an anesthesiologist at the Clinica Ustedes from 1995-98, I worked closely with doctors and patients in every type of medical and surgical specialty including OB-GYN, neurosurgery, thoracic surgery, plastic surgery, urology, orthopedics, pediatrics, orthorynolaryngology, and others.

Creativity and skill in program development: From 1990-91, I was a General Medical Doctor at the Los Angeles Health Center in Mexico. In that capacity I was in charge of the Infant/Maternal Program (PAMI), and I totally reorganized this program which covered approximately 1,000 very low-income families.

Proven teaching skills: From 1989 to 1991 at the Central Hospital in Mexico, I was an instructor at the Internship and Residency Program of Anesthesia, and I supervised and trained residents. During that time I earned a reputation as a skilled communicator who excelled in teaching difficult and complex concepts. I have also had considerable experience in communicating with the general public; for example, when I was in charge of the Infant/Maternal Program (PAMI), I planned and delivered at least 14 educational lectures for the community in the preventive medicine area, and I directed public information and public relations related to two huge vaccination campaigns.

Demonstrated ability to excel in academic production: I offer a proven ability to perform in the academic arena, including preparing and delivering professional papers. For example, I lectured in November 1997 at the Central American Congress of Anesthesia on "Experience with Vecuronium (Norcuron R) in Anesthesia for Cardiovascular Surgery," and I am eager to contribute to the academic community through professional papers and conferences. I have attended numerous professional conferences from 1992 to 1994 which included a course in intensive therapy, a course in intensive care, a course in regional anesthesia, a course in clinical considerations in anesthesiology, a course providing an update in intensive therapy, a course in respiratory therapy, and other courses dealing with anesthesia and cardiology, neuromuscular relaxants, as well as with the changing roles of medical versus surgical management in the 1990s and the new century.

Knowledge of foreign languages

With the population becoming increasingly Hispanic, I feel that my language skills could be valuable. I speak Spanish fluently, since it is my native tongue, and I speak Italian and French on a basic level.

Excellent personal and professional reputation and stable family life

Finally, I believe that my stable family life and excellent moral character would be assets to the medical profession and to the communities that I would be serving. Happily married with one child, I have spent the last two years getting reestablished in the United States after getting married in 1998 to an American. My husband is totally supportive of my career, and he has a mature understanding of the sacrifices he will need to make in order for me to pursue my career goals in internal medicine and cardiology. Upon your request, I can provide outstanding personal and professional references which will attest to my dedication to hard work and long hours. For example, I worked <u>three</u> jobs from 1995-1999, averaging more than 80 hours per week, while maintaining the highest quality in every aspect of my work. I hope you will favorably consider me for a residency in internal medicine; I sincerely feel I could make valuable contributions to your fine "teaching hospital."

PLEASE SHARE WITH US SOMETHING ABOUT YOURSELF THAT MAY NOT BE ADDRESSED ELSEWHERE IN YOUR APPLICATIONS AND WHICH COULD BE HELPFUL TO THE ADMISSIONS COMMITTEE AS WE REVIEW YOUR FILE.

I would like the committee to know that my decision to enter medicine was influenced by my older sister, Natalie, who was born with birth defects. When I was growing up, I saw my family sacrifice other things in our lives for medical priorities as they searched tirelessly for doctors who could help. Natalie overcame the physical deformities as well as suicidal depression and other psychological obstacles and is now a respected Ph.D. in Psychology.

I also admired my grandfather who was a doctor and realized at an early age that I wanted to be a rural doctor like him. Living with Natalie I saw that medical and psychological/mental problems often go together and I realized that I wanted to combine my interests so that I could help not just the physical illnesses suffered by my patients but the whole patient.

Part Seven: Miscellaneous Other Essays and Personal Statements For Scholarships, Internships, Fellowships, and Other Purposes

Sometimes it's necessary to write an essay or personal statement for a special purpose, such as obtaining a scholarship. In this section you will find essays and personal statements used to apply for a variety of programs, including fellowships, internships, and apprentice programs. One of the internship applications required a resume, which you will see on the next page, but you will also find several other examples of resumes used to apply for undergraduate school and graduate programs in a later section of the book.

You will notice that the essay questions for scholarships do not vary from the essay questions used for general admissions. We wanted you to show you, however, some essays written for the purpose of obtaining scholarships and fellowships.

Paige McNeal

1110 Hay Street, Fayetteville, NC 28305   (910) 483-6611

GOAL

To qualify for an internship in the International Management Program and work in one of the three objective areas shown on my resume.

EXPERIENCE

INSTRUCTOR. Gaither Community College, Clarkston, TN (1997-present). Am a popular instructor of the Stained Glass Course as well as an instructor in the Adult Continuing Education Department.

EDUCATION

Completing **B.S. degree in International Business Management,** Tennessee School of International Business, Clarkston, TN.
* Maintaining 3.6 GPA while working 20 hours a week in the job above.

OBJECTIVE 1

Small business management and pet grooming expertise: *Qualified to teach pet care/grooming through two years of working in a pet shop.*
* Expert in all aspects of boarding, grooming, and preparing pets for shipment domestically and internationally.
* Qualified to teach professional pet grooming.
* Skilled in small business management including marketing, finance, and inventory control.
* Proven pet expert with experience in all aspects of pet care.

OBJECTIVE 2

Cooperatives: *Qualified to teach cooperative set-up and management through extensive work with one of the country's largest crafts co-op.*
* Was involved in forming "from scratch" a not-for-profit cooperative.
* Increased membership from 25 to nearly 50 artists and craftsmen.
* Was the guiding hand in assuring that all financial and marketing matters were handled expertly.
* Aggressively marketed support for the cooperative in terms of grant money and grant aid; was successful in obtaining funding from the city and from the Arts Council.

OBJECTIVE 3

Office management and computer operations: *Qualified through working for five summers in jobs which required excellent typing, filing, office operations, and computer operations skills.*
* Offer proven ability to troubleshoot software and hardware problems.
* Am able to relate well to others and have been successful in teaching computer skills and office operations to others.

LANGUAGES

Speak Spanish fluently and have a good understanding of Italian.

TRAINING

Received Certification upon completion of a one-year Business Program, Faison Technical Community College.
Currently enrolled in Spanish II, Principles of Marketing; Gaither Community College.
Completed courses in computer applications and Windows.

APPLICATION FOR SUMMER INTERNSHIP
Paige McNeal
SSN: 000-00-0000
Country Choice: Bolivia

My reasons for wanting to work in an internship in Bolivia are many. Although I have enjoyed life and have enjoyed various luxuries, I have always worked hard and feel that I have many talents and occupational skills which could be helpful to people in other cultures, and especially to those in developing cultures.

Of Hispanic descent, I speak Spanish fluently and understand Italian, and I am very comfortable in multiracial and multi-cultural situations. I feel I could contribute as an intern in three areas primarily:

1. **I can teach skills in business management,** especially small business management. Based on my experience in a pet shop, I am well qualified to teach others how to board and groom pets professionally as well as how to ship pets domestically and internationally.

2. **In developing countries, many vendors could benefit from my knowledge and experience related to the organization and management of cooperatives.** With more than five summers of experience working in the largest nonprofit arts and crafts co-op, I was involved in forming "from scratch" this nonprofit co-op. More than 50 artists are now involved in the cooperative of which I am a current board member. I am skilled at handling the start-up, administrative, and marketing matters which must be handled correctly if a co-op is to get off the ground. I have been successful at obtaining funding from the Richmond and the Arts Council for this cooperative, and I would be able to guide others in obtaining funding for their cooperatives.

3. **Finally, I am an expert at many matters of home economics.** I would delight in teaching others my excellent dressmaking and alteration skills, and I would also enjoy teaching my cooking skills to others.

What I hope to do in Bolivia specifically
I think of myself as an extrovert; therefore, I want to meet and visit with the people of Bolivia in order to win their friendship, learn their ways of life, and show them methods of improving themselves. Helping them improve their lives will be the challenge I see for myself.

I look forward to working with the other interns and with individuals from international agencies in order to ensure the successful completion of each project. I believe working with numerous individuals from various agencies will require patience, flexibility, and adaptability on my part as well as the ability to listen carefully and communicate in an effective manner. I am confident my fluency in Spanish and my ability to effectively communicate my point of view will make me a valuable part of the summer internship program in Bolivia, and I hope I am selected for one of these internships.

ESSAY FOR THE JOHN
MOTLEY MOREHEAD
SCHOLARSHIP TO THE
UNIVERSITY OF NORTH
CAROLINA AT CHAPEL
HILL

1) What do you consider to be your most significant achievement to date in its value to your school or larger community? Why was it important to others?

My most significant achievement was the project I undertook to earn the Eagle Scout award in Boy Scouts. I chose to transform a playground at my church which had been neglected for a long time and which was in an essentially abandoned and unsafe state. At the time, our church was experiencing personnel changes and the budget was being slashed. Although the funds to repair the playground were minimal, it was not a major priority, and I undertook the project because I felt the work would not get done otherwise. I directed a project in which we repaired broken equipment, trimmed trees, erected protective fences for safety, and built a new piece of play equipment. Although I could have undertaken a higher-visibility project, I am happy every time I see smiling children playing there.

2) Describe a situation from your life in which you either initiated an important undertaking or were called upon to be a leader. How did you respond to that situation? What did you learn from your successes or failures?

I was recently called upon to be a leader when I was asked as a junior to become Captain of the Terry Sanford Tennis Team. I began playing tennis only a few years ago, as I played mostly baseball, soccer, and basketball as a youth. From the first time I picked up a tennis racquet, I decided that I wanted to learn to hit that little yellow ball in a skillful manner. I made the Terry Sanford Tennis Team "by the skin of my teeth" in my freshman year, but I was in the 7th position without the hope of much playing time. Nevertheless, I made practices religiously so I was ready to play when one of the starting six couldn't play. I was proud that I lettered in tennis even in my freshman year. In my sophomore year, after working hard on my game, I moved up to the #6 position—not a giant step forward, but a legitimate playing spot. I again lettered in tennis in my sophomore year and was selected to the All Conference Team. In my junior year, Coach Bowman asked me to become the team's captain. To both my tennis colleagues and to the coach, my dedication to (and love of) the sport is well known, and I was recognized for my "work ethic" by several people during last year's end-of-season get together. Now as captain, I realize that the team looks to me for leadership, and all the players know that I am extremely disciplined and committed to the hard work and long workouts that it takes to get good at tennis. I have many challenges ahead of me in tennis, including improving my current ranking in North Carolina Boy's 18s. However, the biggest challenge ahead of me is related to my high school team rather than to my personal advancement. Playing in the #4 spot on the team this year, I am also playing on the #1 doubles team, and I feel a responsibility to do all I can—both as a leader and individually—to help my team become the state champions. I believe that a leader must always set an example, and I strive to be the best team captain (and player) I can be.

One of the criteria for the Morehead Award is "evidence of physical vigor." Please describe the ways in which you fulfill that criterion.

I have been blessed with a great appetite for sports as well as unusual stamina, and I play sports year-round. I have been a member of the Terry Sanford soccer team in my freshman, sophomore, and junior year, and this year I volunteered to be backup goalie when the backup quit. As the season progressed, I became the starting goalie on Terry Sanford's varsity soccer team, which won the conference tournament. I lettered in tennis in my freshman, sophomore, and junior years; I was named All Conference in my sophomore year; I compete year-round in tennis tournaments, and I currently serve as tennis team Captain. I play tennis whenever I have free time, which is usually on Friday and Sunday afternoons. On a classic soccer team, I play traveling soccer during a season which runs February-May with 4 tournaments in the fall and summer. I also participate in basketball and baseball on city league teams.

ESSAY FOR THE JOHN MOTLEY MOREHEAD SCHOLARSHIP TO THE UNIVERSITY OF NORTH CAROLINA AT CHAPEL HILL

What nonacademic plans or goals do you have for Grade 12?

My main goal is to improve my tennis ranking in the state, which is currently #61, and I am hard at work preparing for the North Carolina Qualifier in June. It is my goal to be ranked in the top 20 in the state in the Boys 18s next year. The Terry Sanford tennis team reached the state semifinals in both my freshman and sophomore years. During my senior year I have a strong desire to help the Terry Sanford Tennis Team win the state championship in tennis, because I believe Terry Sanford could have the best team in the state next year. In soccer, I believe we also have a good chance to advance far in the state playoffs, and my minimum goal in soccer is to help my team win the conference regular season title.

EXPLAIN WHY YOU HAVE CHOSEN TO ATTEND A MILITARY ACADEMY.

I made the decision to apply to a military academy during my junior year. I thought about the type of career I wanted and decided I wanted to be an officer in the military. A military academy, rather than a prestigious private college or public university, is the best place to prepare myself for that career.

I want to be a military officer. I believe a career in the military provides the fastest path possible to a position of responsibility and leadership. I have been a leader in the Boy Scouts and on my high school football and wrestling teams. I have won numerous awards for my leadership in both athletics and sports, and I am drawn towards leadership positions and aspire to that as a career. I understand that with leadership comes responsibility—responsibility to your employees, to your duty, and to your mission. There is no career that brings these aspects together better than that of a military officer, especially so soon after graduation.

ESSAY WRITTEN IN APPLICATION FOR A SPECIAL SCHOLARSHIP AWARDED TO A FEW COLLEGE SENIORS WHO ARE APPLYING TO A PRIVATE MILITARY ACADEMY

My father, my uncle, and my grandfathers have all served in the military. I enjoy hearing them tell the stories of those times. I can tell that their time in the military was special to them. It was a meaningful time to them when they felt like they were doing something that really mattered. The quality of life we enjoy today was fought for and won by people in the military, many of whom gave their lives. We take for granted so many things that we would not have, were it not for people who were willing to stand up for and defend for our way of life. I would be proud to be part of that history and tradition. Although my family is not wealthy, I have enjoyed many privileges since my birth, and I want to give something back to society. Becoming a military officer and serving my country will enable me to "give back."

Since middle school, and even before that, I have concentrated on both my studies and athletics. I have excelled at both. I consider my ability to combine both scholarship and athletics to be a strength that I should cultivate, and I believe my time management and organizational skills will equip me with some of the skills I will need in order to adjust to the fast-paced life of a military cadet.

I consider myself to be courageous, and I have been recognized for heroism by my coaches and teachers. I believe military academies seek those who possess courage and fortitude, and military academies provide opportunities to build upon those strengths in college and after graduation as an officer in the Army.

There are so many options available for young people today. I know that applying to a military academy is "going against the grain." Most of my friends are heading off to top-notch public and private universities and are anticipating the challenges of dating and joining a fraternity. My goals are different.

It's easy to get distracted in today's society with its emphasis on so many surface things. I admire the emphasis at the academies on thinking strategically and committing to a career that's certainly not the easy path. I saw General Schwarzkopf speak on television at the Republican National Convention. What an inspiring leader! He's a product of West Point and is one of my heroes. That's the type of leader I want to be. Becoming a strong leader in public service is why I want to attend a military academy.

Part Eight: Letters and Resumes
to accompany application materials

A resume may enhance your chances of admissions. In this section you will see samples of effective resumes for students seeking admission to college and undergraduate schools as well as graduate schools and PH.D. programs.

Sometimes you may wish to send a resume along with a letter requesting a letter of reference. Even people who know you may not be aware of all you do, so a resume may give them valuable information for the reference letter you are seeking.

Date

Dr. Karen Masterson
Vice Chairman, Resident Affairs
Emory University School of Medicine
Department of Anesthesiology
Atlanta, GA 33498

**LETTER REQUESTING
ADMISSION TO A
MEDICAL RESIDENCY
PROGRAM**

Dear Dr. Masterson:

With the enclosed materials I am making formal application for a residency in anesthesiology. You will see from my Personal Statement accompanying this application that I offer expertise and personal qualities including the following:

- Extensive professional experience as an anesthesiologist
- Proven teaching ability
- Creativity and skill in developing new programs
- Reputation for scholarship and desire to contribute to the advancement of knowledge in the field of anesthesiology
- Numerous professional honors and distinctions
- Expertise related to foreign languages
- Stable and supportive family life
- Proven capacity for hard work and long hours
- Outstanding personal and professional references

I have made the decision to submit this application to your fine institution only after careful consideration of the opinions of colleagues as well as my analysis of the information contained in brochures and other literature discussing your mission and needs. I feel certain that I could be an asset to you, but I also feel that your institution would provide numerous advantages to me and to my family. I would welcome the opportunity to participate in teaching and clinical research while working in a position whereby I could keep myself continually updated and receive special training. The "mother city" of your institution is one that I feel my family and I would enjoy living in very much, and we would welcome the opportunity to contribute to community activities.

I look forward to exploring with you the possibility of my becoming affiliated with your fine institution as a resident in anesthesiology, and I can guarantee you that I could make enormously valuable contributions in that role.

Thank you in advance for giving my application your kind and thorough consideration.

Yours sincerely,

Kathryn Wallace

May 15, 2001

Dr. Elmer Spielberg
Dean of College of Arts and Sciences
Georgia Central University
Macon, GA 33456

Dear Dr. Spielberg:

I am writing to make a formal request that you review my recent application for admission to the Graduate School of Public Administration. My application for admission was denied on May 2, 2001, and I am respectfully requesting that you review my application and consider granting me a provisional admission so that I could demonstrate in summer courses that I am a viable candidate, outstanding scholar, and dedicated to a career in the public administration field. I would also like to provide information not previously available to the admissions committee.

As a graduate of Georgia Central University with a B.S. in Business Administration, I wish you to know that I worked in demanding jobs while financing my college education. While I achieved only a 2.4 GPA in my undergraduate program, you will see from my enclosed resume that I excelled in my job during that time with Hechts. I was recognized with awards for sales and customer service.

Since graduating with my B.S. degree, I have distinguished myself in the private sector through my sales and sales management abilities. Both with IBM in my prior job and currently with the Merck Pharmaceutical Division, I have achieved the highest levels of productivity while becoming known for integrity and fair dealings. While at IBM, I earned the distinction of Top Sales Executive and earned membership in the company's highly prestigious leadership club for the most talented sales managers. In my current job with Merck Pharmaceutical, I have been recognized for achieving the highest sales production in the Division and was chosen to be the computer trainer in that division because of my superior computer knowledge.

Although I am excelling in private industry, I feel strongly that I would like to make major contributions to the public sector. My goal is to become a city manager or town manager, and I feel that my proven management gifts as well as my highly refined communication skills could make valuable contributions to governmental efficiency. My desire to enter the public sector is certainly not motivated by financial reasons. Undoubtedly I could make more money in the private sector, and I have certainly enjoyed financial success based on my major achievements.

Since my track record demonstrates that I can succeed and excel in anything I take on, I respectfully request that you consider my strong desire to contribute to the public sector and review my application to the M.P.A. Program. I would be content with a provisional admission so that I could prove my scholastic abilities and academic prowess. Please give my application for admission a favorable re-review.

Sincerely,

Maynard Jackson

JOANIE SMITH

1110 Hay Street, Fayetteville, NC 28305 • preppub@aol.com

Employer: Bank of America
From: 8/99 *To:* Present
Location: Richmond, VA
Nature Of Business: Finance/Banking
Job Title: Consumer Banker III (was promoted from I through III)
Number and Titles Reporting to You: 0
Salary: Starting: $25,000   Ending: $28,000

Responsibilities: Was recruited by Bank of America during my senior year of college, and completed an intensive four-month training session after graduation; began as a Consumer Banker I, progressed rapidly to Consumer Banker II, and then earned an unusually rapid promotion to Consumer Banker III.

Sales Achievements:
- At two different banking centers, was a major reason why both achieved record sales results; have earned a reputation as an ambitious go-getter with a knack for developing trust.
- Consistently exceed all performance goals while developing and implementing aggressive personal goals related to portfolio management, daily product sales, telemarketing, and outside sales; am skilled in cross selling products including brokerage products.
- Received the distinction of having the highest number of securities sales referrals; won this honor in tough competition with my peers throughout the district; also exceeded the sales performance of my companion consumer banker ranked 2nd in the state.

Management Responsibilities:
- Serve as acting banking center manager during the manager's absence, and supervise employees in handling a wide variety of banking operations; have worked with colleagues and employees to help them refine their sales skills.

Consulting Experience:
- Am aggressively helping Bank of America reposition itself as a "full-service financial institution" that can provide all financial management and investment services; have become respected for my strong consulting skills and expert knowledge of financial products including investments, savings, and protection and credit products.
- Routinely deal with executives from various industries, and have become skilled at analyzing a company's financial situation from a strategic point of view; am routinely sought out by numerous customers for my advice/recommendations related to areas including portfolio management, asset growth, and risk diversification.

Highlights of other experience:
Gained early management experience while working every summer since I was 16; began as a Camp Counselor and was promoted to Program Director and Counselor-in-Training for the Christian Camp in High Point, which served 300 children aged 7-18 per session.
- At college, worked as a tutor in anatomy and physiology and as a waiter.

HONORS
COLLEGE: Dean's List every semester. Intramural basketball, volleyball, and soccer.
HIGH SCHOOL: Appointed Marshal of 11th grade class. Varsity basketball starter both 11th and 12th. 1st team All-Conference tennis player 12th grade. President of Fellowship of Christian Athletes. Active in my church, United Methodist Church and youth group member.

CRAWFORD JAMES PHILMONT

1110 1/2 Hay Street · Fayetteville, NC 28305 · (910) 483-6611

RESUME TO ACCOMPANY COLLEGE APPLICATION

OBJECTIVE

To enroll in a university where I can excel academically in earning a B.S. while contributing to university life through involvement in clubs, sports, and extracurricular activities.

PSAT/SAT

SAT scores junior year were 1290 (640 math; 650 verbal).

EDUCATION

Lassiter High School, Philadelphia, PA, 1997-2001.
Cum Laude National Latin exam, May 2000.
Latin Scholar, American Classical League Magna Cum Laude National Latin Exam, May 1999.

SCOUTING

Rose to the rank of **Life Scout**

COMPUTERS

Highly proficient in utilizing computers with Windows operating system C++ Programmer.
Skilled in using Internet technologies.

SPORTS

Football:
- 12th grade: Senior year positions are fullback and middle line backer.
- 11th grade: Received **Hero Award** given by players and coaches in recognition of my dedication despite an injury in which I tore ACL.
- 10th grade: Was one of seven 10th graders to make the Varsity team; started at **Center** the whole year on a team that made the state playoffs.
- 9th grade: **Team Captain,** Junior Varsity team; started as fullback and middle line backer.
- 8th grader: **Team Captain** and **Defense MVP** on a team that was the undefeated conference champions, Fuller Middle School.
- 7th grader: Only 7th grader to start on the Fuller Middle School team and one of only five 7th graders to make the team.
- 3rd-6th grades: Played on City of Phily Youth League, 3-year starter.
- Named **Defense MVP** and **City All Star.**

Wrestling:
- 11th grade: Wrestled at 160 lbs. **Team Captain.** Received the **Delbert Smith Memorial Award** given by players and coaches in recognition of "outstanding courage and hard work" in finishing 3rd in the conference despite a grueling recovery from an ACL injury.
- 10th grade: Received the **Coach's Award** given by the wrestling coach to the player who most exemplifies the work ethic and positive attitude sought in dedicated wrestlers. Also received the **Outstanding 10th grade Wrestler Award**. Wrestled for Senior High School Varsity Team at 171 lbs. Was 28-6 overall on a varsity team which was the undefeated (7-0) conference champion.
- 9th grade: Lettered at 150 lbs.

WORK

WEB-BASED BUSINESS ENTREPRENEUR. Philadelphia, PA. (1999-present). Have established a web-based business which recruits web surfers who allow advertisers to send information to their computers.

MICHAEL MCHALE
P.O. Box 56611, Fayetteville, NC 28305   (910) 483-6611
SSN: 000-82-2196

OBJECTIVE

To pursue the study of law with the goal of gaining technical knowledge which I can combine with my exceptionally strong public speaking, analytical, and writing skills in order to play a key role in the formulation and implementation of national, state, and local policy concerning land use and environmental issues.

EDUCATION

Bachelor of Arts (B.A.) degree, Political Science and Political Philosophy, Augusta State University, Augusta, GA, 2000.
* Was awarded a $1,000 scholarship to attend Augusta State University; worked every summer to finance my education.
* As a senior, took a graduate course in Environmental Law; authored a highly praised paper on sustainable forestry and the law.
* Elected Senator, Student Government Association, freshman year.

**HIGH SCHOOL
EDUCATION**

Graduated from Allison Smythe High School, Willington, GA, 1994.
* Was inducted into the Key Club, a service organization.
* Member, German Club.
* Member, Drama Club, and was chosen for several lead roles; and gained a reputation as a talented public speaker.
* Played football freshman year; played soccer sophomore, junior, and senior years and was **All Conference** my junior and senior.

LANGUAGE

Speak and read Spanish with moderate ease.

LICENSES

National Registry of Emergency Medical Technician (EMT) A 555555.
* Winter Emergency Care Technician.
* Professional Ski Patroller, licensed by National Ski Patrol, 1996.
* Extensively trained in the Fundamentals of Search and Rescue (FUNSAR), National Association of Search and Rescue.

COMPUTERS

Proficient with software including MS Word and Excel.

EXPERIENCE

PROFESSIONAL SKI PATROLLER. Jackson Hole Resort Company, Jackson Hole, WY (1998-present). Am one of 28 ski patrollers who perform a wide variety of tasks related to keeping mountains skiable at this fast-growing resort 50 miles near Salt Lake City.
* Participate in avalanche patrols and work with explosives.
* Have refined my decision-making skills handling emergencies.

CARPENTER. Traditional Finishings Plus, Willington, GA (Summers 1996-98). In summer jobs during college, worked in construction companies performing trim work and constructing concrete form.

SENIOR COUNSELOR. YMCA Camp Moosehead-Boys Summer Camp, Willington, GA (Summer 1996). At this 60-year-old boys camp, supervised 14 boys full time while supervising sailing and aquatics.

ADRIAN SUMMERS

1110 1/2 Hay Street, Fayetteville, NC 28305   910-483-6611

GOAL

To obtain a degree in political science while excelling academically and contributing to student life through my strong communication, debating, and public speaking skills.

EDUCATION

Graduate from Xavier High School, Xavier, FL, 2002; top 5% of class.
- My mother died when I was 12, and I work nearly 25 hours a week to help my father, who is a janitor in the school system.
- Active band member; play saxophone and marching baritone.

RESUME TO ACCOMPANY A COLLEGE APPLICATION

LANGUAGE & TRAVEL

Fluently speak and read German.
Have traveled extensively throughout Europe.
- Knowledgeable of German customs and culture; lived in Germany.

COMPUTERS

Proficient with Windows operating systems and Microsoft Word software. Gained familiarity with numerous programs through a course I took in college called "Toolbook Multimedia 3.0."

EXPERIENCE

SALES REPRESENTATIVE. The Body Piercing Store, Xavier, FL (Summers 1998-present). Began with the company in a part-time sales position during my sophomore year of high school, and have always ranked in the top third of sales producers in the company.
- Supervise up to two sales clerks, and have trained numerous sales professionals on effective techniques related to closing the sale and customer service.
- Have been trained to perform minor jewelry repair.
- Was credited with playing a key role in the growth of sales at the company's Greensboro location.
- Have been entrusted with the responsibility of opening and closing the store as one of the responsible "key holders."
- Have become skilled at conducting comprehensive inventories.
- Refined my teaching and communication skills in this business which places me in daily contact with up to 75 customers of ear piecing and body piecing services; the company's services must be explained precisely with a view to clarifying medical and legal issues related to piecing while earning the consumer's confidence.

WAITRESS (part-time while in high school). Fisher's Paradise, Xavier, FL (part-time during the school year, 1998-present). Work up to 25 hours a week at a family restaurant, and am known for my sunny disposition and professional style of interacting with customers.

CASHIER (part-time while in high school). McDonalds Restaurant, Xavier, FL (part-time during the school year, 1998-present). Learned to work well with others and refined my time management skills.

PERSONAL

Work well in environments which require an individual who is able to make prudent decisions in unusual circumstances. Am a positive individual with an upbeat personality.

KEVIN D. MCPHERSON

1110 1/2 Hay Street · Fayetteville, NC 28305 · (910) 483-6611

OBJECTIVE

To enroll in a university where I can excel academically in earning a B.S. while contributing to student life through involvement in clubs, sports, and extracurricular activities.

PSAT/SAT

SAT scores on the December 2000, test were 1300 (700 math; 600 verbal).
PSAT scores on test taken in fall 1999: 1290.

EDUCATION

Michigamee High School, Marysville, AK, 1997-2001. Ranked in top 1% of class; curriculum emphasizes AP and Honors courses.

- Nominated for inclusion in *Who's Who Among American High School Students,* 1998 and 1999.

Sophomore Year: Inducted into National Honor Society. Member of the Math Club.

Junior Year: Was honored by being named a **Marshall** at high school graduation 1999.

SCOUTING

Received the respected **Eagle Scout Award**, Boy Scouts of America, March 24, 1998.

- Earned Eagle Scout Award when I was fourteen; one of the youngest ever in my district.
- Won top prize (a tent) for being Top Salesperson in troop's annual fund-raiser.
- Inducted into Order of the Arrow, an elite camping membership by peer election.

COMPUTERS

Computer enthusiast proficient in using Windows, Microsoft Word.

SPORTS

Tennis: Lettered two times in Varsity Tennis (freshman and sophomore years); am expected to be a key member of the tennis team in my junior and senior years.

- Named **Captain of Varsity Tennis Team** as a junior, spring 2000.
- Selected **All Conference** in my sophomore year.
- Our Varsity Tennis team reached the **final four in the state dual team playoffs** in both my freshman and sophomore years; our only loss each year was to the eventual state champion team in the semifinals of the playoffs.
- Alaska ranking: In 1998, was ranked #100 in the Boys 16 age group in the state; advanced to #64 in my age group in Dec 1999.

Soccer: Played on my school's junior varsity team in my freshman and sophomore years.

- As a high school junior, **lettered as the starting goalkeeper on the Varsity Soccer team.**
- Our Varsity Soccer team was **Conference Tournament Champion,** finished second in the regular season, and made the state playoffs in my junior year.
- Starting striker (forward) on Force Blue, a Classic Traveling team.

PATRICK JAMESON

1110 1/2 Hay Street • Fayetteville, NC 28305 • (910) 483-6611

SAT/PSAT

SAT scores on the March 2001 test were 1420 (740 verbal; 680 math) PSAT scores on test taken in fall 2001: 138 (67 verbal, 71 math).

EDUCATION

Senior, Bristol High School, Bristol, TN; will graduate June 2002.
* Named Scholar Finalist in the College Board's National Hispanic Scholar Recognition Program.
* In top 10% of class; curriculum is mostly AP and honors courses
* One of only three juniors invited on high school's Quiz Bowl team
* Competing member of my school's Forensics Team, and compete in the Extemporaneous Category.
* Member, Chess Club and Science Club.
* Nominated for *Who's Who Among American High School Students*.

SCOUTING

Received **Eagle Scout Award**, Boy Scouts of America, spring 2001.
* Since earning my Eagle Scout Award and becoming 18, have become an Assistant Scoutmaster in Boy Scout Troop 71.
* Was inducted into the Order of the Arrow, an elite camping group.

COMPUTERS

Computer enthusiast proficient in using Windows, Microsoft Word; proficient with Versacad and am currently mastering Autocad.

SPORTS

Judo: Currently Green Belt.
Wrestling: member of the varsity wrestling team, junior year.
Cross country: member of the cross country team, senior year.
Cycling: Cycling enthusiast and expert bicycle repairman.
Soccer: Played soccer on city teams as a youth in grades 3-10.
Camper and **hiker.**
Enjoy **basketball** and **baseball.**

MUSIC

Highly competent guitarist; took guitar lessons briefly and then mastered the guitar through practice; have taught myself to play the piano.

CHURCH

Strong religious foundation; attend church and Sunday School regularly.
* Serve as acolyte; member of United Youth Fellowship.

TRAVEL

Have traveled in Mexico and Jamaica as well as throughout the U.S.

WORK

BIKE MECHANIC. The Bicycle Shop, Bristol, TN (2001-present). In my senior year, work part-time from 4-7 every weekday after school and from 10-5 on Saturday as a bike assembler, mechanic, and repairman.
Other work experience: Worked as a freelance book reviewer for local publishing company, evaluating manuscripts.

LANGUAGES

Completed accelerated AP courses in Spanish and German.

PERSONAL

Love reading and usually read several books a month in spare time. Pride myself on my strong character and high standards of behavior.

COVER LETTER TO ACCOMPANY APPLICATION FOR A PH.D. PROGRAM

On this and the opposite page, you will see the cover letter and resume which accompanied an application for a Ph.D. Program.

Dear Dr. Smythe:

With the enclosed materials, I am making formal application to the Ed.D. in Educational Leadership Program at University of Nevada.

You will see from my enclosed resume that I have an M.ED. in Special Education and have gained a statewide reputation as an expert in the field of exceptional children's programs. In my current job with Webster County Schools, I supervise 95 teachers, teacher assistants, speech pathologists, and psychologists while directing the day-to-day operations of programs for special populations of children.

I was quite excited to see a question on the application related to my work in a program of significance with public schools, and I have written about my experience as a change agent implementing a new educational approach called Combined Education within the Webster County Schools.

I am committed to spending the rest of my life involved in the design and implementation of programs which will be "user-friendly" to teachers and students in the public schools, and I offer a "track record" of contributions to educational development within Nevada. I have been active in developing programs for transition from school to work for handicapped students, and I strongly believe the handicapped can be prepared and trained to become productive employees.

I would be delighted to make myself available to you for a personal interview, if you feel this is desirable or necessary. I am confident that I could become a distinguished alumnus of the doctoral program at UN, and I feel certain that my experience in teaching and administration would enrich the learning environment of the other doctoral students. Thank you in advance for giving my application every consideration.

Sincerely yours,

Nancy J. Vetstein

NANCY J. VETSTEIN

1110 1/2 Hay Street, Fayetteville, NC 28305 • 910-483-6611

OBJECTIVE

To apply to the Doctoral Program (Ed.D.) in Educational Leadership in order to gain insight and knowledge that will enable me to continue, at even higher levels of leadership, my "track record" of contributions to educational development within Nevada and the nation.

EDUCATION

Certificate in Educational Administration and Supervision, University of Nevada, 1986.
M.ED. in Special Education, University of Nevada, Reno, NV, SC, 1974.
B.A. in History and Art, University of Nevada, 1971.
Extensive continuing education in areas related to Combined Education, Strategies for Teaching SLD Students, Mastery Learning, and other areas.

AFFILIATIONS & COMMUNITY LEADERSHIP

- Member, Liaison Committee, Kibler Mental Health Agency
- Active supporter, CARE Center, Muscular Dystrophy Association
- Advisory Board Member, Partnership Training, University of Nevada
- Member for 20 years, national and state Council for Exceptional Children

EXPERIENCE

DIRECTOR OF EXCEPTIONAL CHILDREN'S PROGRAMS. Webster County Schools, Reno, NV (1994-present). Was promoted from Supervisor to Director, and now manage 95 teachers, teacher assistants, speech pathologists, and psychologists while directing the day-to-day operations of programs for handicapped children.
- Developed innovative new workshops and training opportunities for teachers on writing IEPs and transition education; gained considerable experience in writing federal grants.
- Worked closely with the Office of Civil Rights in collecting data related to transportation.

SUPERVISOR, EXCEPTIONAL CHILDREN'S PROGRAMS. Webster County Schools, Reno, NV (1988-94). Became knowledgeable about laws governing Exceptional Children's Programs while coordinating staff development workshops, chairing the Administrative Placement Committee, supervising Educational Diagnostic Centers, and overseeing services provided through the Homebound/Hospital and Vision Impaired Programs.

INSTRUCTIONAL SPECIALIST. Webster County Schools, Reno, NV (1982-88). Supervised the Behavioral Emotionally Handicapped Programs which included training teachers in writing and implementing behavior management plans.
- Authored the Behavior Management System in use in Webster County.

COLLEGE INSTRUCTOR. University of Nevada, Reno, NV (1979-80). On a part-time basis, taught the Introduction to Special Education Course, the Testing & Measurement Course, and the Gifted & Talented Course.

PERSONAL

Outstanding references upon request. Proven ability to work with others.

Date

Exact Name of Person
Exact Title
Exact Name of Company
Address
City, State, Zip

Dear Exact Name of Person (or Dear Sir or Madam if answering a blind ad):

With this letter and the enclosed resume, I would like to initiate the process of applying for a fellowship with your organization and to acquaint you with my outstanding professional knowledge and skills.

As you will see from the resume, I am a well-educated and self-motivated professional with a background of community service and effectiveness in leadership roles both in professional settings and in community action environments. My educational background includes two master's degrees: most recently a Master of Library Science and an earlier Master of Adult Education along with a B.S. in Business Administration, all earned at the University of Washington in Seattle.

My background as a Media Specialist at area elementary schools led to my acceptance for this position at the high school level. At Easterling High School I have been selected for numerous additional duties including School Grants Coordinator and School Technology Specialist. In the former role I have become highly familiar with researching and writing grant applications while in the latter I apply my knowledge of the latest technology utilized in libraries to instruct other faculty members and conduct staff development workshops. In addition to serving the school as Audio-visual and Reference Librarian, I also was chosen as ACT Test Center Administrator to hire and train staff as well as making preparations for testing.

If you can use an articulate and mature professional with a wide range of abilities and knowledge, I hope you will call me soon for a brief discussion of how I could apply for fellowship opportunities within your organization. I will provide excellent professional and personal references at the appropriate time.

Sincerely,

Bonnie L. Bertolaet

BONNIE L. BERTOLAET

1110 1/2 Hay Street • Fayetteville, NC 28305 • (910) 487-5023

RESUME TO ACCOMPANY
APPLICATION FOR A
FELLOWSHIP

OBJECTIVE   I am seeking a fellowship based on my outstanding professional skills, proven leadership ability, and desire to make significant contributions in my field.

EDUCATION   **Master of Library Science**, University of Washington, Seattle, WA, 1990. **Master of Adult Education**, University of Washington, Seattle, WA, 1982. **Bachelor of Science in Business Administration**, University of Washington, Seattle, WA, 1980.

EXPERIENCE   **MEDIA SPECIALIST (AV/Reference Librarian).** Easterling High School, Seattle, WA (1993-present). Since August 1995-present, have served as the **ACT Test Center Administrator**; hired and trained staff to administer the ACT Assessment Test; prepared facilities and materials for test day.
- Instructed students in the use of reference books, library materials, and electronic information sources.
- Purchased books, computer software, and equipment for the media center.
- Supervised student library assistants; co-sponsored library club.
- Cataloged and processed library materials.
- Conducted fundraisers.
- In an additional duty as **School Grants Coordinator,** compile and disseminate information about grants; assist with the application process; and plan grant writing workshops.
- As **School Technology Specialist,** instruct faculty in the use of technology; conduct staff development workshops.

MEDIA SPECIALIST. Dudley Elementary School, Seattle, WA (1991-93). Instructed students in the use of the media center and information skills; purchased books and equipment for the media center; planned activities to promote reading.

LIBRARY ASSISTANT & GRADUATE ASSISTANT. University of Washington, Seattle, WA (1989-90). As a Library Assistant, handled general circulation desk responsibilities and serial maintenance.

Highlights of other experience:
GRADUATE ASSISTANT. University of Washington, School of Education, Seattle, WA. While obtaining my Master of Adult Education, assisted professors in the Department of Educational Administration and Supervision; performed typing, filing, and other clerical tasks; assisted in the preparation of seminars for principals and school administrators.
- Conducted research for Assistant Dean of the School of Education.

PERSONAL   Known for strong personal qualities: **Congenial:** Work well with others; **Conscientious:** Committed to excellence in any job I take on; **Resourceful:** Take the initiative when I see a task which needs to be accomplished.

Date

Exact Name of Person
Title or Position
Name of Company
Address (no., street)
Address (city, state, zip)

**COVER LETTER TO
ACCOMPANY RESUME
SEEKING A TENNIS
SCHOLARSHIP**

This is the type of cover
letter and resume you send
in your junior year.
The resume which
accompanied the resume
is on the facing page.

Dear Exact Name of Coach:

With the enclosed resume highlighting my tennis achievements, scholastic honors, and personal qualities, I would like to formally introduce myself and tell you that I would like to explore the possibility of playing on your tennis team as an incoming freshman in the class of 2002.

Currently an Honor Roll junior with a straight-A average, I believe I will have the grades and SAT score to be admitted to the school of my choice on academics alone. I have already scored a 1290 on the SAT and am hoping to improve on that score when I take the SAT again in the spring. A junior at Converse High School, I have a class rank of #8 out of approximately 300 students.

You will see from my resume that I offer a track record of accomplishments in tennis, and I sincerely believe I have the talent and drive to become one of the world's all-time best tennis players. My most recent rankings are #1 in GA, #1 in the Southern Section, and #12 nationally.

In this letter of introduction, I not only want you to know that I am a top scholar and athlete but also that I pride myself on my strong character and personal reputation for reliability, morality, and stamina. I am confident that I have the skills and personal qualities needed to become one of the world's greatest tennis professionals.

I will be playing in the Easter Bowl in Palm Springs, CA, in April 9-15, in the Penn Supercircuit Tournaments Feb-May, and in the Nationals this summer. I enclose a detailed schedule of my upcoming tournaments in the hope that I might have the opportunity to meet you during the months ahead.

I am in the process of identifying the schools to which I will be applying, and I would be appreciative if you could give me some indication, in writing or by phone, about whether you would like to explore the possibility of my playing for you. I know of your fine reputation and would be honored to talk with you about how my talents might fit into your program.

Sincerely,

Jorge Gonzalez

JORGE GONZALEZ

1110 1/2 Hay Street, Fayetteville, NC 28305   (910) 483-6611

Height: 6' 0"   Weight: 155 lbs.   DOB: 8/13/84

GOAL

(1) To continue to develop my skills as a tennis player and (2) to make a significant contribution to the reputation and winning record of a respected university.

RANKINGS

	State (GA)	Southern	National
2001:	No. 1 (16s)	No. 1 (16s)	No. 12 (16s)
2000:	No. 4 (16s)	No. 39 (16s)	No. 41 (16s)
1999:	No. 1 (14s)	No. 1 (14s)	
1998:	No. 1 (14s)	No. 1 (14s)	No. 60 (14s)
1997:	No. 2 (12s)	No. 3 (12s)	

Resume used to explore the possibilities of a tennis scholarship at a major university

GAME DATA

- *Left-handed* player
- *Best surface*: hard
- *Best shots:* serve and volley
- *Style:* all court

SCHOLARSHIP

- *Class rank:* #8 out of 300 students; currently a junior
- *Honor Roll student* at Converse High School, Converse, GA
- SAT scores: Verbal 620; math 670; retaking SAT spring 2001

SCHOOL LEADERSHIP

- National Honor Society
- Junior Class Marshall
- Member of Key Club
- Member of Spanish Club (Secretary)
- Recipient of Kiwanis Scholarship Achievement Award
- Voted "Best All Around" in 9th grade, Converse Junior High
- Named Outstanding Freshman, faculty award

TENNIS HONORS

- *Invited by USTA to represent the U.S.* in the Coffee Bowl
- *Fourth Place in The National Indoors in B18s*, Dallas, TX, 2001
- *Third Place in The Nationals in B16s*, Kalamazoo, MI, 2001
- *Finalist in The Nationals in B14s*, San Antonio, TX, 1999
- Played in *Rolex Orange Bowl International Championships*, 2001; one of only two Americans to reach Round of 32
- *Southern Closed Singles Champion*: 2001, 1999, 1998,
- GA State 4A High School *Singles Champion*, 2001
- GA Qualifier *Singles Champion*: 2001, 1999, 1998
- GA Qualifier *Doubles Champion*: 2001, 2000, 1999, 1998
- Played in *Easter Bowl Championships*, 2001, 2000, 1998, 1997; finished in **top 16** in Boys 16s, 2001
- Played in *Junior Orange Bowl*, 1999
- *GA Junior Davis Cup Team*, 2001, 2000, 1999
- Recipient of *GATA Junior Tennis Council Award* for contributions to GA Junior Tennis, 2001, 1999
- Named *Mid-South 4A Conference Player of the Year*, 2001, 2000
- Named *MVP, Converse Senior High School Tennis Team*, 2001

Part Nine: Letters of Reference
How to Request Them and What They Should Look Like

You often need to write a letter asking an individual to provide a letter of reference for you. In this section you will find models to follow in requesting letters of reference, and you will see what those letters of reference should look like.

Teacher Recommendation forms are provided by many institutions, and the teacher/faculty member is advised as follows: "You may simply attach this form to a letter, but we urge you to make sure that each of our questions has been amply addressed. Specific illustrative examples are especially helpful." Here are typical questions asked on teacher and faculty recommendation forms:

1. What do you know of this student's intellectual qualities? What are your impressions of the student's academic priorities? We are especially interested in any evidence you can give about the nature of his/her motivation for academic work—the breadth and depth of intellectual interests—the originality, independence and sensitivity he/she displays in course work—the quality of performance as compared to that of his/her classmates.

2. Which personal qualities stand out in the applicant? Are there any features in the applicant's background that will help us better understand his/her academic or extracurricular performance? Are there any personal strengths, weaknesses, or problems about which you feel we should be aware?

3. In your best estimate, how will the applicant respond to an academically competitive environment?

4. Please use this space for any additional comments about the applicant and his/her candidacy.

5. Do you have any reason to doubt this student's academic integrity?

6. How would you compare this applicant to his/her entire class?

One prominent institution asks this question of teachers and faculty:

Please write a summary appraisal (limited to one page) of this candidate, assessing his or her academic and personal qualities, and promise as a Brown student. We are particularly interested in evidence about character, relative maturity, integrity, independence, values, and the things he or she is enthusiastic about, and any special talent or quality he or she possesses. Avoid *listing* student activities which are available elsewhere. We are interested in specific events and unusual circumstances which will give us added insight into the strengths and weaknesses of this candidate. Special biographical information is sometimes helpful. (Photocopied reports are acceptable; and should be attached to this form.)

Because the candidate recommendation forms are so time-consuming for those preparing them, we strongly support asking teachers to write a "form letter" for you which can be duplicated many times if you are applying to multiple institutions. An example of a letter to a teacher asking for a generic letter of reference is on page 170.

February 27, 2001

Mr. Charles E. Cartwright
Strickland Place
2555 Faygill Road, Suite A
Martinsburg, WA 11111

LETTER REQUESTING A REFERENCE TO ACCOMPANY AN APPLICATION FOR ADMISSION

Dear Chuck:

I am contacting you to see if I could impose upon your kindness again to provide recommendation materials needed for my graduate school applications.

Out of respect for your time, I have grouped all required references and have tried to reduce your time to an absolute minimum. You were kind enough to prepare a letter of recommendation for me on November 14, 2000.

I am providing a copy of the personal statement I would like to send to Austin School of Medicine, so that you will know of my strong interest in this graduate program. A resume also is enclosed.

The admissions process at all schools is well underway, and I am hoping that I can pick up the completed references on Monday, March 15, 2001, by midafternoon. Please note that, where applications are to be mailed by the recommender, I would like to actually drop those in the mail myself unless you object. This relieves you of the burden of mailing anything.

I would like to convey my heartfelt thanks in advance for your help.

Yours sincerely,

Mark Offit
Work: 483-6611
Home: 483-2233

Date

To Whom It May Concern:

This letter is a recommendation that Riley Lightfoot be accepted for admission in the School of Veterinary Medicine.

As a mature woman, Riley is able to define, plan, and apply herself towards achieving goals. She is an exceptionally hard worker with the stamina required to maintain a heavy schedule when necessary. She is also realistic and aware of time or personal limitations.

She is intelligent, gregarious, and articulate. Her training and work as a counselor will give her the ability to relate to and effectively communicate with clients facing difficult decisions concerning their animals.

In my association with her in the field of wildlife rehabilitation, I am continually impressed with her pursuit of additional knowledge through attendance at various classes offered, attendance at national wildlife rehabilitation symposiums, and personal communication with other experienced individuals or professionals in the field. She has a high moral and ethical commitment to animals in her care and makes every effort to ensure diets, housing, and supportive care is not just adequate, but optimum.

It is my belief that Riley would be an excellent student and would graduate to become an excellent member of the veterinary profession.

Please feel free to contact me if you require additional information.

Very truly yours,

Gertrude Stein
Animal Care Inc., Founder/Director
Board of Directors, National Wildlife
Rehabilitation Association

July 18, 2001

Mrs. Rachel Garjesik
Rural Route 1
Bristol Heights, TN 22333

Dear Mrs. Garjesik:

I am writing this letter to ask if you would prepare one letter of recommendation to accompany my college applications this fall which I could use in mailing to all the universities to which I apply. My guidance counselor, Mr. Dawson, has given me some advice as to how I can make this request simple.

I plan to apply to several Ivy League schools as well as Stanford University, the University of North Carolina at Chapel Hill, and West Point. I have already taken my SAT (740 verbal, 680 math) and SAT II subject tests. I had an interview at Harvard University on June 28 and am traveling briefly to West Point this summer.

What I ask is this: would you please prepare one letter of recommendation (dated August 2001 is fine) for me with the salutation "To Whom It May Concern" (Mr. Dawson's suggestion), make copies on Bristol High School letterhead, and place a copy in each attached envelope.

I know this is a lot to ask a teacher to do over the summer break. However, I am proud to be one of the few students who can actually spell and pronounce your name correctly. Plus, I wanted to submit this request to you before school starts and you are mobbed by the rest of the seniors. Thank you for your consideration of my request.

Yours sincerely,

Patrick Teague

BRISTOL HIGH SCHOOL
885 Bristol Avenue
Bristol, TN 88455
(888) 483-6611

Mason Hicks, Principal   Anne Gilbert, Assistant Principal

August 2001

Dear Sir or Madam:

In my opinion, Patrick Teague would be an excellent candidate for a place in your freshman class of 2005. Because Patrick is a young man of outstanding character, strong capabilities, and exemplary citizenship, I feel he would truly be an asset to any academic community.

Through his academic career, Patrick has proved himself to be a self-disciplined, high achiever. He is a very creative, well read, and articulate student. He is extremely motivated to succeed and has consistently maintained A/A- averages in honors and advanced placement courses. As his transcript will show, he earned 4s on the advanced placement tests in Spanish and American History. Because of his strong academic record and his excellent communication skills, he was chosen to be a member of the Quiz Bowl team. He has also participated in forensics since the eighth grade.

While maintaining high academic standards, Patrick has pursued other extra-curricular interests. He has shown great perseverance and leadership ability by achieving the rank of Eagle Scout. During his years in scouting he has demonstrated a love of outdoor activities and has learned survival skills. He also enjoys the sport of bicycling.

Patrick is a young man of high principles. He is honest, trustworthy, and highly dependable. He is well liked and respected by his fellow students. He has been raised in a Christian home and has always participated actively in church activities. He has served regularly as an acolyte and has been an active participant in the youth fellowship group which is service oriented.

In addition to his high level of intellectual creativity and academic promise, Patrick is a true young gentleman with impeccable manners and a gracious style of interacting with others. He is known for his warmth of personality and sense of humor as well as for his concern for others.

I feel confident that Patrick would have the self-discipline and stamina to succeed in a rigorous academic environment, and I also feel certain that he could one day become a distinguished alumnus and very successful human being.

Sincerely,

Rachel Garjesik

TO: ADMISSIONS COMMITTEE

FROM: Barbara Moore, R.N., D.O.N.

DATE: 24 May, 2001

RE: Reference for Mark Offit

LETTER OF REFERENCE

As Director of Nursing at Harriet House, I became acquainted with Mr. Offit in 1998. Since that time he has unselfishly volunteered his time during summer months, holiday vacations, and weekday afternoons. His caring and compassion reveal a temperament well suited to the practice of medicine, and his positive attitude has endeared him to the staff and patients of our 159-bed facility. Although absolute reliability seems to be an uncommon quality these days, he has proven herself to be a committed soldier in every task he has undertaken. I have developed the highest respect for his character and wish to comment on his aptitude for the medical profession.

Experience in care giving

Under my direct supervision, Mr. Offit assisted patients with Alzheimers, AIDS, diabetes, and brain stem injuries. He was quite capable and effective in engaging patients with exercise, wheelchair aerobics, range of motion, hand-eye coordination, and sensory stimulation. He worked in one-on-one development involving music and intellectual stimulation and generously donated his time to write personal letters.

Exceptional creativity

I have had many opportunities to observe Mr. Offit's creativity and resourcefulness. For example, on his own initiative he organized and managed outings such as picnics, fishing activities, museum outings, and shopping trips. He also started "wheelchair aerobics" in which participants would exercise parts of their bodies using their own resistance and a ball. His imagination inspired many popular arts and crafts activities which provided a subtle form of physical therapy for patients while also engaging their spirits in tasks which they found to be fun and socially satisfying.

Outstanding leadership, communication, and problem-solving skills

Because of his mature judgment and excellent communication skills, Mr. Offit was invited to participate in several operational areas not normally participated in by volunteers. For example, he sat on the grievance committee and assisted in finding solutions to a wide range of problems where residents' expectations were not being met. The facility also named him its Restorative Aide, enabling him to be a member of the Restorative Walking Team and the Restorative Feeding Team. He also became involved in orienting new patients to the facility, and he was highly effective in both of those roles because of his vibrant personality and personal charm.

Attention to detail

Documentation is a key part of any medical program because the progress of each patient must be closely monitored. Mr. Offit demonstrated thoroughness in his attention to detail and fastidiously prepared daily records, monthly schedules, as well as the facility's newsletter.

Page two of recommendation letter for Mark Offit

Hands-on approach to patient care

Personal care is a vital part of patients' needs, and Mr. Offit has always demonstrated a meticulous approach in helping patients with personal matters including oral care, hair care, and bathroom care. I believe it is enormously useful for future doctors to have an understanding of the "behind-the scenes" details of patient care, and he has displayed a cheerful disposition while attending to every kind of personal hygiene task.

A true desire to enter the medical profession

As I have watched Mr. Offit transform into a young man during the last nine years, so too have I watched him strengthen in his desire to become a doctor. On numerous occasions he has shown an insatiable appetite for knowledge about the types of care our facility provides to patients with Alzheimers, AIDS, diabetes, cancer, and brain stem injuries. I have observed him over the years demonstrate a true yearning to be involved in caring for the sick and diseased in our society. I feel certain that he will become a fine physician, and I have no doubt that he will be an asset to the medical field. He has had ample opportunity to observe the hardships involved in being a doctor—the long hours and uncertain schedules, for example—and I believe his capacity for hard work and excellent time management skills should go a long way toward helping him excel as a doctor.

Signed:

Anita Hill, R.N., D.O.N.

LETTER OF REFERENCE

ABOUT THE EDITOR

Anne McKinney holds an MBA from the Harvard Business School and a BA in English from the University of North Carolina at Chapel Hill. A noted public speaker, writer, and teacher, she is the senior editor for PREP's business and career imprint, which bears her name. Early titles in the Anne McKinney Career Series (now called the Real-Resumes Series) published by PREP include: *Resumes and Cover Letters That Have Worked, Resumes and Cover Letters That Have Worked for Military Professionals, Government Job Applications and Federal Resumes, Cover Letters That Blow Doors Open,* and *Letters for Special Situations.* Her career titles and how-to resume-and-cover-letter books are based on the expertise she has acquired in 20 years of working with job hunters. Her valuable career insights have appeared in publications of the "Wall Street Journal" and other prominent newspapers and magazines.

Judeo-Christian Ethics Series

BACK IN TIME
Patty Sleem
Published in large print hardcover by Simon & Schuster's Thorndike Press as a Thorndike Christian Mystery in November 1998.
(306 pages)
"An engrossing look at the discrimination faced by female ministers."– *Library Journal*
Trade paperback 1-885288-03-4— $16.00

SECOND TIME AROUND
Patty Sleem
"Sleem explores the ugliness of suicide and murder, obsession and abuse, as well as Christian faith and values. An emotional and suspenseful read reflecting modern issues and concerns." – *Southern Book Trade*
(336 pages)
Foreign rights sold in Chinese.
Hardcover 1-885288-00-X—$25.00
Trade paperback 1-885288-05-0— $17.00

A GENTLE BREEZE FROM GOSSAMER WINGS
Gordon Beld
Pol Pot was the Khmer Rouge leader whose reign of terror caused the deaths of up to 2 million Cambodians in the mid-1970s. He masterminded an extreme, Maoist-inspired revolution in which those Cambodians died in mass executions, and from starvation and disease. This book of historical fiction shows the life of one refugee from this reign of genocide.
(320 pages)
"I'm pleased to recommend *A Gentle Breeze From Gossamer Wings*. Every Christian in America should read it. It's a story you won't want to miss – and it could change your life."
— Robert H. Schuller, Pastor, Crystal Cathedral
Trade paperback 1-885288-07-7— $18.00

BIBLE STORIES FROM THE OLD TESTAMENT
Katherine Whaley
Familiar and not-so-familiar Bible stories told by an engaging storyteller in a style guaranteed to delight and inform. Includes stories about Abraham, Cain and Abel, Jacob and David, Moses and the Exodus, Judges, Saul, David, and Solomon.
(272 pages)
"Whaley tells these tales in such a way that they will appeal to the young adult as well as the senior citizen."
– *Independent Publisher*
Trade paperback 1-885288-12-3— $18.00

WHAT THE BIBLE SAYS ABOUT...
Words that can lead to success and happiness *Patty Sleem*
A daily inspirational guide as well as a valuable reference when you want to see what the Bible says about Life and Living, Toil and Working, Problems and Suffering, Anger and Arguing, Self-Reliance and Peace of Mind, Justice and Wrong-Doing, Discipline and Self-Control, Wealth and Power, Knowledge and Wisdom, Pride and Honor, Gifts and Giving, Husbands and Wives, Friends and Neighbors, Children, Sinning and Repenting, Judgment and Mercy, Faith and Religion, and Love.
(192 pages)
Hardcover 1-885288-02-6—$20.00

Business & Career Books

RESUMES AND COVER LETTERS THAT HAVE WORKED
Anne McKinney, Editor
More than 100 resumes and cover letters written by the world's oldest resume-writing company. Resumes shown helped real people not only change jobs but also transfer their skills and experience to other industries and fields. An indispensable tool in an era of downsizing when research shows that most of us have not one but three distinctly different careers in our working lifetime. (272 pages)
"Distinguished by its highly readable samples...essential for library collections." – *Library Journal*
Trade paperback 1-885288-04-2—$25.00

RESUMES AND COVER LETTERS THAT HAVE WORKED FOR MILITARY PROFESSIONALS
Anne McKinney, Editor
Military professionals from all branches of the service gain valuable experience while serving their country, but they need resumes and cover letters that translate their skills and background into "civilian language." This is a book showing more than 100 resumes and cover letters written by a resume-writing service in business for nearly 20 years which specializes in "military translation." (256 pages)
"A guide that significantly translates veterans' experience into viable repertoires of achievement." – *Booklist*
Trade paperback 1-885288-06-9—$25.00

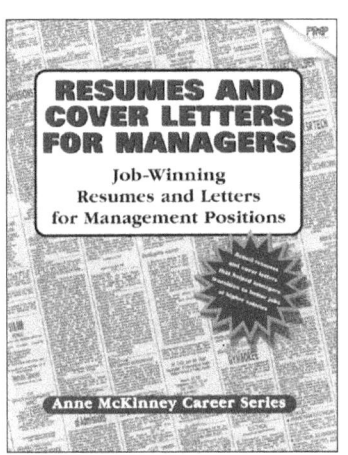

RESUMES AND COVER LETTERS FOR MANAGERS
Anne McKinney, Editor
Destined to become the bible for managers who want to make sure their resumes and cover letters open the maximum number of doors while helping them maximize in the salary negotiation process. From office manager to CEO, managers trying to relocate to or from these and other industries and fields will find helpful examples: Banking, Agriculture, School Systems, Human Resources, Restaurants, Manufacturing, Hospitality Industry, Automotive, Retail, Telecommunications, Police Force, Dentistry, Social Work, Academic Affairs, Non-Profit Organizations, Childcare, Sales, Sports, Municipalities, Rest Homes, Medicine and Healthcare, Business Operations, Landscaping, Customer Service, MIS, Quality Control, Teaching, the Arts, and Self-Employed. (288 pages)
Trade paperback 1-885288-10-7—$25.00

GOVERNMENT JOB APPLICATIONS AND FEDERAL RESUMES: Federal Resumes, KSAs, Forms 171 and 612, and Postal Applications
Anne McKinney, Editor
Getting a government job can lead to job security and peace of mind. The problem is that getting a government job requires extensive and complex paperwork. Now, for the first time, this book reveals the secrets and shortcuts of professional writers in preparing job-winning government applications such as these:
The Standard Form 171 (SF 171) – several complete samples
The Optional Form 612 (OF 612) – several complete samples
KSAs – samples of KSAs tailored to jobs ranging from the GS-5 to GS-12
Ranking Factors – how-to samples
Postal Applications
Wage Grade paperwork
Federal Resumes – see the different formats required by various government agencies. (272 pages)
Trade paperback 1-885288-11-5—$25.00

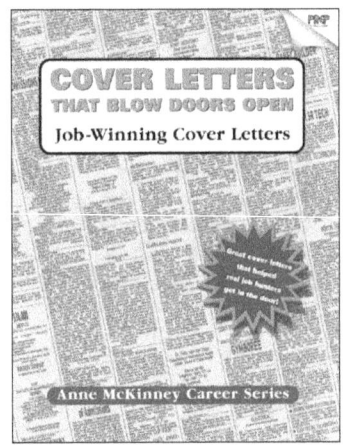

COVER LETTERS THAT BLOW DOORS OPEN
Anne McKinney, Editor
Although a resume is important, the cover letter is the first impression. This book is a compilation of great cover letters that helped real people get in the door for job interviews against stiff competition. Included are letters that show how to approach employers when you're moving to a new area, how to write a cover letter when you're changing fields or industries, and how to arouse the employer's interest in dialing your number first from a stack of resumes. (272 pages) Trade paperback 1-885288-13-1—$25.00

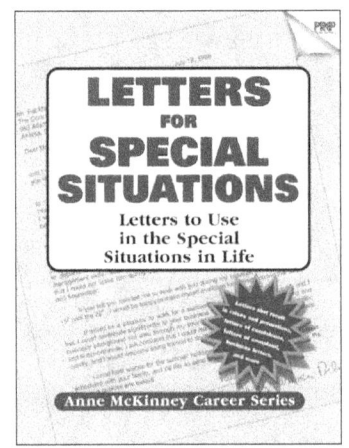

LETTERS FOR SPECIAL SITUATIONS
Anne McKinney, Editor
Sometimes it is necessary to write a special letter for a special situation in life. You will find great letters to use as models for business and personal reasons including: letters asking for a

raise, letters of resignation, letters of reference, letters notifying a vendor of a breach of contract, letter to a Congressman, letters of complaint, letters requesting reinstatement to an academic program, follow-up letters after an interview, letters requesting bill consolidation, letters of reprimand to marginal employees, letters requesting financial assistance or a grant, letters to professionals disputing their charges, collections letters, thank-you letters, and letters to accompany resumes in job-hunting. (256 pages)
Trade paperback 1-885288-09-3—$25.00

PREP Publishing Order Form

You may purchase any of our titles from your favorite bookseller! Or send a check or money order or your credit card number for the total amount*, plus $3.20 postage and handling, to PREP, Box 66, Fayetteville, NC 28302. If you have a question about any of our titles, feel free to e-mail us at preppub@aol.com and visit our website at http://www.prep-pub.com

Name: _____

Phone #: _____

Address: _____

_____

E-mail address: _____

Payment Type: ☐ Check/Money Order ☐ Visa ☐ MasterCard

Credit Card Number: _____ Expiration Date: _____

Check items you are ordering:

☐ $25.00—RESUMES AND COVER LETTERS THAT HAVE WORKED.

☐ $25.00—RESUMES AND COVER LETTERS THAT HAVE WORKED FOR MILITARY PROFESSIONALS.

☐ $25.00—RESUMES AND COVER LETTERS FOR MANAGERS.

☐ $25.00—GOVERNMENT JOB APPLICATIONS AND FEDERAL RESUMES: Federal Resumes, KSAs, Forms 171 and 612, and Postal Applications.

☐ $25.00—COVER LETTERS THAT BLOW DOORS OPEN.

☐ $25.00—LETTERS FOR SPECIAL SITUATIONS.

☐ $16.00—BACK IN TIME. Patty Sleem

☐ $17.00—(trade paperback) SECOND TIME AROUND. Patty Sleem

☐ $25.00—(hardcover) SECOND TIME AROUND. Patty Sleem

☐ $18.00—A GENTLE BREEZE FROM GOSSAMER WINGS. Gordon Beld

☐ $18.00—BIBLE STORIES FROM THE OLD TESTAMENT. Katherine Whaley

☐ $20.00—WHAT THE BIBLE SAYS ABOUT... *Words that can lead to success and happiness*. Patty Sleem

New titles!

☐ $16.95—REAL-RESUMES FOR SALES. Anne McKinney, Editor

☐ $16.95—REAL-RESUMES FOR TEACHERS. Anne McKinney, Editor

☐ $16.95—REAL-RESUMES FOR CAREER CHANGERS. Anne McKinney, Editor

☐ $16.95—REAL-RESUMES FOR STUDENTS. Anne McKinney, Editor

☐ $16.95—REAL ESSAYS FOR COLLEGE & GRAD SCHOOL. Anne McKinney, Editor

☐ $10.95—KIJABE An African Historical Saga. Pally Dhillon

_____ **TOTAL ORDERED (add $3.20 for postage and handling)**

Discounts on large orders. (910) 483-6611 for more information.

THE MISSION OF PREP PUBLISHING IS TO PUBLISH
BOOKS AND OTHER PRODUCTS WHICH ENRICH
PEOPLE'S LIVES AND HELP THEM OPTIMIZE THE
HUMAN EXPERIENCE. OUR STRONGEST LINES ARE
OUR JUDEO-CHRISTIAN ETHICS SERIES AND OUR
BUSINESS & CAREER SERIES.

For a brief free consultation, call 910-483-6611
or write to
PREP, Department Essays, Box 66, Fayetteville, NC 28302.

QUESTIONS OR COMMENTS? E-MAIL US AT PREPPUB@AOL.COM
OR VISIT OUR WEBSITE AT WWW.PREP-PUB.COM

www.ingramcontent.com/pod-product-compliance
Lightning Source LLC
Chambersburg PA
CBHW081445170526
45166CB00008B/2315